The Fiume Crisis

THE FIUME CRISIS

Life in the Wake of the Habsburg Empire

Dominique Kirchner Reill

THE BELKNAP PRESS OF
HARVARD UNIVERSITY PRESS

Cambridge, Massachusetts
London, England
2020

Library of Congress Cataloging-in-Publication Data

Names: Reill, Dominique Kirchner, author.

Title: The Fiume crisis : life in the wake of the Habsburg Empire /
  Dominique Kirchner Reill.

Description: Cambridge, Massachusetts : The Belknap Press of
  Harvard University Press, 2020. | Includes index.

Identifiers: LCCN 2020018506 | ISBN 9780674244245 (cloth)

Subjects: LCSH: D'Annunzio, Gabriele, 1863–1938. | Habsburg, House of. |
  Nationalism—Italy. | Sovereignty. | Fascism—Croatia. | Rijeka (Croatia)—
  History—20th century. | Europe, Central—History. | Europe, Eastern—
  History—1918–1945.

Classification: LCC DR1645.R54 R45 2020 | DDC 949.702/1—dc23

LC record available at https://lccn.loc.gov/2020018506

For French and Peter,
my favorite people

Contents

A Note on Names

As is true with so many histories of central, eastern, and southeastern Europe, most of the personal names and places in this book have multiple versions that coexisted in the time period under study and were determined mostly by the language one spoke. For personal names, I have opted to use the one most commonly found in the documents consulted. So, for example, when referencing the 66-year-old head of the tobacco factory, I use the Germanized version of his name, Koloman Termatsits (which he used when engaging with local administrations), instead of the Hungarian version, Kálmán Termatsits (which he used when writing to his superiors in Budapest). For place names, I have chosen to use the version that would help a reader find the location on an English-language map today: so Vienna instead of Wien, Venice instead of Venezia, Istanbul instead of Constantinople, Opatija instead of Abbazia, Zadar instead of Zara, Split instead of Spalato, and so on.

The one exception is the name for the city the book focuses on: Fiume, which today is known as Rijeka. Fiume and Rijeka mean "river," in Italian and Croatian, respectively. For centuries, people called the town by either name. I use Fiume for historical reasons, not nationalist ones. Early twentieth-century Fiume does not delimit the same city as today's Rijeka. The Fiume in this book is the semiautonomous city-state and the suburbs it controlled; its official name was "Fiume," as Italian was one of the official languages, while Croatian was not. Today's Rijeka includes this urban space as well as others that in the early twentieth century were administered by different states using different official

languages and different laws, such as Sušak and Kantrida. During the
period covered by the book, Sušak was a separate town administered
by Croatia-Slavonia, and Kantrida was a sleepy seaside village administered by the Austrian half of the Habsburg Empire. Fiume was its own
city, administered by a mixture of self-made statutes and laws issued
by the Hungarian Kingdom of which it was part. To understand the
hows and whys of the Fiume Crisis, it is crucial to respect these structural differences of the past. Hence the use of the name Fiume for the
period under study. When discussing today's city, I call it Rijeka.

The reader will notice very quickly that wherever possible I have indicated the age and profession of every person named in the book,
from the rebellious schoolchild, to the lowliest housecleaner, anxious
baker, resourceful housewife, desperate retired dockworker, to the head
of Fiume's provisional government. I did this intentionally to show how
this history affected all age groups and every economic class, not just
the veterans and young paramilitary men who have peopled most of
the new histories of Europe's immediate postwar.

One last note on a naming choice that may perhaps seem odd. I use
"the Kingdom of Serbs, Croats, and Slovenes" and the adjective Serb-
Croat-Slovene instead of the more commonly used (and less awkward)
terms Yugoslavia and Yugoslav. The country formed in 1918, which included most of what is today Slovenia, Croatia, Bosnia-Herzegovina,
Serbia, Montenegro, Kosovo, and Macedonia, was not officially called
Yugoslavia until 1929, though the name was used in unofficial communications. That is not the primary reason for my choice. The real reason
is that between 1918 and 1921 the issue of how the Kingdom of Serbs,
Croats, and Slovenes would be organized, how centralized it would
be, and what sort of state or national identity it would have was hotly
contested over issues of post-imperial dissolution and post-WWI state-
making. The kingdom itself did not get a constitution until 1921, did
not have a single currency until 1923, and did not have its own citizenship law until 1928. I use the official name instead of the unofficial one
to acknowledge this context, even though it leads to some awkward
moments. I use Yugoslav and Yugoslavia when they are specifically referenced in primary sources or when I am discussing the unitarian
"Yugoslav" national political or cultural ideology.

Maps

Rijeka (Fiume) Today

Fiume within the Habsburg Empire

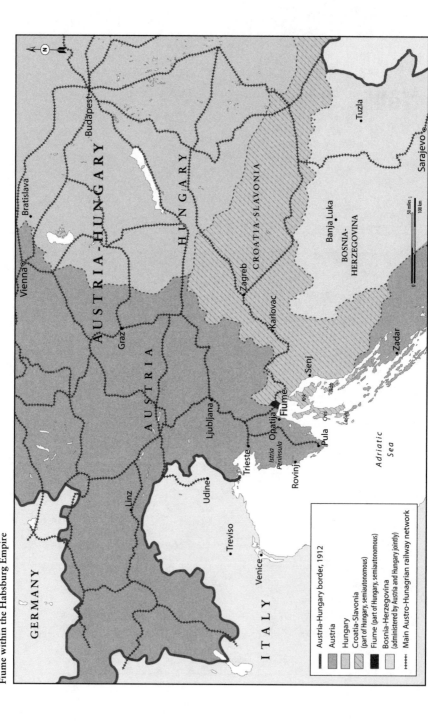

GERMANY

AUSTRIA-HUNGARY

AUSTRIA

HUNGARY

ITALY

Vienna

Bratislava

Budapest

Graz

Linz

Udine

Treviso

Venice

Ljubljana

Trieste

Istria
Peninsula

Opatija

Rovinj

Pula

Fiume

Senj

Karlovac

Zagreb

CROATIA-SLAVONIA

Banja Luka

BOSNIA-
HERZEGOVINA

Tuzla

Sarajevo

Zadar

Krk

Cres

Rab

Lošinj

Adriatic

Sea

N

50 miles
100 km

Austria-Hungary border, 1912

Austria

Hungary

Croatia-Slavonia
(part of Hungary, semiautonomous)

Fiume (part of Hungary, semiautonomous)

Bosnia-Herzegovina
(administered by Austria and Hungary jointly)

Main Austro-Hungarian railway network

FIUME 1919 – 1924

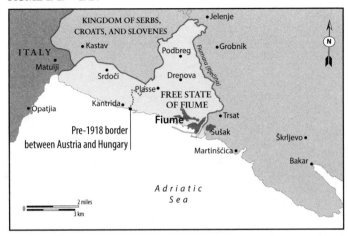

FIUME 1924 – 1941

FIUME 1947 – present

The Fiume Crisis

Introduction

The Christmas of Blood

Christmas 1920 was not what locals had come to anticipate in Fiume, the industrial port town in the northeast corner of the Adriatic Sea. Usually Fiume's bustling mixture of culinary activities left visitors engaging in endless debate about which cultural heritage predominated in the town. The aroma of walnuts and poppy seeds made children beg their parents to buy yet one more Hungarian-inspired *oresgnaza* roll. Butchers stocked extra ground beef and pork for the beloved cabbage-covered *sarma* pockets featured on dinner tables throughout Croatia and the Balkan beyond. Fishmongers boasted about how well their slithery, fat eels fried up for the *bisato* enjoyed all along the Adriatic and Italian coastlines. The sound of geese honking reassured cooks that their main course was waddling its way into the city center on time for the sauerkraut with which they planned to pair it. And wine merchants kept sherry on hand for the small but determinedly British community who enjoyed their traditional trifle. Catholic and Protestant Fiumians usually spent this period doing last-minute shopping, decorating trees, hanging mistletoe, lighting incense to clear out old spirits from their homes, preparing the yule log, distributing food and clothes to the needy, and marveling at the enormous nativity scenes featured in the churches, where many attended midnight mass. For the roughly 5 percent of the population that had either celebrated Chanukah two weeks before or would celebrate Orthodox Christmas two weeks later, all these preparations meant profits, also something to celebrate. Christmas was perhaps the time when Fiume's Mediterranean, central European, Balkan, and commercially oriented cultural mosaic came together most successfully.

But at Christmas 1920 all this disappeared. The city was under siege. Its food and energy supplies had been completely cut off for days. There was a strict curfew. Shops were closed. Markets were empty, houses of worship deserted. By December 24, the rumblings of artillery could be heard, a portent of the bombs that would be lobbed onto the town two days later. While much of Europe was enjoying its second year free of the shrapnel of war, Christmas 1920 in Fiume was no festival of lights, songs, and holiday treats. It was a time of cold, darkness, whispered apprehension, and destruction.

Why was Fiume attacked on Christmas? Not because of any religious conflict or at the behest of an expansionist neighbor. The reason was more prosaic. It was attacked on Christmas because newspaper distribution and readership throughout Europe and the Americas was at its lowest during the holiday. The fear of media attention is understandable, for the country attacking the town of circa fifty thousand inhabitants was none other than the neighboring Kingdom of Italy, whose population of about thirty-five million was almost entirely Catholic. A powerful Catholic country attacking a relatively small, mostly Catholic town during Christmas was bad enough, but the reason for the attack was seemingly unfathomable: Italy attacked Fiume to make it accept its internationally determined status as a sovereign city-state and stop demanding annexation to Italy. The attack was intended to force Fiume to accept its independence, or, to put it another way, to force Fiume to stop calling itself part of Italy.

What Fiume should be and what state it should belong to had been of global concern as early as November 1918. The issue haunted the diplomats of Europe and the United States. Theories about what would become of Fiume splashed across the headlines of the world's newspapers. Before World War I, Fiume was a semiautonomous city-state within the Habsburg Empire, a prosperous port city that linked with Habsburg railway lines to bring colonial goods to Europe's heartlands and central European products and peoples to global markets. After World War I, with the Habsburg Empire dissolved, no one could agree

The main pedestrian thoroughfare of Fiume's city center, the Corso (Croatian Korzo), October 29, 1918. This picture was taken two years before the Christmas of Blood, immediately after the Habsburg administration disappeared. Note the Italian flag waving from the clock tower and the double-headed eagle statue at the top, a symbol of the city's long Habsburg history. With its electric lighting, broad promenade, storefronts, and an abundance of bakeries, the Corso was a special attraction during the Christmas season, a place where chestnut sellers abounded.

who should control this tantalizing port city. For over two years, dip-lomats haggled, financial elites bribed, and nationalist activists shouted to ensure that their interests counted most. In 1920, an agreement was finally reached between the Kingdom of Italy and the Kingdom of Serbs, Croats, and Slovenes: no state would absorb Fiume; it would be an in-dependent city-state. In response, Fiume's city representatives insisted again (as they had since the beginning) that Fiume should determine its own future and that what it wanted was not independence but an-nexation to Italy. Though eager to annex Fiume since the end of World War I, Italian government officials feared alienating the other resistant Great Powers over it (especially the United States, which bankrolled much of Italy's budget). And so, Italy had consistently threatened to blockade Fiume unless it accepted whatever fate international diplo-mats decided for it.

For over two years, these threats had just been words, and month after month, the town defied international pressure and the many pro-nouncements from Paris, Rome, Belgrade, Zagreb, London, and Wash-ington, DC. Would the Italian state really lay siege to a city simply because it wanted to be Italian rather than be made independent or joined to the Kingdom of Serbs, Croats, and Slovenes, as Woodrow Wilson insisted it should? Would Italians really allow the town (of which almost half the body politic were considered Italian) to suffer hunger, cold, and military violence just because they wanted to be joined with their Italian brothers against Serb, Croat, and Slovene aspirations? Precisely as Fiume's deft publicists had hoped, public opinion in Italy answered with a resounding "No!" The Italian government tried every-thing to avoid making their threats against Fiume real. But when Fiume refused to recognize the final border agreement between the Kingdom of Italy and the Kingdom of Serbs, Croats, and Slovenes, tolerance for Fiume's intransigence ended. Italy's attack on Fiume was made as strategically, reluctantly, and quietly as possible. Hence the Christmas attack, which surprised everyone, most especially the Fiumians.

Fear of media coverage of the attack was compounded by the fact that one of Italy's most beloved celebrities, 57-year-old poet-soldier Gabriele D'Annunzio, had made annexing Fiume to Italy his pet cause.

Throughout 1918 and 1919, D'Annunzio had made speeches in Italy calling Fiume a "martyr city," painting Fiumians as sacrificial victims battling the forces of international diplomacy to heal "the mutilated victory" Italy had endured at the close of World War I. When his speeches failed to move the Italian government, D'Annunzio went to Fiume in September 1919 along with several hundred raucous followers who proclaimed themselves the "shock troops" of Italy's inevitable move to add the city to the Italian motherland. A year later, in September 1920, with the Italian government still refusing to take Fiume as its rightful prize, D'Annunzio supplanted the local Fiume government and declared himself the duce of Fiume, insisting that he was holding it as a regency until Italy claimed it as its own. D'Annunzio had been a press darling since the age of 17, when he had falsely publicized his own death to build interest in his poetry. His Fiume adventures made him even more famous, bringing fascination with his persona to a fever pitch. By 1920, newspaper readers everywhere identified Fiume with D'Annunzio and vice versa. Key figures in the Italian government and military, however, believed that Fiume locals were not so enamored of their charismatic poet-dictator, his intemperate followers, or their hardline motto that saw only two options—Fiume's annexation to "Italy or death." The Italian military pursued a strategy—often used when facing a dictator—of turning up the pressure on the local civilian population in the hope that they would oust D'Annunzio on their own and then submit to the international agreements laid out for them. It was winter, after all. How and why would fathers, mothers, grandparents, poor and rich, young and old, cope without the electricity, coal, water, wood, medicines, and food necessary to survive the dark, wet, cold month of December? Would they really risk all this (and Christmas, too) just to serve an unhinged poet-dictator? If Fiumians were surprised that the Italian armed forces bombed their town, they were not alone. The Italian army and navy were surprised as well, having expected the locals to resolve the situation before things came to this point.

By December 26, D'Annunzio's soldiers consolidated their positions in the municipal core, blowing up all the bridges with direct access to the city from the east and barricading the major thoroughfares from the west and north. Civilians without proper residency papers were ordered to leave (though most did not), those with weapons were commanded to relinquish arms (though most did not), and some outspoken Fiumians were imprisoned (in case they took advantage of the situation to instigate revolt). When the siege failed to bring Fiume to its knees, the Italian military command bombed D'Annunzio's headquarters while Italian soldiers simultaneously pushed into the city. Invasion meant Italian soldiers penetrated Fiume through the apartment-lined streets and the terraced gardens that clung to the steep inclines of the coastline. Here locals really could have proved dangerous. The countless windows could have served as prime guerrilla attack positions for thousands of fathers, mothers, and children intent on saving Fiume from its invaders. Gunfire, grenades, or even domestic weapons like rocks, scissors, knives, and scalding liquids could have been launched with little hope of retaliation from the hesitant, encroaching army below. However, when the Italian forces moved through backyards and under balconies, they were met not with desperate resistance but with Italian flags on windowsills, eyes peeking through shutters, and uneasy silence.

Bombs landed on barracks; on the governor's palace, where D'Annunzio was holed up; and on private residences on the outskirts of town. Many homes were destroyed by D'Annunzio's troops, who used far more dynamite than required to blow up the bridges connecting the city to the east. All the bombing—whether by D'Annunzio's dynamite or Italy's cannons—brought only cowering reserve from the tens of thousands of Fiumians caught in the crossfire. In essence, Fiumians resisted neither their poet-dictator nor their invaders, watching warily while protecting themselves as much as possible. It was not until December 28 that the recently ousted municipal representatives succeeded in convincing their duce to surrender, abdicate, and allow locals to negotiate a peace with the Italian military command. On New Year's Eve, Italy's war on Fiume was officially over; the city agreed to kick out D'Annunzio and his troops, and Fiume accepted the independence international diplomats had designated for it.

A staged photograph of D'Annunzio's troops preparing to obstruct Italian military forces from entering Fiume. Note the relatively small number of men available to keep the Italian troops out. Note also at top right the woman looking on from her window: for many Fiumians the Christmas of Blood was a strange and unintelligible spectacle.

In his hyperbolic style, D'Annunzio called the attack on Fiume the "Christmas of Blood" (Natale di sangue), even though only thirty-two people died (five civilians and twenty-seven soldiers, ten of whom were fighting for D'Annunzio, seventeen for Italy). Perhaps the term felt accurate for the parents of 12-year-old Alpalice Almadi, crushed in her home by Italian bombs, or the family members of 36-year-old Antonia Copetti and 39-year-old Antonio Kucich, but the blood spilled by Italy's attack pales in comparison with the mortality rates suffered in the recent world war. Even measured against other historic Christmas tragedies, Fiume's Christmas of Blood feels particularly misnamed, given how reluctant Italian invaders were to cause bloodshed and how successfully locals remained outside the fray. Fewer newspapers around the globe reported on the 1920 Christmas attack than would have a week earlier or later, but those that did skipped over the low body count

The destroyed bridges that had connected Fiume to the lands to its east, including the railway bridge providing access from Fiume to Zagreb-Budapest and the thoroughfare bridge connecting Fiume to the Croatian satellite town of Sušak.

and described it as a case of Italian "fratricide," a shameful sign of poor leadership from both the Italian government and D'Annunzio. The reports predicted that Fiumians would need "some time for the sad impression of these days to be erased."[1] Contrary to these assumptions, however, just two days after fighting ceased, a local journalist was stunned and a little disgusted to see that "the City has returned . . . to normal. Some public offices are open, lots of shops are swarming with people, especially those featuring foodstuffs. . . . [People talk] with passion, but without distress, . . . as if . . . the bombardment was of a Chinese city on the part of the Russians, instead of Fiume on the part of Italian cannons!"[2]

The 1920 Christmas attack and all that led up to it are remembered most not in the city's courtyards, cafés, and living rooms but in Italy. For Fiumians, much bigger, bloodier, and more terrifying moments were to come. In 1922, Italian Fascists would lead a coup d'état against the independent Fiume government. In 1924 Benito Mussolini would annex Fiume to Italy, leading the many thousands of Fiumians who identified as Croatian or Slovene to be victimized legally, politically, culturally, and sometimes physically as never before. In 1943, Fiume would be occupied by Nazi Germany, and the circa 2 percent of its population that was Jewish would be almost totally annihilated, suffering the highest mortality rates of any Jewish community within the Kingdom of Italy's borders.[3] In 1944, heavy bombing by Anglo-American planes and retreating German forces would leave hundreds dead and almost all of the city's industrial buildings and its port razed to the ground. In 1947, Fiume would be annexed to Josip Broz Tito's Yugoslavia and would go officially by the Croatian version of its name, Rijeka ("river"; *fiume* in Italian also means "river"). At the end of World War II, many thousands of the city's Italian population would flee, fearing either retribution for Italian Fascism's crimes or what living in a socialist, Yugoslav nation-state would entail.[4] In the 1950s and 1960s, a herculean effort at rebuilding and repopulating the town would be undertaken, one that rested on the backbreaking labor of locals in a time of economic want and community trauma. Finally, in the 1980s, Rijeka's economy began to crumble like so many other industrial ports, leading to a steady population loss. Though many families living there can trace their histories back to before World War I, the hungry, missed Christmas of 1920 and everything that led up to it have been overshadowed by everything that followed.

In Rijeka today, D'Annunzio's Christmas of Blood is little more than an anecdote discussed in blogs, analyzed in academic journals, or featured in newspapers as a Christmas-season curiosity. Historians of the town, both within Croatia and beyond, have focused on tracing how the city's prewar political elite lost control to the relatively small number of extreme Italian nationalists in the postwar.[5] D'Annunzio and the Christmas of Blood, with all the nationalist rhetoric and attempts at the mass expulsion of "national others," is seen as a harbinger of what was to come, with most pointing to Mussolini's Fascist regime—and its aggressive centralization and Italianization campaigns—as the true death

The urban area of Fiume, probably taken in 1920 from the hillside community of Trsat (within Croatian-held Sušak). From background to foreground: the mountains on the eastern coast of the Istrian Peninsula; Kvarner Bay, Fiume's main port (the small number of ships is due to years of maritime blockade); the city center; and residential neighborhoods tucked throughout the city's slopes.

knell for Fiume's unique poppy-seed-, eel-, *sarma*-, and sauerkraut-eating world. The Christmas war did not signal the immediate end of this multicultural port city, and in Rijeka the story is not D'Annunzio, his legionnaires, or the Christmas of Blood, but instead the long-term Italian nationalist forces that eradicated the multicultural world that celebrated Christmas before 1920 with Italian, Hungarian, Croatian, Slovene, Austrian, Czech, Romanian, and British delicacies.[6]

In Italy, everything related to 1919–1920 Fiume, D'Annunzio, and the Christmas of Blood is seen as fundamental to explaining what happened after World War I. D'Annunzio's September 1919 arrival in Fiume (called the "Marcia di Ronchi"), the behavior of his followers (the so-called legionnaires), and the Christmas of Blood are key points in an exten-

D'Annunzio leading his troops in the "Eia! Eia! Eia! Alalà!" war cry to celebrate the anniversary of their arrival in Fiume. The war cry always ended with right arms raised to proclaim an enthusiastic willingness to fight. Though no women or children participate in the cheer here, on numerous other occasions the few women volunteers in D'Annunzio's corps participated actively in such rallies.

sive narrative used in classrooms, television programs, films, books, and academic research projects to explain how Italy fell into Fascism between the end of World War I and Mussolini's March on Rome in 1922. D'Annunzio's charismatic performance as a leader speaking to an adoring crowd from a balcony while professing disdain for all that was orderly, feminine, bourgeois, or "liberal moribund," coupled with his promised return to Italian imperial potency, has been regularly identified as Mussolini's model for his rise to power. As George Mosse and Emilio Gentile convincingly argue, D'Annunzio introduced a new way of doing politics, cementing a sacralization of mass-oriented nationalism that helps explain why so many across the world saw totalitarianism as essential to the spiritual and material survival of their communities.[7] Mussolini's Fascist squads copied the veteran-obsessed, ruthless esprit de corps of D'Annunzio's legionnaires down to the Roman salute and the "Eia! Eia! Eia! Alalà!" war cry.[8] And it was more than just imitation: when D'Annunzio left the public eye after the Christmas of Blood, many of his followers joined the Fascist movement, and there is a direct lineage of nationalist activism from D'Annunzio's Fiume to Mussolini's Italy.

Even the aspects of D'Annunzio's time in Fiume that the Fascists did not adopt have sparked a seemingly insatiable interest within Italy. Discussions of how D'Annunzio counted among his collaborators not just soon-to-be Fascists but also anarcho-syndicalists, monarchists, Catholic socialists, futurists, homosexual poet-aviators, feminists, cosmopolitan anti-imperialists, and nationalist republicans are regularly used to explain the complexity of Italy's postwar period, as well as to show how Italian nationalism was not necessarily, nor even primarily, fascist oriented. "Fiume" in these histories is not a place but a moment—one where a rainbow of disparate elements of the Italian political, social, and cultural world vied with each other to challenge the conservative liberal values of the traditional Italian ruling elite, when Fascism was one such element but by no means yet the predominant one.[9] The amalgam of influences and imaginaries encapsulated in this version of D'Annunzio's Fiume episode has been called "the Festival of the Revolution" (La festa della rivoluzione) and likened to Woodstock. Historians of the more bizarre elements of D'Annunzio's Fiume adventure argue that hundreds of Italians came to Fiume in 1919 hoping to experience an alternative cultural world much as Americans came to a dairy farm in 1969 New York—albeit one that was lighter on the music and heavier on the politics.[10] Through this lens, the Christmas of Blood marks the moment it first seemed clear that cultural revolution within Italy was doomed except for those willing and able to engineer a militaristic takeover of the state. In this sense, Mussolini's rise to power was a second act to the failure of D'Annunzio's supposedly fun-loving experimental romp that ended with the Christmas of Blood.

There is quite a disconnect in these two histories. Within Rijeka and among those who study it, the stories that explain how the city and its inhabitants changed have taken center stage. Seen from this light, Christmas 1920 interrupted a world but did not transform it. Within Italy and among those who study it, the symbolic power of Fiume for Italian nationalists and the experience of the Italians who went to Fiume with D'Annunzio eclipses all else. What Fiume was before, what its residents experienced, and the role locals had in their city's steady rebellion against Wilsonian diplomacy is lost. Instead it is D'Annunzio defying the Italian state (to Roman salutes and applause) and what the Italian state did or did not do to neutralize this symbol that matter. Somehow the fact that locals had been stubbornly challenging the entire Paris Peace Treaty process almost a year before D'Annunzio and his legionnaires arrived is forgotten, along with the traumas Fiumians suffered and the strategies they employed to avoid suffering still more.

Broader European histories have taken their cue from Italian historiography. In the outpouring of recent work on the immediate postwar period (thanks to the centennials of World War I and Fascism, questions about the future of European democracy and nationalism, and doubts about American diplomatic leadership), Fiume à la D'Annunzio and the proto-fascism argument have served as an example of how World War I was the rupture point that introduced much of what we wish had not happened in Europe. Adherents of Mark Mazower's thesis in *The Dark Continent* that European liberalism's impotence explains the popularity of charismatic, chauvinist, and totalitarian movements use D'Annunzio's Fiume as a vivid example of how parliamentarianism failed to stabilize Europe during the interwar period.[11] Robert Gerwarth's *The Vanquished* supports this point and continues a long tradition of painting D'Annunzio's legionnaires as emblematic of the birth of a violent paramilitary nationalism that explains not just Mussolini's rise but Hitler's as well.[12] Adam Tooze posits a strange mix of US imperialism and isolationism as the mise-en-scène that allowed events like D'Annunzio in Fiume to turn into the diplomatic media circus they became.[13] And Pankaj Mishra even begins *Age of Anger* with a prologue describing D'Annunzio's Fiume "as a watershed moment" that led to a long line of "terroristic politics of the frustrated" whose most recent installments can be found in ISIS, Brexit, the European far right, Donald

Trump's policies, and other current irrational xenophobic political movements.[14]

There can be no doubt that the frenzy around D'Annunzio and his legionnaires had an adverse effect on Italy's post-WWI democratic culture.[15] But perhaps the most terrifying part is how much he and his band of irregulars hijacked the Fiume story by convincing everyone that what happened there was a "historical moment for Italy." They erased "the other" from the consciousness of contemporaries, supplanting it with images of themselves. And most alarming of all, the historical narrative still locates Fiume in the history of charismatic, sacralized, paramilitary politics, a mini prefiguring of what would happen in Italy. Nowhere is the city's ethnic diversity (so different from almost completely Italian-speaking Italy) apparent. Nowhere are questions raised about why a town would condone or perhaps cheer a charismatic Italian nationalist leader and his paramilitary devotees when at least 50 percent of its population did not use Italian as its mother tongue. Rarely has a nationalist movement so successfully blotted out those elements that did not fit its self-narrative. D'Annunzio's version of his time in Fiume has leaked its way into our general histories of the interwar period, even though it was more pomp than circumstance. What Fiume represented beyond D'Annunzio, how it continued for years in fighting Wilsonian diplomacy, and all that did not fit with Italian nationalist propaganda have been erased.

The danger of this approach goes still further. Fiume's "non-Italian others" were not cleansed from the city or suppressed en masse by D'Annunzio's legionnaires. Fiume was not a "bloodland," and though it was a "shatterzone of empires," the shards started cutting much later than elsewhere, in part because Fiume's internal dynamics did not so quickly give up the imperial ghost.[16] The horrific interethnic violence, rape, fire, and fury experienced in places like the Baltics, Ukraine, Macedonia, or Anatolia were not found in "paramilitary Fiume." And even though Fiume was represented as "more Italian than Italy"—as *italianissima*—by Fiume publicists well before D'Annunzio arrived, after his arrival Fiume's residents still included a higher percentage of non-Italians than anywhere in mainland Italy. D'Annunzio's legion-

A photograph from 1920 in the Fiume city center of some of D'Annunzio's legionnaires, here mostly Arditi soldiers (collars open) and artillerymen (collars closed).

naires played up the image of ruthless soldiers for the cameras, but unlike their German post-WWI Freikorps counterparts, D'Annunzio's legionnaires did not leave behind an unforgettable and unforgivable history of hurt. Nationalist outbursts threatening violence against Croatians, Slovenes, and Hungarians can be found in Fiume's historical record both before and after D'Annunzio, with stores vandalized, street brawls, and attempts to expel those who countered the Italian annexationist platform. But what is most shocking about these moments is not that they happened, but how few and ineffectual they were.

The real story of postwar Fiume is not how bodily violence destroyed the city's "others," but how city policies engineered a vision of "Italian Fiume" that obligated locals to play up Italianness and downplay everything else. Fiume bureaucrats and financial elites consciously manipulated the city-state's infrastructures to make a professed citywide Italianness sustainable for a deeply heterogeneous society. These local initiatives set the stage and kept the curtains open for D'Annunzio to demand "Italy or death" without much pushback from the real Fiume. And with local diversity cut out of the picture, it is easy to ignore the places D'Annunzio's charisma fell on deaf ears. Bringing the local back into the story triggers new questions, particularly about how a postwar city administration could silence ethnic tensions in a Wilsonian nationalizing world. Even more important is the question of why so many in Fiume seemed willing to hitch their star to an Italian annexation agenda, given that they were unlikely to be seen as national insiders by the nation-state they were working so hard to join. What were the issues, arguments, and hopes that convinced non-Italians to hide under all the italianissima propaganda to make Italian annexation happen?

This book seeks to answer those questions by moving away from what led up to D'Annunzio's Christmas of Blood and focusing instead on the forces that help explain why, after the fighting ended, the city transitioned back to everyday life so quickly. Fiume's concerted effort against Great Power politics owed its longevity less to Italian nationalist sentiments and more to local efforts to navigate the obstacles and opportunities of imperial dissolution. Historical accounts of the Fiume-D'Annunzio crisis have overlooked the fact that Fiume was a semiautonomous city-state within the Habsburg Monarchy, where local government had a significant role in determining how its residents could live and prosper. When we look at the economic, legal, and social administration of the city before and after Christmas 1920, we see that the city's reminders to Wilson of its "right to self-determination" were anchored in its day-to-day continuance of the administrative infrastructure established under the Habsburgs. With the Austro-Hungarian Monarchy dissolved in 1918, Fiumians adapted the vestiges of that empire to their newly isolated position and used them to push for a geopolitical reordering that satisfied their interests.

How could a city keep an even course against the will of the Paris Peace Conference when half its population used the language of the lands to its west while the other half preferred the languages of the lands to its east? This book shows that the reworking of the residual imperial infrastructure kept Fiume residents invested in their common future so that the city could be linked to the richest state in the region (the Kingdom of Italy) rather than isolated as an international city-state or married to the fledgling and industrially underdeveloped Kingdom of Serbs, Croats, and Slovenes. Far from being an example of how extreme nationalism stalled international efforts to create a stable nation-state order in post-1918 Europe, Fiume shows that the strongest impediments to Wilson's plans were the long-standing imperial frameworks and mindsets that persisted after the empires that created them had vanished. Fiume elites' goal was to keep imperial structures and mindsets going by substituting the Italian monarchy for the dissolved Austro-Hungarian one. This history of 1918–1921 Fiume challenges the increasingly accepted notion that people after World War I pushed for national self-determination to get out of empire. Instead, the Fiume Crisis was a move to continue empire under the aegis of nation.[17]

The argument that the successor states of Austria-Hungary functioned much like smaller versions of their Habsburg predecessor is not new. Already in 1951 in *Origins of Totalitarianism*, Hannah Arendt likened (albeit in passing) the postwar successor states to mini-versions of the Habsburg Monarchy of which they had all been a part.[18] In *The Habsburg Empire*, Pieter Judson argues that "each of these self-styled nation states [formed from the ruins of Austria-Hungary] in fact acted like a small empire."[19] Arendt and Judson came to these conclusions by looking at how nationalist politics in postwar Poland, Czechoslovakia, or Hungary affected state loyalties, political movements, and the many xenophobic campaigns that resulted from them. As Judson beautifully puts it, "The Habsburg Empire was gone, but the production of politics around cultural difference as the primary way for people to make claims on their state continued with a vengeance."[20] Investigation into the day-to-day workings of postwar Fiume reveals that this is as much true as it is false. Yes, inhabitants in a successor state like Fiume manipulated a politics of cultural difference as they tried to determine where they should sit geopolitically in the new Europe. To Wilson's firm refusal to annex Fiume to Italy, locals before D'Annunzio and then alongside him repeated incessantly that the city was italianissima. However, behind this claim of cultural difference, local administrations manipulated older Habsburg state infrastructures to keep Fiume's diverse linguistic and ethnic populations together, with locals actively participating in continuing imperial practices. Many Fiumians were even explicit that the Kingdom of Italy should function as a direct substitute for the Habsburg Empire.

The ethnic intolerance and nationalist impulses D'Annunzio was shilling may have been the stories of the moment in contemporary newspaper accounts—and many subsequent histories—but for those on the ground at war's end, bodily survival and efforts to return to prosperity were the most important issues. Navigating regime change after an empire disappears is no easy feat, as reports from the former Soviet and Yugoslav blocs have reminded us, but local enterprises managed to keep Fiume's diverse population interdependent enough to support the city's drive against Wilson's plan for Europe. And like the many difficulties Eastern Europeans face today, the successes of Fiume were pronounced in some areas and particularly lacking in others. Though my work rejects the nationalist extremism argument in explaining the hows and whys of the Fiume Crisis, it does show how the experience of regime change set loose many of the energies that led locals to turn to extremist solutions in the coming decades.

The Fiume Crisis has three interrelated aims. First, in its critical retelling of an extraordinary event of the interwar period, it disputes commonly held assumptions about the rise of charismatic fascism in Europe. Second, it re-peoples the history of Fiume, pushing aside the vision of the Italian occupiers and foregrounding the experiences of the kaleidoscope of communities and individuals who called Fiume home. To do this, I have delved into the mundane, into how people lived within, around, and against the state structures they encountered daily in a time of political uncertainty, economic scarcity, and widespread regional upheaval. Chapters on money, law, citizenship, and education and propaganda dissect how and how successfully the city government kept its populace united, fed, and loyal enough to let it continue defying Wilson and pushing for annexation to Italy. These chapters show how locals kept their worlds operating as stably as possible by continuing to use and promote the imperial infrastructures of the former Habsburg

A mother and her children stand alongside Fiume's port, with working men in the background, probably taken in 1920. Though Fiume's industrial port suffered enormously during the period 1918–1921, hosting many more military vessels than commercial ones, its small-owner sailboat trade network in fish, wine, olive oil, and regional agricultural produce continued, sometimes legally, often illicitly.

Empire. Certainly they revamped economic, legal, and cultural institutions to the specificities of time and place, but locals seemed to believe in the efficacy of the newly vanquished imperial models and kept what they could. Seen thus, the immediate post-1918 period is far from the anti-imperial "Wilsonian Moment" that Erez Manela and others have described.[21] Not only did imperial mindsets continue, they may actually have been strengthened, for it was now the former imperial subjects promoting the system, not a metropole forcing them to do so.

Of course, the process of transposing prewar imperial economic, political, and cultural structures was not always smooth. Newly cut off from the vast Habsburg Hungarian Kingdom, Fiume had far fewer resources at its disposal. Habsburg Hungary had encompassed a political

and economic unit of over one hundred thousand square miles inhabited by twenty-one million people. Little eight-square-mile Fiume, with
its fifty thousand inhabitants, had grown because it had access to the
vast financial, commercial, and administrative networks Hungarian
rule provided. Left to its own devices after 1918, Fiume had limited
human, material, or diplomatic resources. The few personnel left in
Fiume were not talented or experienced enough to confront the deba-
cles they faced. Corruption and nepotism abounded, and some of the
new members of the city's government hoped that the city could be
"made Italian" in ways that implied intimidation and violence. But
amazingly, though lacking assets and ruled with a newly nationalist-
oriented government, Fiume's body politic, desperate for a return to
normalcy, took up the reins when and where the state failed. Fiume
from 1918 to 1921 presents the strange phenomenon of a state pulling
itself together as much from below as from above. But not everything
could be negotiated within the framework of a ghost imperial state.
Noting where Fiume's city institutions failed at navigating the immediate postwar period gives us greater insight into why so many
Fiumians, coming from so many different ethnicities and creeds,
supported Italian annexation instead of continuing as they had been
since 1918.

Indeed, the way the city refurbished Habsburg imperial models exposes how particular (and potentially non-nationalist) Fiume's vision
of its future was. If Italian annexation were really the only goal, why
not just replace existing laws and structures with those of the state they
wanted to join? Wouldn't making Fiume work Italian-style have made
the city's incorporation into Italy real in lived terms, rendering Fiume's
contested borders moot, or nearly so? Instead, Fiume's governing elites
spent the years between 1918 and 1921 consolidating a functioning post-
Habsburg, Fiume-specific state system that was Italianized more in
appearance than in content. Local bureaucrats and financial elites were
well aware of the paradoxical methods they were employing. Hiring
practices changed after 1918 expressly to protect Fiumians' jobs against
Italian competition in case incorporation into Italy was achieved.[22]
Leading figures in Fiume's maritime business circles demanded that

laws be attuned to local interests as soon as possible so that once another government (that is, Italy) took over, firm structures that fore-
stalled "national interests" would already be in place.[23] In many respects, Fiume's bid and means for realizing Italian annexation were
closer to a plan to continue autonomy within a large, expanding
kingdom than a move toward national unification. Much as they had
done for decades under the Habsburg Monarchy, Fiumians between
1918 and 1921 struggled to preserve and bolster their autonomy in a
(future) big state, but now under the auspices of nationalism.

By showing a Fiume less entangled with its Italian occupiers, this
history connects Fiume's story with one faced by more than half of
postwar Europe. Looking at Fiume this way emphasizes the consequences of the sudden dissolution of the Romanov, Habsburg, Hohen-
zollern, and Ottoman empires. Over half of Europe's residents found
themselves suddenly without a governing body to administer their
economy, their laws, or their benefits. Wallets were filled with crinkled
currencies of states that no longer existed. Law books spouted principles of now-extinguished monarchies. Citizenship papers that had qual-
ified their holders for state services became worthless memorabilia. No
maps existed of where states began or where merchants could trade. In
these twilight years between the world that was and the world that
would be, everyday Europeans in Fiume and beyond struggled to survive and prosper. Fiume's on-the-ground history is emblematic of the
demands and strategies employed in a world whose ruling empires had
dissolved without new states ready to replace them.

This, then, is the third aim of *The Fiume Crisis*, to re-situate Fiume
in its postwar cultural and geographical context—a Europe without
continental empires. Before 1918, approximately 318 million people lived
within diverse landscapes organized around the infrastructure of continental empire. And like the circa 64 million who had had to defer to
the German kaiser Wilhelm II when his automobile passed, the 52 million who had recited loyalty oaths to the Austro-Hungarian kaiser-könig
Franz Josef when picking up their identity papers, the 181 million who
had used coins engraved with the face of the Russian tsar Nicolas II,
and the 21 million who had publicly acknowledged the sultan in

Istanbul, Mehmed V, for his sponsorship of the building of each new railway station, post-1918 Fiumians found themselves immersed in the workings of a state with no head left to defer to and no deep imperial coffers to keep it going.

Fiume, the smallest of the postwar successor states, offers the perfect opportunity to unearth the tense, pragmatic drama of what it meant to live in the ghost state of empire. Excavating one of the most famous examples of postwar nationalist revolt against Wilsonian diplomacy reminds us that we need to proceed carefully when assuming it was nationality politics that set in motion so many of the difficulties of the postwar successor states. This history of Fiume encourages us to rebel against much of what we have assumed and offers new ways to analyze the postwar histories whose failures would haunt Europe in the decades to come. But before we can understand how the realities of living in a post-state world change our understanding of post-WWI Europe, we must see clearly how the stories we have loved reading and retelling for nearly a hundred years have concealed this reality. Only then can we recognize how an on-the-ground history of this hotspot city challenges how we understand not just what happened there but also what happened throughout post-imperial Europe.

1

Concealing Histories

The Different Fiume Stories

Some stories are just too good not to tell. And Fiume after World War I is one of them. It was a diplomatic debacle that paralyzed the Paris Peace Conference and led indirectly to Japan holding a mandate over part of mainland China. It helped cause the collapse of two Italian governments. It was one of the first places in Catholic Europe to give women the right to vote, not to mention having open homosexuals in charge of military units. Pirates procured food when supplies ran low. Anarchosyndicalists helped write the city's new constitution. Celebrated artists and scientists came to pay their homage to the city's fight against the Great Powers. Cocaine flowed freely among those with the money to pay for it. It all ended with a "Christmas War" in which very few died. And it marked what many see as the birth of charismatic fascism. Unsurprisingly, many historians of interwar Europe use the Fiume Crisis to spice up their narratives. Who can blame them? After all, the spice is real, although much of it was created to keep Fiume in the news in the first place.

The story everyone loves to tell has three different beginnings, depending on which version is being told. The diplomatic debacle story begins in the New York offices of Woodrow Wilson's advisers before the war was even over. The journalistic fanfare and the women's rights story begins in Fiume as soon as fighting ended in late October 1918. The fantastical proto-fascist adventure tale begins in September 1919 when Gabriele D'Annunzio made his entrance. The different start dates indicate the separate morals of each story, the reasons we are still telling them. As such, perhaps it is best to tell them separately, in the order of their different beginnings, so that we can see what is there and what is missing.

Story One: The Diplomatic Debacle and Wilson's Plans for Europe

It is hard to say how much Woodrow Wilson knew about Fiume before he started drafting the Fourteen Points in December 1917. Though he had been to Europe before, he was more drawn to the imposing quads of medieval Oxbridge colleges than to the grit of modern Mediterranean port life. As a voracious reader deeply concerned with America's position in the world, however, he probably noticed that a place called Fiume kept being discussed in economic circles. Before 1917, when Fiume appeared in the *New York Times*, it was usually in pieces about international economic competition and transatlantic immigration. In 1883, for example, readers learned that there was "considerable gossip" about shipments of crude oil in barrels to "Fiume, in the Adriatic," as previously transporting oil that way had seemed like a disaster waiting to happen.[1] In 1896, Wilson's eye might have caught his surname in a Fiume story announcing that "the Wilson Line steamship *Vasco*" had arrived in New York from "Fiume, Austria," carrying well over two thousand tons of beet sugar.[2] In 1904, more than one person thumbing through the dailies probably paused at the headline "Japan Orders Torpedoes in Italy." Reading further, Americans probably felt surprise upon learning that "Japan has sent to Fiume three experts to watch the construction of torpedoes which are to be delivered to the Japanese Government in the next three years."[3] In 1905, an editorial informed all who would listen that Hungary was going to make Fiume its mass emigration port, guaranteeing to send to the United States "not less than 30,000 emigrants a year."[4] In 1910, Fiume's role in moving emigrants across the Atlantic created a worldwide rate war, with the "the Austro-Hungarian Government" offering steamship lines a 20 percent discount if they made Fiume their port of call for shipping Europeans to the United States.[5] The message of these articles and a slew of others could be summed up as follows: Fiume equals new industries, oil, steamships, agricultural export, a torpedo factory, a train hub, an emigration center, big state subsidies, and a money maker.

A careful reader might have noticed that the "where" of Fiume was hazy. Let us remember what those articles were conveying: Fiume was Austria's beet sugar port; Japan sent experts to Fiume, in Italy, for its torpedoes; Hungary contracted with steamship companies promising thirty thousand emigrants out of Fiume a year; and the Austro-Hungarian government lowered the fares for transatlantic travel by 20 percent if you departed from Fiume. Was Fiume part of Austria, Italy, Hungary, or Austria-Hungary? The city was undoubtedly important for the world's increasing globalized trade and immigration. But for someone like Wilson—elected president of Princeton University in 1902, governor of New Jersey in 1910, and president of the United States in 1912—there was probably no need to sort out these complexities. It was enough to know Fiume meant a bustling port, global industry, and plenty of emigrants.

In 1917, as Wilson was preparing what he described as the "objects of the war and the possible basis of a general peace," not knowing where places were, especially busy industrial ports like Fiume, was not just foolish, it was dangerous.[6] In November 1917 Wilson assembled a commission of "experts" in New York City, known as "the Inquiry," to study all the territories that would potentially come under discussion at a peace conference, including Fiume.[7] Wilson wanted "a guaranteed position" on where borders should be made. As he told his Inquiry advisers in December 1918, "Tell me what's right and I'll fight for it."[8] Six specialists were assigned to figure out where Fiume belonged, with another four weighing in when the Paris negotiations got rough.

Wilson's experts included linguists, political scientists, historians, and lawyers. But for Fiume, they were mostly geographers. Fiume was as perplexing to international diplomats as it was to readers of the *New York Times*. This had not always been so. From the revolutions of 1848 until the restructuring of Habsburg lands in 1867, Fiume was administered by the Kingdom of Croatia-Slavonia, even though much of the

town's government and trade were conducted in the lingua franca of
Adriatic urban culture, Italian. This changed in 1867 when Hungary
decided it wanted an industrial Mediterranean port to compete with
Italy's Venice and Austria's Trieste. Through some rather devious diplomacy, Hungarian politicians and Fiume business elites convinced the
Habsburg emperor, Franz Josef, to reinstate the corpus separatum, the
city's pre-Napoleonic status. The 7.56-square-mile city core, with its
relatively deep-water port, would be removed from Croatian oversight
and function as a semi-independent city-state governed by an Italian-
language municipal council and a Hungarian governorship directly responsible to Budapest.[9] Since then, Fiume existed outside the strictures of regional governance. It was administered by the city's economic
elite and directives from far-off Budapest. The Fiumara (called the Eneo
in Italian, the Rječina in Croatian, and the Recsina in Hungarian)—a
small river flowing to the Adriatic through a valley east of the city
center—was designated as the border between Hungarian corpus separatum Fiume and the Kingdom of Croatia-Slavonia to its east. With
the new designation, Hungarian money came flowing in, helping to set
up railways, expand ports, install tram lines, and build state-of-the-art
factories, refineries, institutes, banks, a hospital, and an emigration
center. All that building and investment quickly attracted people from
all over the Adriatic, as well as from central, eastern, and southeastern
Europe.[10] By 1890, over half of Fiume's population had been born outside the city. Before Hungary reinstated the corpus separatum, Fiume
was a smallish port town of seventeen thousand. Once separated from
the lands, laws, and policies surrounding it and pumped full of money
and opportunities from the metropole, Fiume became an international industrial port—the ninth largest in continental Europe—with
triple the population (over fifty thousand) when Wilson's experts began
studying it.

Fiume's rise might have been the result of economic, political, and
administrative separation from the regions surrounding it, but this divide did not extend to daily life. Fiumian and Hungarian officials tried
to bolster administrative separateness from the neighboring Croatian
and Slovene countrysides by restricting the languages of trade and ed-

View of the Dead Canal, the small-boat harbor situated between Fiume and
Sušak where the Fiumara emptied out into the Adriatic until the river's outlet
into the sea was diverted in the mid-nineteenth century. To the right, the wood
emporium. In the distance, the bridge connecting the two towns with the Croatian hill town of Trsat above. To the left, Fiume's riverbank, a site of informal
regional trade.

ucation to either Italian or Hungarian. Nonetheless, people of all tongues
congregated, worked, and invested in the city, speaking the city's
local Fiumian (Italianate) dialect, standard Italian, Croatian, Slovene,
Hungarian, German, Czech, Romanian, and Yiddish.[11] This cosmopolitan language culture was not the remnant of pre-1867 networks, but,
like the rest of the city's changes, the result of Fiume's boom. And as
Fiume's population grew, so, too, did that of the cheaper outskirts in
the Austrian-held lands to its west and the Croatian-held lands to its
east. Most of these outskirts were agriculturally oriented suburbs
that fed the industrial core with food and labor. But just across the Fiumara River to Fiume's immediate east, Sušak—a satellite city of circa
twelve thousand inhabitants—flourished under Croatian administrative

guidance. In Sušak, Croatian laws and taxes ordered the city and Croatian served as the primary language of government and education. As the Kingdom of Croatia-Slavonia was also part of Hungary's Crown of St. Stephen, movement—whether of peoples or goods—was very easy between the city, Fiume, and its satellite, Sušak.[12]

Italian/Hungarian Fiume and Croatian Sušak grew in tandem, connected by two bridges and a railway line that went from Fiume through Sušak and on to Budapest via Zagreb. Port workers, fishermen, vegetable sellers, schoolchildren, and domestic servants crossed back and forth over these bridges every day. Affluent businessmen looking for the nicest views and the best topographies built their villas on both sides of the Fiumara. Industries, too, expanded their warehouses along both sides of the river.[13] At the beginning of the twentieth century, Fiume was Hungary's second-biggest capital producer (after Budapest), and Sušak was Croatia's second biggest (after Zagreb).[14] By 1918, when Wilson's team of geographers were trying to decide where Fiume should sit on a map, they also had to decide whether Fiume should be treated as just the tightly defined entity the Hungarians had nurtured or as the center of a larger region that included Sušak and the other nearby villages that were growing year by year.

Wilson's geographers consulted histories in English, German, French, and Italian; geographical analyses; and Austro-Hungarian statistical reports.[15] The Inquiry also studied the treatises that the Italian and the Serb-Croat-Slovene delegations at the Paris Peace Conference had written to explain why Fiume should be given to Italy or to the newly forming Kingdom of Serbs, Croats, and Slovenes, respectively. The Italian delegation wanted Fiume counted as a separate entity. The Serb-Croat-Slovene delegation wanted Fiume, Sušak, and the remaining hinterlands to be counted as one metropolitan area. Both delegations saw the dispute of how to define Fiume's borders as intrinsically linked to which entity would have a greater "ethnic right" to claim its incorporation into its respective state. If Fiume was limited to just its core, without Sušak and the remaining hinterlands, then the majority of the population would be composed of those who spoke Italian as their mother tongue. If Fiume were extended to include Sušak and the hinterlands, there would be a majority of those who spoke Croatian or Slovene as their mother tongue. Along with academic specialists, Inquiry experts also commissioned journalists and American military personnel to travel to Fiume to assess the city's infrastructure and local sentiments.[16] The reports regularly noted that "nationality in Fiume is poorly defined," with "numerous cases in which families were divided" between national loyalties. American on-the-ground reports echoed the opinion that Fiumians desired "a more or less autonomous form of government. The degree of autonomy proposed varies from the complete independence under international guarantee . . . to the limited form of a 'free port' under the mandatory of either Italy or Jugoslavia."[17]

Geographically speaking, the Inquiry specialists spent an absurd amount of time explaining why they did not consider the Fiumara River a real divider between Fiume and Sušak. Multiple American reports insisted that Sušak was not a satellite city but a "mere suburb." In these analyses, the Fiumara was downgraded from its status as a river that powered Fiume's many mills to little more than a "creek."[18] Wilson's chief territorial adviser in Paris, Professor Isaiah Bowman, probably explained the Fiume-Sušak issue to the president much as he did in the textbook he published while the final peace treaties were being signed: "Many persons talk loosely of Sušak as if it were another city separated from Fiume by a river. As a matter of fact, only a shallow brook separates the two; Sušak is as much part of Fiume as Brooklyn is a part of New York."[19] There is something amusing about comparing 1919 Brooklyn, with its two million inhabitants, to Sušak, with its circa twelve thousand, but the point was clear to all who participated in the US intelligence meetings: Fiume was not a singular, isolated place. It was the Manhattan to a larger, interdependent, metropolitan area, and Sušak was no Newark, but just another borough within a similar New York river-city system.

The Inquiry experts went through all the reasons *New York Times* readers would have assumed Fiume was part of Austria, Italy, Hungary, or Austria-Hungary and came up with the answer that, after the war to end all wars, it was in everyone's best interest that Fiume should belong to none of those lands. The Inquiry assured Wilson (with reams of

paper, maps, and statistics to back it up) that with the Habsburg Monarchy dissolved in October 1918, Fiume should be added to the new
Kingdom of Serbs, Croats, and Slovenes. Just as they had argued in
their preliminary reports, the six geographers assigned to the Fiume
case said that nationality could not determine what state the city should
be joined to, as no matter where Fiume sat on a map, many, if not most,
of its inhabitants would be living in a national state with which they
would not identify. Commercially, however, Fiume's role in the viability
of the new Kingdom of Serbs, Croats, and Slovenes was easy to understand. The Inquiry experts supported Wilson's opinion that the Austrian-
held port of Trieste should be incorporated into the Kingdom of Italy.
But in their minds that needed to be balanced by giving the Hungarian
port of Fiume to the Kingdom of Serbs, Croats, and Slovenes. Not only
would this help the struggling new kingdom to prosper; it would keep
the landlocked markets of Austria, Hungary, and Czechoslovakia from
falling under Italian monopoly. As they put it concisely in the little
"Black Book" defining US peace aims in January 1919, Fiume should
belong to the Kingdom of Serbs, Croats, and Slovenes because it was
"vital to the interests of the latter, and likewise assures to the more remote hinterland, including Austria and Hungary, the advantages of
two competing ports under the control of different nations."[20] These
were precisely the kinds of free-trade arguments Wilson appreciated,
and he went into the Paris Peace Conference convinced he had a strong
"guaranteed position" on Fiume.

Wilson received the first determination on Fiume from his experts in
January 1919 and then a supplementary (but almost identical) judg-
ment in March 1919. But he had given his Fourteen Points a year earlier,
when the Austro-Hungarian Monarchy still existed and Italy was among
the Entente allies losing most in the battle against it. Wilson's January 1918 Fourteen Points led everyone in Europe to expect him to
take a different position on the Fiume issue. The Wilson whom Europeans expected in 1919 was the one who had promised in 1918 that "in
determining all such questions of sovereignty the interests of the population concerned must have equal weight with the equitable claims of
the government whose title is to be determined."[21] He added that "the

Picture taken from the uppermost reaches of Sušak, showing, left to right, Sušak, the Fiumara River's outlet to the sea, the Delta (where the border post between Sušak and Fiume was located), the Baross port (dedicated to the import and export of wood), the Dead Canal (which functioned as a small boat port), and Fiume's main port. Disagreements about whether Fiume functioned as a separate town or as a condominium town with Sušak were not just political but represented strong economic, communication, and trade concerns.

peoples of Austria-Hungary . . . should be accorded the freest opportunity of autonomous development," and "a re-adjustment of the frontiers of Italy" would be promoted "along clearly recognizable lines of nationality."[22] In short, in 1918 Wilson had promised that there would be an "autonomous" determination of government among the lands of Austria-Hungary, as well as an expansion of Italian borders based on nationality arguments. Fiume was a part of Austria-Hungary that already functioned as a semiautonomous city-state. More than half of its population (setting aside the satellite city Sušak) was considered Italian. Given these facts, in 1918 Wilson would surely have been open to letting the Fiumians decide if they should be joined to Italy.

Was it naïveté or cunning on Wilson's part to promise "autonomous determination" even as he hired an army of experts to give him "guaranteed positions"? Hundreds of Wilson scholars have studied his dealings at the Paris Peace Conference, but seen through the lens of the Fiume debacle, the answer seems to be both.[23] Wilson's naïveté stemmed from his belief that nationality numbers and economic rationality indicated which government a people would want. So, in charging the Inquiry to give him hard facts, Wilson thought he was opening the door to "autonomous determination." On the other hand, in assigning his experts to put together a policy book for American peace aims, Wilson also showed his awareness that his Entente allies would be fighting for terms and territories that did not accord with the Fourteen Points values they had agreed to when proclaiming they wanted to make a peace to end all wars.[24] Wilson wanted to be ready to fight off the expansionist aims of his British, French, Italian, and Japanese allies and the secret treaties they had concluded to make the war a profitable undertaking. He saw himself as a lone soldier in the battle to defend the prospects of the newly formed "smaller states" that would have little voice in the day-to-day negotiations. Naively, he thought that acting on the numbers his experts had provided meant he was doing precisely what people on the ground would want.

Strangely enough, it was not the negotiations over Germany, Poland, the Middle East, colonial Africa, or Bolshevik Russia that showcased how the clash between 1918 self-determination diplomat Wilson and 1919 expert-armed Wilson could lead to a breakdown of the Great Power peace negotiations. Instead it was Wilson's confrontation with the Italian delegation over Fiume that led him to threaten abandoning the peace conference in April 1919.[25] Days after Wilson's threat, everyone in Paris would be flummoxed when the Italian delegation actually did depart (the only Great Power walkout during the entire year of negotiations). How could a peace treaty with Germany be pushed through or a League of Nations be founded if the Entente could not stick together long enough to decide something as relatively minor as the fate of Fiume? Things got so bad, in fact, that British prime minister David Lloyd George famously characterized the heated April 1919 weeks of international deadlock over Fiume as "a comparatively trivial issue upon which to wreck a peace settlement for the world."[26]

The Italian delegation left for two reasons: one territorial, the other diplomatic. The territorial issue was that Wilson's denial of Italy's demands seemed based on contradictory arguments. Italian diplomats insisted they should be allowed to incorporate Fiume because half its population was considered Italian and Fiume's government had declared its desire to be joined to Italy according to their "rights of self-determination." If the Paris Peace Conference was about sovereignty, nationality, and the rights of self-determination, why would Fiume not be incorporated into Italy? Time and again, Wilson responded by indicating there was not enough of a majority in Fiume to determine nationality or self-determination rights and thus nationality could not determine its borders. This being the case, Wilson argued, questions of regional commerce and the financial viability of the newly formed successor state of the Kingdom of Serbs, Croats, and Slovenes needed to supersede.

Wilson's position on Fiume galled the Italians because he had already denied many of their other demands on nationality grounds. Italy had not joined the Entente allies in 1914, declaring neutrality. It joined the Entente in April 1915, when France, the United Kingdom, and Russia secretly promised it enormous territorial gains in the northern Alpine region and along the eastern seaboard of the Adriatic (not including Fiume).[27] Wilson respected Italy's claims in the Alps, and France and the United Kingdom seemed willing to respect the 1915 London Treaty terms on the eastern Adriatic seaboard territories. Wilson, however, was not willing to hand over the eastern Adriatic to Italy. His adamant stance was reasonable. Aside from Italian communities in some of the sea towns, the lands in question (most of Dalmatia) were overwhelmingly populated by Serbo-Croatian speakers. Giving Dalmatia and its islands to Italy looked to Wilson like an act of imperialism. Putting hundreds of thousands of Serbo-Croatian speakers under Italian rule because of secret treaties that prewar empires had made did not cohere with Fourteen Points values. Wilson did not just want to take a stand against Italy's demands in the eastern Adriatic; he felt morally obligated to do so.

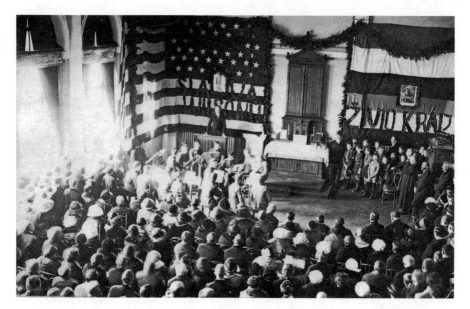

A Serb-Croat-Slovene nationalist rally, probably held in Sušak in spring 1919.
At rear left is an American flag, backward, with a portrait of Woodrow Wilson
and the words "Glory be to Wilson." On the right is a Serb-Croat-Slovene flag,
with a portrait of King Peter I and the words "Long live the king." Though
Italian nationalists had come to hate Wilson by April 1919, Serb-Croat-Slovene
nationalists concerned about the future of Fiume still put faith in him.

For the Italian delegation, Wilson's peace terms seemed like a lose-
lose situation. No Fiume, for pragmatic reasons that discounted nationality and self-determination arguments. Yet at the same time, nationality arguments were being used to prevent the full honoring of the
treaty that brought Italy into the war in the first place. Looking at the
tremendous gains of France and Great Britain in colonial matters and
the border readjustments with Germany, Italian politicians and hundreds of journalists back home agreed: the Paris Peace Conference was
rigged in favor of the strongest Great Powers and against the less
powerful ones. In May 1919, Lloyd George responded to the heavily
publicized Italian charges by suggesting that perhaps "the Italian griev-
ance was not limited to the single question of Fiume but arose from the
fact that they 'were not being treated quite as a great first-class power.'

No one had offered them a mandate."[28] Hoping Lloyd George was right, Wilson and French prime minister Georges Clemenceau joined him in floating the idea of giving Italy a mandate over a large section of southern Anatolia (today's Turkey) and the Caucasus region— territories containing important ports, oil fields, coal mines, and thousands of square miles inhabited by tens of thousands of people—in exchange for a compromise on Fiume. To everyone's frustration, Italian prime minister Vittorio Orlando quickly made it clear he "really did not care a scrap about Asia Minor if he could get Fiume."[29]

As Orlando told the other Great Power delegates, Fiume had come to symbolize the growing sense among many Italians that the peace negotiations were forcing Italy into what many termed "a mutilated victory," echoing a verse Gabriele D'Annunzio had recently coined. Over and over the populist Italian press questioned why Italy had suffered almost a million in military and civilian deaths, along with spiraling debt and inflation, if it were not to get what it had been promised for joining the war. Italian citizens fought in World War I because their country called them to arms. In 1915 the Italian government explained that war was necessary to secure more defendable borders and to "liberate" Italian speakers from foreign (then Habsburg) rule. The Italian delegation refused to sign peace treaties without the territorial advances they had been promised. And an ever-growing sector of Italian voters indicated that the only successful peace would be one where Italian speakers, like those in Fiume, were under Italian rule. Though Italy had not been promised Fiume in the 1915 treaty, the constant reports of the city's "demand to be joined to Italy" convinced many that peace without Fiume was immoral. As Prime Minister Orlando pointed out again and again, "The question of Fiume was raised by the city itself," and thus "Italian public opinion had made Fiume a national question, and that as not only the United States but also Italy's allies had refused to concede this point, it was useless to continue the conversations until he had put the case before Italy."[30]

In the weeks before the Italian delegation left, Wilson's response to these arguments fluctuated between incomprehension, annoyance, and disgust. He trusted the expert reports he had been given countering the

Italian claims and was quick to point out that in 1915 Italy had shown no particular interest in Fiume, regardless of how many Italian speakers lived there. Why should this so-called nationality argument be taken at face value? Was Italy not just making a grab for a monopoly on Adriatic trade? Representatives from the Kingdom of Serbs, Croats, and Slovenes had made that argument often in separate meetings with US, British, and French statesmen throughout the peace conference. Italian delegates had not been present at these meetings because they refused to recognize the new Kingdom of Serbs, Croats, and Slovenes as an Entente ally, citing that until 1918 almost half of this new kingdom's population had been under Habsburg rule and had fought against Italy.[31] This left Wilson to voice Serb-Croat-Slovene claims on their behalf, ones that ran precisely counter to those of the Italians. He insisted time and time again that the new Kingdom of Serbs, Croats, and Slovenes would be defenseless without control of the eastern Adriatic shore, that their commercial prospects would be dire without the port of Fiume, and that if he gave into Italian demands, hundreds of thousands more Croats and Slovenes would be ruled by Italy than Italians would be ruled by them.

With US, British, and French brokering, it seemed a compromise on the eastern Adriatic seaboard was possible. But not over Fiume. When at one of the last joint meetings Italy's prime minister responded to Wilson's intransigence with enraged tears, Wilson decided to give up trying to negotiate and instead to reach out directly to the Italian people. Surely, he thought, he could convince everyday Italians that their state's claims on Fiume were unjust and that they should encourage their statesmen to be satisfied with what they had received for their war sacrifices, instead of pushing greedily for things they did not deserve and would not get.

Wilson's press release to the Italian people on April 23, 1919, was the last straw for the Italian delegation. Never before had a country's leader sidestepped the representatives of an allied country with whom they were negotiating. Such a bad-faith move was something leaders on warring sides did when they believed diplomats were not honestly representing their citizens. Wilson had been warned by his advisers and by

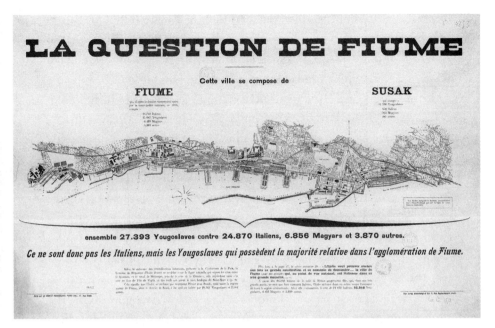

Map of Fiume-Sušak produced by the Serb-Croat-Slovene delegation during the Paris Peace Conference, published in 1920 and distributed to the international press and the French, US, and UK delegations. The map emphasizes that Fiume and Sušak are one interdependent unit, with a majority Slavic-speaking population. Below the numbers of Yugoslavs versus Italians, Hungarians, and others, it states, "It is therefore not the Italians, but the Yugoslavs who are the majority in the urban area of Fiume." The use of "Yugoslav" as a nationality category instead of Serb, Croat, or Slovene was typical for the time to emphasize the unitary quality of the "South Slav nation" (the meaning of "Yugoslavia" in English), but Yugoslavia was not the official name of the country until 1929.

the leaders of France and the United Kingdom that this would have explosive consequences, but he thought it was worth a try. He had visited Italy briefly in early January 1919 and had been touched by the hundreds of parades in his honor, the flowers, and the "Viva Wilson" signs that had greeted him. He was sure that if he could reason directly with the Italian public, he could convince them he was fighting for exactly what they had celebrated in him: a world of peace, justice, and protection of the small and big alike. In Wilson's mind, it was Italy's delegation that was blocking justice, and the Italians could do something about it. And so, brimming with sentimentality and certainty, Wilson told Italian readers that Fiume "must serve as the outlet and inlet of the commerce, not of Italy, but of the lands to the north and northeast of that port: Hungary, Bohemia, Roumania, and the states of the new Jugo-Slavic group."[32]

Within hours of the publication of Wilson's appeal, the entire Italian delegation left the Paris Peace Conference. They had already threatened to leave over Fiume, but now that Wilson had flouted diplomatic norms and insinuated that the Italian government did not represent the wishes of the Italian people, there was little reason to stay. Wilson was not overtly perturbed by their departure. As he told his chief press secretary, he did "not care so much" except "for the effect it may have in Germany" (which was preparing to come to Paris to sign the Versailles Treaty).[33] What shocked and dismayed him was that Italians did not respond as he had hoped; they almost unanimously sided with their government against Wilson. Immediately upon arriving in Rome, the Italian delegation called for a vote of confidence in Parliament, which it received overwhelmingly, along with acclaim from hordes of Italians who jeered Wilson in the streets of Rome, Florence, Milan, and Turin.

The Italian delegation returned to the peace treaty negotiations a few weeks later, partly to have some say in how the spoils of the German, Ottoman, and Austro-Hungarian territories were to be distributed, and partly out of fear of economic retribution from US creditors. But the Fiume issue was even more unresolved now that the Italian delegation could say confidently that they were doing exactly what their compatriots wanted. Wilson continued to insist that Italy would not get Fiume "so long as I am here," and the Italian delegation kept pushing for the platform "lands of the 1915 Treaty + Fiume."[34] Every time negotiations were resumed, they failed. Italians at home eventually became so frustrated with their government's deadlock in Paris that they voted Orlando out in June 1919, replacing him with a more economically oriented, US-friendly government under the leadership of Prime Minister Francesco Saverio Nitti. And when the situation was still unresolved a year later, Nitti's government, too, was pushed out. Meanwhile, Wilson had to bow out of the Fiume negotiations when it became clear that the US Congress would not support much of what he was doing in Paris.

In November 1920, without Wilson there to support it against Italy's claims, the Kingdom of Serbs, Croats, and Slovenes agreed to much of what Italy wanted in terms of the 1915 treaty. It was decided that neither state should have Fiume, which was declared a city-state under League of Nations and Italian supervision.

Wilson's leadership over the Fiume debacle in Paris did not resolve where Fiume should sit on a map, but it had other consequences. First, after the Italians left, in order to keep the Paris Peace Conference together, Wilson became much more amenable to other thorny questions of Great Power expansion, especially regarding Japan. Before the Italians left, the president had been adamant that Japan should not gain control of Germany's former concessions in mainland China. But the United Kingdom and France had promised Japan control of this territory to get it to join the Entente war effort in 1914, much as they had promised Italy most of the Adriatic to hasten its entry. Wilson's arguments against Japan's demands were strikingly similar to those he had made against the Italians: national sovereignty trumped prewar international treaties, and it was unjust to put nearly one hundred thousand Chinese under Japanese control. With the Italians absent, the pressure to keep the peace conference together long enough to sign the German treaty made Wilson relent as he had refused to do with the Italians.[35] As Wilson's chief geographic adviser put it, "The purely local problem of Fiume involved the purely local problem of Shantung [Shandong]!"[36] Without the Fiume debacle, Germany's holdings on the Shandong Peninsula would probably have returned to China rather than become a Japanese mandate. Not only would this have changed the lives of over one hundred thousand Chinese, it would have avoided triggering the anti-imperialist outcry in China that many argue was the first time Chinese nationalism had been linked with global anti-imperialism.[37]

Another consequence of the Fiume debacle hit Wilson closer to home. The United States counted almost four million American citizens who were Italian born. In January 1919, many Italian-Americans had cheered Wilson for what his Fourteen Points seemed to promise for their brethren back home. By April 1919, when Wilson's message about Fiume was made public, these same Italian-Americans condemned him for

anti-Italian prejudice. Senator Henry Cabot Lodge, along with other
rival political leaders, jumped on the Fiume bandwagon to gain the
support of these newly disaffected Italo-American communities, calling
out in Congress and on the pages of American newspapers that "if Italy
is of opinion that it is necessary to her safety and for her protection
that she should hold Fiume, I am clearly of the opinion that it should be
hers, especially as the people of Fiume, I understand, have voted to join
with Italy."[38] Thanks in part to Lodge's rabble-rousing, Fiume exacerbated Wilson's many difficulties in shoring up support at home for his
peace plan.

   More broadly, the question of how the Fiume issue could have risked
"wreck[ing] a peace settlement for the world" has led historians to ask
whether Wilson could ever have pulled off a Fourteen Points peace and
the League of Nations he envisioned. Clearly, his combination of naïveté and cunning about how justice would be determined did not
help. But there was something deeper going on. Why did the complete
breakdown of negotiations occur around Fiume and not Alsace-
Lorraine, Ireland, Syria, the Polish corridor, Palestine, or even Shandong? At the time, a member of Wilson's Inquiry team remarked that
"having fornicated with France and England for four months, Wilson
is attempting to re-establish his virtue at the expense of Italy."[39] In
short, Wilson ignored most of his Fourteen Points values in negotiations with the United Kingdom and France, but with Italy he reclaimed
his moral ground. Historian Daniela Rossini notes this same motive
force behind the Fiume debacle but expresses it the other way around:
Wilson let the Fiume question become an "issue to wreck world peace"
because he did not believe in the Italian government's capacity to oppose
American will.[40]

   It is true that many of Italy's demands were entirely imperialist, but so
were those of France, the United Kingdom, and Japan. The real reasons
for Wilson's intransigence were, first, that he saw Italy's political institutions as backward, and, second, that Italy depended on US money
and grain. Wilson did not fight as hard against France, the United
Kingdom, and Japan, even though their aims were equally (if not more)
imperialist and land-grabbing.[41] Fiume became for Wilson the symbol

of his willingness to stand up against imperialism and old-style secret diplomacy precisely because he saw Italy as the one imperial power he could beat. He fought for right when he knew he had enough might. In situations in which US might was less clear, right became less of a priority. Looking at the diplomatic history of the Paris Peace Conference through the lens of the Fiume debacle, Wilson's plans for Europe and a world without war seem even more doomed than they are usually depicted. He did not fail just because no one else fought by his side. He floundered because he fought over small things he thought he could win, while shying away from many of the controversies that would loom so large in the century that followed.

Story Two: Self-Determination and the Press

Of the three stories regularly told about Fiume, the on-the-ground story is the least coherent: it pops up out of nowhere onto the world stage in October 1918 and disappears behind the D'Annunzio extravaganza story in September 1919. But many of the international clashes around Fiume were fueled by a sense that what was happening on the ground made the city's future impossible to determine. As mentioned, American military personnel in the city reported Fiumians' desire for "a more or less autonomous form of government . . . [perhaps] under the mandatory of either Italy or Jugoslavia." Italian diplomats explained that "the question of Fiume was raised by the city itself." Serb-Croat-Slovene diplomats emphasized that only by assigning Fiume to their kingdom could the city be secured its own "right to live." When D'Annunzio and his followers entered Fiume in September 1919, they insisted they had abandoned everything and marched to the port city because "Fiume is today the symbol of liberty," the liberty, in other words, to make Fiumians' *own* push for Italian self-determination real.[42] These reports fed the strategies against Wilsonian diplomacy and supported the tale of D'Annunzio's proto-fascism, propelling Fiume into the larger narrative of interwar Europe. In a sense, there would have been no "Fiume stories" without this founding lore of Fiume as a local problem that could not be solved or ignored.

The local version of the saga begins with the end of the Habsburg Monarchy. The fact that no one can say precisely when that happened explains some of the confusion about the events of autumn 1918.[43] On October 16, in order to make a separate peace with the Entente, Habsburg emperor Karl conceded autonomy to the peoples of Austria, as required by Wilson's Fourteen Points. Two days later, on October 18, 42-year-old Fiume-born businessman Andrea Ossoinack—the official Fiume representative to Budapest's Hungarian parliament—announced that "since Austria-Hungary in its offer of peace has accepted people's rights to self-determination as proclaimed by Wilson, also Fiume as a corpus separatum claims for itself this right."[44] Ossoinack's fellow Hungarian deputies dismissed his declaration, reminding him that Emperor Karl had promised autonomy to the peoples of *Austria*, not Hungary, and thus the promise did not extend to Hungary's internal political situation. Austria-Hungary might have sued for peace, but only the peoples of Austria had been granted autonomy, and Fiume was part of Hungary, not Austria.

Four days later, on October 22, rallies were held in Zagreb, Croatia, demanding the formation of a separate Slovene-Croat-Serb state (that would include Fiume), led by a Zagreb-based national council and severed completely from Hungarian control.[45] The next day, on October 23, hundreds of Habsburg soldiers stationed in Fiume attended a rally supporting the Zagreb declaration in Croatian-held Sušak (a ten-minute walk from their Fiume barracks). The soldiers returned to Fiume hoisting the blue, white, and red flags of the South Slav national movement. When Hungarian police forces in Fiume tried to compel the soldiers to relinquish the flags, an armed conflict ensued that led to mutinies, looting, and attacks on the Fiume jails to free prisoners and destroy police files.

Five days after that, on October 28, the foreign minister of Austria-Hungary contacted the United States to negotiate a separate peace from Germany. The next day, Hungarian military personnel and administrators in Fiume formally renounced control of the city and invited representatives from Zagreb's National Council to take the place of the Hungarian governorship to restore order to Fiume. The 50-year-old

Fiume-born lawyer, publicist, and South Slav national activist Rikard Lenac was proclaimed *veliki župan* (county prefect) of a jointly administered Fiume and Sušak, where "fellow citizens" were reassured in both Italian and Croatian that "in the name of Zagreb's National Council of Slovenes, Croats, and Serbs . . . all citizens are guaranteed inviolable and honorable rights to personal freedom and property, without distinction of nationality."[46] One day later, on October 30, members of Fiume's municipal government and leading Italian national activists declared the formation of their own Italian National Council, electing the prominent 69-year-old local physician Antonio Grossich as its president. The 28-year-old Fiume-born lawyer Salvatore Bellasich led the public rally, proclaiming that the "Italian National Council of Fiume . . . demands for itself the right to the self-determination of peoples. Basing itself on that right, the Italian National Council proclaims Fiume united to her Motherland, Italy . . . [and] puts her decision under the protection of America, mother of liberty."[47] That same night, Fiume's Workers' Council (whose leaders gave speeches in Italian, Croatian, and Hungarian) also demanded Fiume's rights to self-determination, but instead of supporting either national council, the Workers' Council called for a citywide plebiscite, open to all men and women above the age of 18, of any nationality, who could prove city residency of at least one year.[48]

It is difficult, if not impossible, to clarify this confusion. Between October 18 and October 30, four different Fiumian entities declared four different forms of Fiume "self-determination," all using Wilson's Fourteen Points to justify their actions. On October 18 Ossoinack (a longstanding voice of Fiume's business elite) declared Fiume a legally independent state entity, using Emperor Karl's pronouncement and Fiume's status as a semiautonomous, Italian-speaking city as his rationale. On October 29 Lenac (a successful lawyer with a thriving firm on Fiume's main thoroughfare) declared Fiume part of the newly forming Kingdom of Serbs, Croats, and Slovenes, based on the Zagreb National Council's claims that Fiume was a natural "ethnographic" part of mainland Croatia. Lenac's declaration was backed by the departing Hungarian administration, mutinous Habsburg troops still stationed in

the city, arriving Serb troops, and local and regional South Slav national activists. On October 30 Grossich (Fiume's most famous scientist,
head surgeon of its city hospital, and, through marriage, a member of
one of the city's most prestigious families) declared Fiume temporarily
independent until it could be formally joined to the Kingdom of Italy,
basing this on the fact that, with Hungary out of power, the Fiume
municipality was the only legitimate governing body that could determine the future of this "naturally" Italian city. Grossich's declaration
was backed by the Fiume municipal council, local and regional Italian
national activists, and (within days) shiploads of Italian soldiers newly
docked at Fiume's port. At the same time, the Fiume Workers' Council
(backed only by the many hundreds attending its rally) declared Fiume's independence, demanding that its political future be determined
by plebiscite under the protection of the Socialist International.[49] Again,
the question of where Fiume belonged arose, but this time the ques-
tioners were not readers of the *New York Times* or diplomats in Paris.
Local Fiumians had a variety of answers of their own.

There were many ways this situation could have turned out, as we
know from the numerous other disputed multiethnic areas after World
War I. An all-out bloody battle could have erupted, as happened in
Ukraine, Transylvania, and Anatolia. Diplomats could have immediately ruled on which claimant would be recognized internationally, as
happened in Alsace-Lorraine, the Sudetenland, and South Tyrol. A local
plebiscite could have been held to determine borders, as happened in the
Schleswig and Carinthia regions. But none of these happened in Fiume,
mostly for geographic reasons: as it was surrounded by mountains and
situated right on a sea, navies were able to reach it faster than armies.
Within days of the four different self-determination movements going
public, Italian, French, British, and American ships descended on Fiume's port, all trying to ensure that the others would not hold too much
sway over the final determination of where Fiume should sit on the map.

By mid-November 1918, Fiume witnessed a strange smorgasbord of
uniformed men walking its quays, promenades, and alleyways, all supposedly joined in an Inter-Allied coalition to keep peace until the Paris
peacemakers decided what to do. Some initiatives ensured that mili-

tary forces worked together—for instance, by assigning joint US, Italian, French, and British patrols of the city and its immediate hinterlands. But more often than not, the different troops worked separately. This was especially true because the Italians sent far more troops than anyone else, with the French sending more than the British and Americans combined, but far fewer than the Italians. This imbalance rendered joint patrols impossible and ensured that clashes of national interests, expectations, stereotypes, and separate commands jostled against each other and kept Fiume's day-to-day Inter-Allied occupation unstable.

Fiume did not serve as a passive checkerboard where the drama of Italian, French, British, and American interests played out. Instead, local activists tried to align themselves with the different Entente powers that had descended on the town in order to further their agendas. Fiumians pushing for annexation to the Kingdom of Italy—spearheaded by the Italian National Council, veterans who had volunteered to fight for Italy during the war, and activists working for regional nationalist groups such as Trento-Trieste—easily convinced the Italian military command that the city's cultural heritage and economic future depended on being joined to Italy.[50] The French military command heard most from those in favor of annexation to the Kingdom of Serbs, Croats, and Slovenes, with arguments emphasizing how Fiume was culturally more Slav than Italian not just because of its urban makeup but thanks to the daily interactions between the city, the port, and the hinterland, which was predominantly Croatian and Slovene. French troops also were regularly warned that economically consigning Fiume to Italy would upset a balance of Adriatic and greater Mediterranean trade (a major concern for the French).[51] American and British military personnel heard from both of these factions but also were the particular target of outspoken locals who wanted Fiume turned into an international city-state. Businessmen and even socialists tried to convince American and British representatives that the city—with its history of relative autonomy and peoples of different creeds and heritages united by a Mediterranean, trade-oriented, Italianate culture—could only prosper if its port and commerce were open to all and its communities not forced to live within the strictures of any one nation.[52] These three paths for Fiume's postwar period were not equally matched in on-the-ground local enthusiasm (as mentioned earlier, the pro-Italy platform was by far the most widespread), but all three camps tried to secure Inter-Allied backing. Soon global tensions among the Allied commands were replicated in local tensions over Fiume's fate. And the global press reporting from the standpoint of the diverse Allied commands painted a confusing picture of "what Fiumians want" to their many readerships.

The first political consequences of the Inter-Allied troops' arrival were the ousting of the National Council of Slovenes, Croats, and Serbs from Fiume's Governor's Palace, the partial silencing of the socialist-oriented Workers' Council, and the installation of the Italian National Council as the de facto government of postwar Fiume. None of these initiatives were voted in. Fiumians did not unseat either national council—for that matter, they had not installed them; both were self-proclaimed governmental entities.[53] The Serb-Croat-Slovene group had taken the power given to it by the exiting Hungarians and had con-solidated its offices thanks to the military support of the ex-Habsburg (mostly Croatian) troops and the entering Serb troops arriving in the region. The Italian National Council had anchored itself in and ex-panded around the preexisting municipal government. It was the ar-rival of troops from the Kingdom of Italy (the first of the Inter-Allied forces to disembark onto Fiume soil) that had consolidated the power of the Italian National Council. Italian soldiers basically escorted the *veliki župan* Rikard Lenac to Sušak and replaced the Serb-Croat-Slovene flags on the Governor's Palace with Italian ones. In early No-vember 1919, the Inter-Allied commands set up two different national councils on either side of the Fiumara River, recognizing the Italian Na-tional Council as Fiume's provisional governing body and the Serb-Croat-Slovene National Council as Sušak's—both without a plebiscite. None of the Inter-Allied commands supported the call by Fiume's Workers' Council for international recognition of Fiume as a "free, in-dependent republic under the protection of the Socialist Interna-tional," and socialist participation in both governments was limited.[54]

The two national councils ruled on opposite banks of the Fiumara River, but neither Fiumians, Sušačani (residents of Sušak), nor the troops stationed in the region lived in separation. The bridges connecting Fiume to Sušak remained open, with Inter-Allied officers checking papers just as Hungarian officials had done previously. Schoolchildren, workers, family members, and the entire marketplace continued to cross back and forth as they always had. Fiumians with different aspirations for the city's future lived and worked together. Italian, French, British, American, and Serb troops socialized with a variety of Fiumians and Sušačani in the cafés, bars, bakeries, and squares on both sides of the bridge.[55] Fiume's multiethnic tapestry remained, made even more varied by all the different tongues spoken by Inter-Allied troops, not just Italian, English, and French but the many dialects of the Serb troops stationed outside Sušak and the languages of France's colonial "recruits" from Southeast Asia.

In the ten months that Fiume was occupied by Inter-Allied forces, political activity exploded. The Italian National Council did whatever possible to appear as the only legitimate governmental organ. Antonio Grossich was made president for his prestige: the world-renowned inventor of the first on-contact antiseptic, an elderly liberal associated with Fiume's decades-long battles for increased autonomy within the Hungarian state, and a man deeply committed to his Italianness and, by extension, the Italianness of Fiume, Grossich offered much to reassure locals and onlookers alike.[56] The simultaneous reconfirmation of 43-year-old Fiume-born Antonio Vio Jr. as mayor was more surprising. In 1915, the wartime Hungarian government had installed Vio as Fiume's mayor, convinced he would do Budapest's bidding by limiting pro-Italian sentiments among the populace and facilitating Hungarian centralization efforts. Vio counted among his family many who preferred the annexation of Fiume to the Kingdom of Serbs, Croats, and Slovenes.[57] Nonetheless, he pledged his commitment to annexing Fiume to Italy, and members of the Italian National Council reconfirmed him to underscore that the newly formed Italian National Council was a continuance of prior Fiume self-government mechanisms, not something made up from scratch.

With Grossich as president and Vio as mayor, everything else administrative was done to make the Italian National Council look and feel like a state. Grossich headed a delegation of Fiume politicians who traveled to Rome in January 1919 to meet with Wilson and plead their case. In March 1919, another Fiume delegation went to Paris to meet with all the Great Power representatives. As it became clearer that Wilson was set against Fiume's annexation to Italy, in April 1919 Grossich declared that Fiume had been "virtually united to Italy since October 30, 1918," and using the state powers vested in him, he declared Fiume part of Italy, to be governed by the Italian National Council on behalf of the king of Italy.[58] The Inter-Allied command quickly repudiated Grossich's declaration, insisting that Fiume could not decide to be added to Italy; only the Great Powers could make such a decision. The Italian National Council, however, kept pushing, changing flags, stationery, laws, and currency to make clear to all that a sovereign Fiume demanded annexation to Italy.

One of the Italian National Council's prime goals was to prove—to experts, Entente diplomats, the global press, the Inter-Allied command, and even the regular Inter-Allied soldiers—just how "Italian" Fiume was. Publicity initiatives went into overdrive. Telegrams were sent almost daily to Paris containing so-called data about Fiume's Italianness. In December 1918, the Italian National Council created a press office whose stated purpose was to reveal to the world (and *especially* readers in the Kingdom of Italy) "the obscenities, the vulgarity, the lies, and the deceptions disseminated by Yugoslav journalism against our interests."[59] The Italian National Council, its press office, and politically motivated private citizens sent newspapers in Italy and Italian diaspora communities in Europe and the Americas salacious accounts of how the "barbaric Slavs" threatened to wipe out their culture, take advantage of their women, and destroy the very essence of everything Dante stood for and Italians the world over cherished. The Italian National Council even supplied postcards to the numerous Inter-Allied soldiers hoping that they would "spread pictures of Fiume to their respective countries, thereby making clearer the reasons why Italy has the right to these lands."[60] Any means to manipulate how Fiume's population could be seen as "Italian" were up for grabs and Fiume's Italian National Council grabbed them.

FIUME - L'Eneo che divide Sussak da Fiume

One of the postcards produced by the Italian National Council to promote a vision of Fiume as absolutely separate from Sušak. The writing on the bottom says, "Fiume—The Eneo [Fiumara] which divides Sušak from Fiume." The angle of the photograph makes the river look much larger and broader, contributing to the sense of division between the two towns.

At this point the women's rights aspect of the Fiume story begins. When municipal elections were announced for September 1919, the Italian National Council realized that the best way to increase the number of Italians voting was to double the number of those eligible. Suddenly and unexpectedly, women were given the right to vote, a right not uncommon in the socialist-inspired republics that sprang up after the Bolshevik revolution, but unheard of in the neighboring Kingdom of Italy and the Kingdom of Serbs, Croats, and Slovenes. Fiume publicists made much of women voting, talking frequently of their unquestioned dedication to making Fiume part of Italy. Local newspaper articles quickly saw women's suffrage as an ideal publicity stunt: articles spotlighted women born "in the time of Napoleon" who hobbled their way to the polls, like 91-year-old Fiume-born widow Anna Gregorig, who told reporters how excited she was to "vote for Italian Fiume."[61]

Fiume's Italian national activists saw women as easily manipulatable and thus useful. For example, 32-year-old Fiume-born Arturo Chiopris registered only women he knew would vote as he wanted them to, filing registration requests for the women of his extended family, close friends, and immediate neighbors.[62] The 44-year-old Fiume-born Alfredo Fletzer branched out further, collecting signatures from housebound widows he assumed would support the cause. Alas, most of their registrations were rejected because they lacked proper documentation.[63] The 22-year-old Fiume-born Pietro Gennari was more persistent, going door to door in hopes of inducing women to vote in favor of annexationist measures. His efforts, however, went less smoothly than Chiopris's and Fletzer's. The widow Anna Candelari apparently "made public her yugophile tendencies," shouting at Gennari that she would "oppose any insinuations that attempted to dissuade her from her decision" against the Italian annexationist platform.[64] Women opposed to government directives used their suffrage rights, too. Their traces are harder to find, however, because the process of voter registration was much easier if government officials thought you would vote as they wanted.

Candelari was not alone, though, in valuing her voting rights. The 57-year-old Maria Sustovich thought voting was so important that she went through the bureaucratic paperwork to add herself to the electoral lists even though the Fiume postal system refused to deliver the necessary documents because she lived within the administrative boundaries of Sušak.[65] Other women used voting as an opportunity not just to assert their political views but to assert which version of their name they preferred to use. The 29-year-old Aurora Kollmann, née Stefancic, broke protocol when registering herself to vote by listing her maiden name instead of her married one. City officials quickly corrected her, crossing out Stefancic and listing her as "Aurora Kolmann, wife of Alessandro."[66] Other women wrote to tell the city government when their names were misspelled or left off the voter registration lists.[67] For many, this new public power was something precious, sometimes to express their views (pro or con) about annexation, and sometimes for reasons that had nothing to do with the geopolitical future of Fiume.

Photograph from elections held in either 1919 or 1921. Fiume publicists eagerly promoted the vision of elderly Fiume women "from the time of Napoleon" delighting in being able to "vote Fiume Italian." The expression of this Fiume lady indicates that perhaps there was some truth to the publicists' claims, though the expressions of those surrounding her raise questions.

Women dominate the on-the-ground stories told about Fiume in the immediate postwar period, but not for the tension surrounding the introduction of women's suffrage. Instead it was the reports about women's interactions with Inter-Allied soldiers that catapulted local events into the world news and then into subsequent histories. Women in these stories (largely supplied to the global press by Fiumians themselves) were doubly symbolic, representing Fiume's authentic, uncorrupted "will" and serving as a touching reminder of the city's helplessness and vulnerability in the face of Great Power politics, Inter-Allied presumptions, and competing national claims. From the arrival of Inter-Allied soldiers onward, journalists focused most of their portrayals of locals' reactions on women. When Italian ships arrived in Fiume in November 1918, reports showed crowds of women covering the ships with "flowers and laurels," "implor[ing] the sailors to disembark," and even boarding and stealing Italian sailors' hats to lure them onto land.[68] Nationalist demonstrations on the part of the Serb-Croat-Slovene faction also placed female enthusiasm front and center, showing girls dressed in Slavic folk costumes welcoming their French and Serb liberators with homespun charm.

Unsurprisingly, fraternization between Fiume's local female population and the Inter-Allied troops was commonplace, spurred on by ladies' interest in postwar companionship, or financial gain, or fear, or a combination of all three. International interest, however, centered on women's "pure" national impulses and the Inter-Allied troops' response. Every history of Fiume before D'Annunzio's arrival focuses on two episodes to explain how things escalated so much that Paris Peace Conference diplomats were ever more convinced that compromise over Fiume was impossible. These same episodes also simultaneously convinced nationalist groups in Italy that occupying Fiume was the only logical next step.

The first incident has such a mundane beginning that it seems absurd that it precipitated the establishment of a special Inter-Allied commission of American, British, French, and Italian generals. The troubles began on July 2, 1919, when two drunk French soldiers stumbled their way home from Sušak to their Fiume barracks by crossing the Fiumara. At some point they bumped into two young Fiume women wearing rosettes in the Italian colors. According to the women, the soldiers tore the rosettes off, trampled them, and then spat in the women's faces while damning Italy. News of an attack on innocent, Italy-loving Fiume women spread quickly, and bands of local Italian nationalists joined with Italian soldiers to make the Frenchmen pay. Three disorderly days later, sixty-seven soldiers had been wounded and nine were dead (including four colonial soldiers from French Indochina). Fighting ended the night of July 6, when soldiers were ordered to stay in their barracks and Italian and French generals made grand speeches reminding all that they had fought together in the war and should stick together in peace. The story was widely reported, and eight days later the diplomats in Paris sent a special commission to Fiume to determine who was at fault for triggering violence within a civilian community along the fault lines of two Entente allies, Italy and France.

News leaked quickly about what the Inter-Allied commission decided in late August 1919. The whole city knew that though British, French, American, and Italian inspectors blamed the escalation on the Italian military, they also pointed out the increased hostility Fiumians felt toward the French for having usurped part of Fiume's port. Both the Italian and French soldiers were deemed too invested in local politics (in part because troops had been stationed there for almost a year without reprieve). The Inter-Allied commission declared that French and Italian military troops should be replaced, the number of Italian soldiers reduced to correspond more closely to those of the other Allied commands, France's naval port moved outside the city limits, Fiume's local militia disbanded, colonial soldiers removed from the urban center, and new elections for city government held (the same elections in which women first voted). The commission's final decree was that "more disinterested" American and British units should oversee city policing to secure equal treatment for all.

The second incident came as a response to the measures enacted by the Inter-Allied commission. On the morning of August 25, in accordance with the commission's decrees, Italian soldiers prepared to leave the city. As they closed up their barracks, the Sardinian grenadiers, who had been in Fiume since November 1918, saw a mass of Fiumians waiting outside. Most of them—or so reports said—were women and children who had covered the streets with Italian flags to force the Italian soldiers to stay, on the assumption that Italian soldiers loved their nation too much to soil its flag. Moved by the dramatic gesture, the soldiers hesitated. But military orders prevailed, and the soldiers pushed the women aside and trampled the flags. A few women were described as then risking their lives by jumping in front of military trucks to halt the evacuation. As reported endlessly in the global press (but especially the Italian), the soldiers swore they would never forget Fiume; they would return. Women cried. Publicists scribbled. By the next day, newspaper readers across the globe knew of the desperate measures Fiume's most innocent would take to make themselves part of Italy.

From August 1919 on, the Fiume on-the-ground story began to be overshadowed by outside (mostly Italian) responses to the sensational accounts. Even today, histories of the Fiume Crisis jump from Wilson's diplomatic impasses in Paris, to Grossich's rebuffed auto-annexation of Fiume to Italy, to friction between the Italian and French troops, to the frantic demonstrations of seemingly guileless (mostly female) Fiumians risking all to be joined to the Italian "motherland." The disjointedness is no accident. As we have seen, Fiume's Italian National Council worked hard to control how the press depicted the city, opting whenever possible to obliterate any visions that did not show Fiume as italianissima.

Modern, scandal-hungry journalists turned the Fiume story from a local event into the international pandemonium it became, but not because any one state had complete control of the media. To the Italian National Council's dismay, accounts emphasizing how Fiume's Italianness had been created by a nationalist city government against the wishes of Fiumians who did not identify as Italian or did not want Fiume joined to Italy were regularly printed in Italy, France, Great Britain, the United States, and the Kingdom of Serbs, Croats, and Slovenes.[69] But these stories did not reverberate with audiences with the same intensity that the melodramatic "helpless-Fiume-that-just-wants-to-be-Italian" narratives did. By the end of summer 1919, a growing number of Italians started caring about Fiume less because of their indignation about Wilson and the Paris Peace Conference and more because Fiume embodied a feminine, pure, and threatened dedication to the Italian national idea, a version that pulled at heartstrings and demanded action.[70] Few worked harder to make this so than the poet-soldier Gabriele D'Annunzio, the man who in most tellings of the Fiume Crisis is considered synonymous with the city itself. On-the-ground tales of Fiume disappear almost completely once D'Annunzio makes his entrance.

Story Three: D'Annunzio and Proto-fascism

"All you have to do is order the troops to shoot me, General."[71]

The short, bald, thin, partially blind 56-year-old man who uttered these taunting words was Gabriele D'Annunzio. And as D'Annunzio stood up in his flashy red convertible, he opened his coat and pointed to his chest to indicate where the shot should pierce him. It was easy to see, since below his coat were the many medals he had been awarded for outstanding military service to Italy in World War I.

The man D'Annunzio taunted was the 56-year-old general Vittorio Emanuele Pittaluga, assigned to control the armistice line west of Fiume for the Italian forces. Pittaluga hesitated. In front of him stood the most popular living Italian—a poet, novelist, playwright, aviator, veteran, and publicist extraordinaire—at the head of a ragtag army several hundred strong, most of them recent defectors from Pittaluga's own troops, the same troops that just weeks before had promised the weeping ladies of Fiume that they would return.[72] Behind Pittaluga stood hundreds of regular soldiers, many of whom had already started to leave their positions to indicate that, if necessary, they would shoot Pittaluga before they let him shoot the taunting hero.

Orders from Rome were clear: it was September 12, 1919, and after the August 1919 Inter-Allied commission report, the Italian government insisted that no insurgent elements were to be allowed entry into the newly occupied territories of the northern Balkans. In fact, orders had recently been made even clearer: specifically, D'Annunzio was not to enter Fiume. Under pressure, Pittaluga relented and D'Annunzio and his troops passed. Inter-Allied commanders followed suit, ostensibly out of fear of the bloodshed that might result with civilians so close.

Without a single shot fired, to the ringing of church bells and with Fiume's president Antonio Grossich bestowing laurel leaves on the entering heroes, D'Annunzio and his motley army wrested control of one of the ten biggest ports in continental Europe from the world's Great Powers. The newsprint wrote itself. And ever since, hundreds if not thousands of histories, memoirs, biographies, commemorations, edited letters, photographic collages, novels, blogs, research papers, and even comic books have recounted the D'Annunzio-Fiume experience. In fact, the interpretations began the day D'Annunzio entered town, for a film crew, photographers, and journalists were all there to record the event. This was exactly why Italian armed forces had been specifically ordered to stop D'Annunzio from reaching Fiume. Everyone knew he might try such a stunt because he had already made the Fiume-Paris debacle and the on-the-ground stories part of his regular repertoire of unapologetically expansionist, bigoted Italian nationalism.

D'Annunzio began taking over the story just days after the Paris Peace Conference began. In January 1919, in response to the first hints that Wilson would not support all of Italy's claims, D'Annunzio published a front-page letter in leading Italian nationalist newspapers explaining that "Italy is big, and wants to get bigger," that her rightful borders encompassed all of the Adriatic, and that any counterclaims were the work of the "lurid Croatians, . . . the rampaging monkeys," who threatened the Italian civilization Italians had fought and died to protect.[73] In the weeks following the Italian diplomats' exit from Paris, D'Annunzio made highly publicized speeches not just demanding that Fiume be joined to Italy but also insisting that Italy needed to liberate itself from the "lies, servility, and cowardice" that subjected it to the unchecked power of "transatlantic [that is, American] gold."[74]

Fiume's on-the-ground story was an important narrative for D'Annunzio. When the July 1919 reports of the skirmishes between Italian and French soldiers came to light, his histrionic rhetoric shifted into high gear. He took the five days of fighting between Italian and French forces and refashioned them as the "Fiumian Vespers," a modern-day reenactment of Giuseppe Verdi's 1855 Italian nationalist opera, *The Sicilian Vespers*. When the pitiful descriptions of Fiume women trying to stop Italian soldiers' retreat hit the newspapers, D'Annunzio began to reimagine his dream to make "Italy bigger." No longer content solely to whip up a fury through his newspaper columns, he decided to lead in person. Though his fifteen-month attempt to rebuild a pure Italy by uniting "martyr Fiume to its motherland" ended in failure, virtually all accounts of this period hinge on the unexpected and shocking adventures of D'Annunzio and his followers. Piracy, free love, nonconformism, drugs, a new constitution based on anarcho-syndicalist principles, the Christmas of Blood: every week it seemed something bizarre, unheard of, and newsworthy was coming out of D'Annunzio's Fiume.

There are many works detailing the story of D'Annunzio and his followers in the port city. I will focus here on the key events from September 1919 to January 1921, an extravaganza that has been given its own "ism": *fiumanesimo* (fiumianism).[75] Precisely what fiumanesimo encapsulated remains elusive, but Renzo De Felice—the grandfather of Italian Fascist studies—describes it as the political, cultural, and social experiences of those who celebrated D'Annunzio's Fiume, whether they actually spent much time in the city or not. According to De Felice, participants in fiumanesimo found it "morally liberating and politically anticipatory of a new political-social order which no one knew how to define concretely, but which tied them all together."[76] Emilio Gentile offers a more specific characterization, emphasizing that though many limit it to the "decadent literary expression and political estheticism" of D'Annunzio himself, in fact, for many it served as "the most original expression of the veteran movements and ideologies" of immediate postwar Europe. Like so many other veterans' movements, fiumanesimo was infused with equal parts anti-parliamentarianism, anti-conformism, anti-materialism, a political theology of mystical nationalism, and the veneration of an aristocracy of soldiers guided by a supreme leader, a duce.[77] Anyone familiar with the early history of Italian Fascism can see why so many find in fiumanesimo the "proto-" to Mussolini's Fascism.

If fiumanesimo is anything, it is an umbrella category of feelings, stylings, attempts, hopes, pleasures, and hatreds experienced by those who enthusiastically followed the fortunes of D'Annunzio's gambol in Fiume. The three key aspects that designate D'Annunzian Fiume as proto-fascism center on how D'Annunzio projected an aura of charismatic, authoritarian leadership that mesmerized his followers; the vibrancy of a restless, disillusioned nationalist veterans' culture that eagerly defied state command; and the myriad of political ideologies that wove into and out of these two phenomena.

D'Annunzio's charismatic hold on his followers in Fiume is perhaps the easiest part of fiumanesimo to explain. His power originated from the fact that he was a beloved celebrity before he reached Fiume. Celebrities are not always charismatic. But D'Annunzio's celebrity was as much a product of his artistic production as it was a by-product of his ability to make the public want to be part of his story. Before World War I, D'Annunzio's charisma only reached middle- and upper-class readers. His sensuous, flamboyantly immoral poetry, novels, and plays aroused attention due to his mastery of the Italian language and all its tropes. But his writing titillated even more because it was both shocking and highly autobiographical. From one piece to another, D'Annunzio filled his audience's imaginations with a moralizing debauchery and narcissism few could imagine anyone wanting to publicize. D'Annunzio's hyperbolic womanizing, his absurd spending, his efforts to avoid money collectors, and his constant presence in the salons of Italy and France kept tongues wagging about his latest cruel phrase. It was all this, as much as his literary powers, that made D'Annunzio a celebrity. People enjoyed imagining what it was like to be him as much as gossiping about him.

It is hard to say precisely when D'Annunzio's charisma moved outside the salons and into the broader public. Some date the transformation to his celebration of Italy's war against the Ottoman Empire in Libya (1912), others to his public commitment to pushing Italy to renounce neutrality at the beginning of World War I (1914). All agree he was already the darling of a growing public when he began publishing from the front in 1915. The *when* of D'Annunzio's transformation might be unclear, but the *why* is not. D'Annunzio's reach spread when he made Italy's need for reawakening through war the centerpiece of his creative efforts. His infamous personal and emotional predilections continued, but they were sidelined. Now his rich repertoire of linguistic nuances, semi-heretical religious imagery, and classical tropes shifted away from Nietzschean dilemmas of the self to a discourse anchored in national combat as rebirthing sacrifice. That a man who spoke and wrote in a manner inaccessible to most could win the hearts of a nation in which over 40 percent of the population was illiterate is remarkable. He did so by going out beyond literary salons to speak to crowds and newspapers, invigorating his fancy phrasings with well-placed obscenities. By 1915, D'Annunzio had learned how to lead a rally, leavening the highbrow language with vulgarisms and modeling his prose on the repetitive formula of call-and-response. The ever-present references to Saint Sebastian, Dante, and the classical masters were still there, but now they included more Bible stories and the gall to publicly call a prime minister "shithead" (Cagoia), all while leading crowds to chant, "Long live the just war! Long live the greater Italy!" His rallies and journalistic rabble-rousing opened up a broader arena, but it only became "national charisma" when the 52-year-old poet and dandy put his body where his words were by volunteering for active service, becoming the oldest lieutenant to serve in Italy's armed forces.[78]

D'Annunzio was not the only Italian intellectual or artist to join up. Many of the Italian Futurists volunteered, as did interventionist socialists like Benito Mussolini. But only D'Annunzio became Italy's jack-of-all-trades action hero. He did not serve on one front; he served on all of them, moving between sea, air, and land as he pleased and the government grudgingly allowed. First he went to sea on a warship. Then he took to the air. In January 1916 he suffered a severe eye injury after a tough landing. He never regained use of the eye but nonetheless demanded to be put back into service a year later. He returned to the air—one of his greatest passions. When morale on the alpine front reached its lowest, D'Annunzio headed to the trenches. By the end of the war, he was a one-man public relations campaign for the Italian military effort, moving between fronts, going where the action was most dramatic and his presence would be most inspiring.

D'Annunzio's service was real. He risked his life many times. But while his comrades in arms fought with weapons, D'Annunzio's contribution was mostly propaganda. He traveled with a pen (and a pressed uniform), writing constantly, describing the many variants of bleak heroism displayed by Italian soldiers. He gave speeches to rally troops, often several times a day. And his responsibilities during missions were more geared to winning the press war than the actual war itself. Thus the fabulous accounts of his "flight over Vienna," during which he and his fellow Italian aviators dropped four hundred thousand leaflets over the capital city of enemy Austria, basically saying, "We could be dropping bombs. . . . Wake up. . . . It's over."[79] Or the by now mythical "Mockery of Bakar" (Beffa di Buccari), where he set loose messages in bottles during an unsuccessful torpedo night raid on a Habsburg naval port just southeast of Fiume that said (more or less), "You thought you were safe in your well-protected harbor. Ha! We Italians will risk everything. . . . You're not safe." D'Annunzio's publications, his speeches, and his outrageous exploits over sea, air, and land made Italy's losing war seem winnable—and a lot less depressing. When Italy finally did win, Italians looked to D'Annunzio as the emblem of the unrelenting bravura that had led them to victory (a much more inspiring idea than the many accusations that the war had been so hard to win because of incompetent leadership, war profiteering, and battlefront sedition).[80] When the peace negotiations over Fiume fell apart, D'Annunzio declared to all who would listen that the only way to save Italy's victory ("the mutilated victory," as he termed it) was to "disobey" (disobbedisco). It was clear to many that this meant Italy should take the Adriatic no matter what the stuffed shirts in parliaments and peace proceedings had to say. They had fought to win the war. Now they had to fight to win the peace.

Undoubtedly fiumanesimo is deeply rooted in D'Annunzio's charisma. But it became a movement—an ism—because of the sheer number and diversity of people who followed him. D'Annunzio did not recruit them directly; his newspaper articles and speeches did that for him. He did not even commit fully to participating in the march on Fiume until a few days before (he could not decide between that and a transcontinental flight to Japan). When he finally got into that red convertible on September 12, 1919, he was so ill with the flu that he had to be held up by the real masterminds, the ones who had organized the deserting troops, stolen the military vehicles, and secured financial support from like-minded industrialists.[81] D'Annunzio's taunt to Pittaluga would not have worked if hundreds of soldiers had not been standing behind him, embodying the unfaltering loyalty Italians felt for everything D'Annunzio signified. And the Inter-Allied command and

Fiume's Italian National Council would not have known to prepare the seamless transfer of military command to D'Annunzio if his entourage in Fiume had not already convinced them he was coming and would not be stopped. Helping D'Annunzio take Fiume was direct insubordination; every person involved believed he or she risked everything to be there. "Disobey to save the nation" had been D'Annunzio's war cry just a few weeks before, and these soldiers thought they were doing just that. It was their enthusiasm and conviction that created much of the proto-fascist fiumanesimo that has fascinated readers ever since.

The men accompanying D'Annunzio to Fiume were a hodgepodge. Most had fought for Italy during the war, some in regiments stationed in Fiume until recently, some at the front, and some native Fiumians who had left their city to fight for Italy's victory and now deserted Italy's military to fight for D'Annunzio. They ranged from the lowliest foot soldier to a few celebrated generals and hailed from all over Italy, from Palermo to Milan. Their uniforms were as diverse as their dialects and accents, marking them as members of Italy's shock troops (Arditi), regular infantry, grenade units, naval units, alpine units, and, of course, the air force. And after newspapers reported the amazing story of D'Annunzio's entry into Fiume, new volunteers began arriving, some who had already left military service, others too young to have seen it.[82] The Italian state tried to block these eager recruits by policing trains, but the challenges dissuaded few. In fact, it seems that the harder it was to get to Fiume, the more important D'Annunzio's action appeared for Italy's future. In one of his most celebrated attacks on Wilson, D'Annunzio had proclaimed, "I dare, not scheme" (Ardisco non ordisco). The men (and some women) who made their way to Fiume in the autumn of 1919 felt they, too, were daring to make Italy great, not just scheming to maintain its position as a second-rate Great Power, as many believed its elected officials were doing.

Though D'Annunzio's followers hailed from everywhere, with widely varied experiences and expectations, the esprit de corps was that of the Arditi, the daredevil shock troops of Italy's trench warfare. During the war, the Arditi regularly participated in suicide missions, jumping over barbed wire into enemy trenches equipped only with knives (often held between their teeth), grenades, and short-range weapons. By 1919, these elite units had an aura of fantastic grandeur. Every Italian recognized their black uniforms, their skull-and-dagger badges, and knew about the mythic, nonconformist camaraderie that bound them together. D'Annunzio's legionnaires (the name his followers were given to characterize them as one unit with one mission, rather than the jumble they actually were) embraced the Ardito spirit, wearing their nonconformist camaraderie like a badge of honor and performing daredevil feats to keep the Fiume campaign afloat. Modeled on the propaganda-oriented exploits D'Annunzio hatched during the war, they also incarnated a manly daring that contrasted so vividly with the diplomats of Paris.

The legionnaires' eccentric antics cemented the fiumanesimo spirit as something real (for its followers), not just an echo of D'Annunzio's rousing words. Some followers formed a pirate crew called the Uscocchi, whose mission (often successful) was to capture Italian commercial ships and either steal their goods or hold them ransom. Another special forces unit, the Desperate (La Disperata), was organized around egalitarian standards, flouting the stuffy classist hierarchies and traditions of old-school military units. They were encouraged to take up nature-oriented, less corrupt, and less civilized lifestyles that included nudism, experimentation with drugs, vegetarianism, and a sexuality we would today call queer or fluid. Some participated in raids outside Fiume, stealing valuable horses and even taking a high-ranking Italian general hostage. Fiume's legionnaires did not see battle until Christmas 1920, but their publicity-prone feats and shockingly un-Catholic rituals made waves in Italy and beyond by demonstrating that the current liberal, parliamentarian leadership of the Kingdom of Italy was helpless even to keep its troops together, while under D'Annunzio's leadership Italy's soldiers could achieve the unthinkable.

How many legionnaires followed D'Annunzio is impossible to determine. Some argue that it was as many as twelve thousand in the first weeks of D'Annunzio's arrival (though this seems highly unlikely). All agree that whatever the number in September–October 1919, it dwindled immediately thereafter, petering out to little more than several

hundred by the end. Ideological positions among D'Annunzio's legionnaires were as varied as their backgrounds and military experience.
Some who followed D'Annunzio to Fiume saw it as a patriotic effort to
save Italy and its monarchy from the corrosive effects of liberal parliamentarianism. Others came because they believed the war could not
end until Italy got bigger and the Mediterranean seaboard surrounding
it became a Mare Nostrum empire reminiscent of ancient Rome and
early modern Venice. Some thought going to Fiume would be a way to
avoid postwar demobilization and thereby guarantee a continuance of
military service—a service that represented for some their first professional experience and only livelihood. Still others followed D'Annunzio
because they believed he stood for a purifying revolution against back-
chamber politics and bourgeois capitalism. Futurist artists, central
European bon vivants, and even the stray anarchist went to Fiume
because they believed that D'Annunzio's impassioned claim that "deeds
make history" (cosa fatta capo ha) would baptize a new world that
pushed old traditions and systems of control aside so that humankind's
true nature (to make art, to make love, to live for life and not profit)
could reign. And some came because following D'Annunzio sounded like
fun: free love, no rules, drugs.

During D'Annunzio's almost sixteen months in Fiume, many entertainments and sports competitions were organized to keep the legionnaires occupied, to raise morale, to ensure they stayed "battle worthy,"
and (always the top priority) to keep the hungry journalistic world fed.
Celebrities including orchestral director Arturo Toscanini; inventor
Guglielmo Marconi; the founder of Futurism, F. T. Marinetti; and even
the founder of Fascism, Benito Mussolini, passed through D'Annunzio's
Fiume to "taste the air" of this new Italy. In his almost daily balcony
speeches from Fiume's Governor's Palace, D'Annunzio promised something to everyone, and his domination of the global press, along with
his famous guests, reassured his followers that it would happen. As time
passed, most followers mutinied and returned home because of dis-
tasteful behavior, lack of funds, boredom, or political directions with
which they did not agree. Those who stayed were bonded in a common
mission to break the Italy they knew in the hope of being part of making

A sports competition organized so D'Annunzio's followers could demonstrate their manly prowess for all to enjoy. Note in the back the range of different uniforms of the observers.

either an Italy that had been or an Italy that would be. And while they all waited, they lived those fifteen months as if Fiume itself were a substitute Italy, already released from the chains of the liberal society they so disdained.

When D'Annunzio marched into Fiume on September 12, 1919, he (like many others) expected that the whole adventure would last a couple of weeks at most. Italy's government seemed weak: attacked from the right by nationalist-imperialist political elements like D'Annunzio and Mussolini and from the left by socialists and workers' strikes in all of Italy's major cities. When the government fell, or so D'Annunzio and his entourage expected, a new government would have little choice but to accept the fait accompli and recognize Fiume's annexation to Italy. That was the plan. That is not what happened.

Initially, Italy's new government, led by the economically minded, US-friendly Francesco Saverio Nitti, also expected D'Annunzio's adventure would end quickly. To engineer this, a compromise option (the so-called modus vivendi) was offered to the leading figures of Fiume's Italian National Council and D'Annunzio's military command. The modus vivendi proposed that in exchange for D'Annunzio leaving and the city ending its demand for annexation, the Kingdom of Italy would commit to protecting the "sovereign rights of the city of Fiume," forestalling any separation "of Fiume and its territory from the mother country [Italy]," and providing for "regular Italian troops to protect the integrity of Fiume while simultaneously respecting its own militia."[83] In short, the modus vivendi promised that Fiume would not be given to the Kingdom of Serbs, Croats, and Slovenes or risk financial, military, or geopolitical isolation if it accepted the independent-state solution.

Initially, it looked as if all parties involved would accept the modus vivendi and D'Annunzio's time in Fiume would end. The majority of the Italian National Council approved it, as did most of the leading political figures of D'Annunzio's command. D'Annunzio, however, wavered, afraid that such a compromise would make him little better than all the two-faced politicians he had spent the last few years maligning. Convinced that the people of Fiume were more attached to him than to ending the international fiasco they had been living in for over a year, he called a plebiscite to decide whether the city should accept the modus vivendi or not. When it quickly became clear that the December 16, 1919, plebiscite would support the modus vivendi, not the continuation of D'Annunzio's "Italy or death" campaign, he called a halt to the voting, declaring the entire proceedings invalid because of corruption and the sad logic of polls.[84] Nitti, furious at this rebuff, scrapped the modus vivendi offer. Confused about what their role in Fiume should be at this point, more legionnaires deserted D'Annunzio. The local Fiume municipal administration looked ever more inward. And D'Annunzio's command began a political rollercoaster ride from December 1919 to September 1920, passing through cycles of monarchism, virulent xenophobic Italian nationalism, internationalism, and anarcho-syndicalism, anything that might shore up support while they waited for the Italian government either to fall or to agree to absorb Fiume into the kingdom.[85]

After almost a year of waiting, things just got even more eccentric. In the summer of 1920, D'Annunzio decided to kick out Fiume's provisional municipal government, form his own state, and ask the 46-year-old anarcho-syndicalist Alceste De Ambris to help write a constitution for an Italian regency headed by himself, the new duce. D'Annunzio called his utopian state the Regency of Carnaro. Its constitution promised that state and industrial relations would be founded on corporatism, egalitarianism, and anti-chauvinism (although throughout the constitution the goal of transforming non-Italian Fiumians into Italians was a clear priority). Instead of a state religion, D'Annunzio proposed that music would serve as the moral compass of the people. He did not stop there. He envisioned his mini utopian regency as a beacon for the oppressed peoples of the world. He commissioned the 28-year-old Belgian poet and musicologist Léon Kochnitzky to found the League of Fiume (also known as the Anti–League of Nations), which claimed to support the rights of unrepresented peoples victimized by Great Power imperialism. D'Annunzio claimed to champion the Irish, Egyptians, Albanians, Croatians, Flemish, Algerians, Indians, Afghans, Cubans, "Blacks of the United States," and "Chinese in California," among many others. (He conveniently forgot all the anti-Croatian speeches he had made, as well as his orders just weeks earlier to expel all "foreigners," especially "enemy Slavs," from Fiume.) Neither D'Annunzio's regency, nor his corporatist constitution, nor his Anti–League of Nations League of Fiume were more than scraps of paper. But the attempts show how the mixed messages his followers heard were a product of a charismatic leader promising everything he could think of to ensure his own success and continued presence in the spotlight.

Fiumanesimo was all things to all those searching for another Italy after the war. And its links to Mussolini's Fascism are unmistakable. First, in real terms, many (but not all) of those who accompanied D'Annunzio to Fiume later joined Mussolini's Fascist squads.[86] It was not just the participants; there was also a continuity in uniforms, salutes, mottos, war songs, and soldierly exaltation of a charismatic duce riling up imperialist enthusiasm in almost daily balcony speeches. As Mussolini's hold on the Italian state tightened, he publicly and administratively recognized D'Annunzio and his legionnaires as the precursors to the Fascist revolution, even offering pensions to those who had volunteered in Fiume. But fiumanesimo was just as non-Fascist as it was Fascist. The bon vivant cosmopolitanism; the comic piracy; the explicit interest in free love, drugs, and queer sexuality; and the forays into anarcho-syndicalism are, as many historians have noted, a potent reminder of how many vibrant, popularly supported options there were for revolution and reform in post-WWI Italy, all squashed when Fascism took over. D'Annunzio's Fiume extravaganza ended in failure, but the enthusiasm it created was an important lesson for many. Mussolini's Fascists immersed themselves in Fiume's symbols and marched on Rome in 1922 with many of the same contradictory motivations as D'Annunzio's followers had had just three years earlier. And with every year Mussolini stayed in power, the elements of fiumanesimo that did not align with Fascism were crushed into an almost mythical legend of the nonconformist Italy that could have been.

What's Missing in the Fiume Stories, and Why Does It Matter?

In some ways it is incredible how much the stories we tell about the Fiume Crisis reveal about immediate post-WWI Europe. The Wilson diplomatic story not only shows why certain decisions came about the way they did but also gives insight into some of Wilson's most fateful weaknesses. Meanwhile, the Fiume on-the-ground narrative exposes the way that much of what mattered in international events depended on how much interest the global media took in local tensions. Finally, the most famous aspect of all—D'Annunzio's Fiume escapade—exposes just how fatal grassroots military veteran dissatisfaction—when coupled with the charisma of a self-proclaimed leader—could be to the liberal parliamentarianism of Europe's victorious Entente. Fiume before 1914 had increasing influence on world commerce and immigration patterns, yet few knew much about it. Fiume after 1918 was one of the hot-spot stories of Europe's interwar period, a potent example of why some initiatives failed and a potential precedent for the nightmares to come.

These stories are all important because they are all true. But something is missing from all of them: Why Fiume? Why did all of these
events happen in a relatively unknown place? This might seem like a
minor question. But there were many economically and politically
important cities in the postwar period whose positions within a nation-
state were contested, and none of them undermined the Paris peace
talks or showcased elements of charismatic proto-fascism. The short
answer to why it was Fiume instead of Trieste, Gdansk, Lviv, Edirne,
Strasbourg, Izmir, Timișoara, or Kaliningrad is that Fiume, though
untethered geopolitically after its empire fell, remained relatively independent for twenty-six months without the bloodbaths of interethnic conflict. The other post-imperial cities either suffered months
(if not years) of civil war or were all completely taken over, whether
by invading armies or new state regimes. Fiume became the locus for
all of these postwar narratives because no one event determined its
trajectory. Its political stability is astounding, considering how many
places in Europe alone—Budapest, Vienna, Munich, Berlin, and Milan,
to name just a few—tottered on the brink of revolution (or else fell
into it) because of postwar economic and political hardships. Fiume's
relative civic peace allowed Paris diplomats to haggle endlessly without
taking action, allowed the press to focus on minor but picturesque
events like the women and their flags, and allowed D'Annunzio
to wax poetic on a balcony stage for fifteen months without doing
much else.

To date, the question Why Fiume? has not received much attention
because the assumption has been that Fiume remained stable in its fight
against Great Power Paris diplomacy, *against* local offenses to Italian
honor, and *in support of* D'Annunzio's mission because the city, or at
least its ruling elite, was overwhelmingly committed to the Italian national cause. In short, thus far, extreme postwar nationalism has explained Why Fiume? But is this really accurate? Undoubtedly D'Annunzio
transfixed many with his fame and his scandalous audacity. And undoubtedly those who left Italy to follow him into the Fiume unknown
responded to precisely that aura. But why did the people of Fiume open
their gates to him, deck him with laurel leaves, and put up with his

profligate ways while they were blockaded and increasingly impover-ished? These questions stem both from the reality that D'Annunzio was essentially a hustler and the fact that these answers make no sense if we look at Fiume itself rather than the diplomats haggling over it, the international press writing about it, and the Italian soldiers marching into it. The question can only be understood and answered when details that have been ignored are confronted, details that quickly make the common belief that it was Italian nationalism that kept Fiume stable virtually untenable.

Perhaps the most important overlooked fact is that Fiume had never been part of the Kingdom of Italy; for most of its history it was a Habsburg-built port city ruled from Hungary and Croatia-Slavonia. The immense implications of this are rarely acknowledged. First, until just one year before D'Annunzio's arrival, the overwhelming majority of Fiume's native sons had been fighting a war on the side of Austria-Hungary *against* Italy. Throughout the conflict and in the years im-mediately after it, World War I was regularly characterized by Fium-ians in their official correspondence and personal letters as a "war with Italy."[87] D'Annunzio was a hero-poet-soldier, it is true. But he was a hero-poet-soldier of those who fought *for* Italy, not against it. One can only imagine what Fiume's widows, orphans, and war wounded thought when they heard D'Annunzio disparaging "the scum that fought for Austria" or boasting about having bombed enemy battalions in which Fiume's sons had fought, some never to return.[88]

Second, not only was Fiume not part of Italy's (or D'Annunzio's) war effort, but more than half the population had a mother tongue other than Italian. They joked, haggled, prayed, flirted, complained, fought, and reminisced in the many dialects of Croatian, Hungarian, Slovene, German, Romanian, Yiddish, and Czech. Fiume was a booming Medi-terranean port with railway lines linking its quays to villages and farm-lands east, north, and south, facts reflected in its population and the languages spoken there. Given this, how much hypnotic pull could Italian nationalism or D'Annunzio's hours-long balcony speeches filled with Dante quotes and Giuseppe Garibaldi nostalgia have had? In this environment, can we really chalk up an entire city's willingness to sacrifice all against Wilsonian diplomacy to Italian nationalism or D'Annunzian charisma?

Third, Fiume was never taken over in the kind of military or dictatorial terms one would expect from troops barracking themselves among civilians. Until 1918, recall that Fiume had been ruled by Hungary under the strange category of corpus separatum, whereby the city was administered locally by a municipal council, a Hungarian-appointed governor, and the royal ministries in Budapest. When the Inter-Allied troops arrived, the Italian National Council became the town's provisional government. The newly formed Hungarian Republic was informed that until annexation to Italy could be realized, "Fiume is constituted as an independent political entity and exercises, through the [Italian] National Council, all public authority."[89] Banks were instructed that all monies collected from taxes, postage, and utilities should go to Fiume state coffers, as the "Italian National Council, with the consensus of the Interallied Command, has . . . taken legal possession of all the offices, institutions, and industrial enterprises of the past Hungarian Government."[90] When D'Annunzio arrived, this still held true. The Italian National Council continued to "remain in office as long as it was necessary," while "all the provisions of a military nature could be taken exclusively by the Comandante [D'Annunzio]."[91] In effect, D'Annunzio took over the position the Inter-Allied command had held, while the Italian National Council continued administering the city. Intrusions into internal administration by first the Inter-Allied and then the D'Annunzio commands happened, but were not appreciated. On the whole, until late 1920, Fiumians continued to administer themselves using the structures and personnel remaining after the dissolution of the Habsburg Monarchy. They were not conquered.

Not much changed even when D'Annunzio declared his stillborn utopian regency and pushed the Italian National Council to the side. Just months before the 1920 Christmas of Blood, Fiumians were informed that unless told otherwise, all state employees were to continue the jobs they had been doing.[92] To be sure, D'Annunzio's soldiers daily committed acts of violence and intimidation against the civilian population. On several occasions, they bashed in store windows said to be owned by "Croatians," or harassed people on the street for not showing enough respect for Italy. But the history of D'Annunzio and his followers in Fiume is not that of the contemporary German Freikorps conquerors in the Baltics or the Green Cadres in Croatia-Slavonia.[93] Fiume was not part of the "bloodlands" trajectory mapped out by Timothy Snyder and Robert Gerwarth.[94] In Lithuania and Estonia, Freikorps troops raped, pillaged, murdered, and burned their way into domination, while for most of the Fiume Crisis life continued much as usual. By studying the Fiume episode as the crux of the Paris Peace Conference or the "proto-" of Mussolini's Fascism, historians have lost sight of all these troubling details and ignored what rendered Fiume so significant. Great Power diplomacy was stalled not because flags were unfurled on camera or because a much-loved poet waxed fantastic about Italian virility. Instead, negotiations could not be finalized because, contrary to expectations, Fiume's resistance to Wilson's dictums did not fizzle out with time or under pressure. Fiume gained front-page attention because, counter to any logic of the time, it just kept on going.

This book investigates how, why, and to what extent Fiume's urban culture retained such a steady course amid all the ups and downs that made it newsworthy. Shifting the gaze from "how the world saw Fiume" undermines the idea that it was extreme nationalism that fueled the city's internal stability. For alongside the many parades proclaiming Fiume italianissima, the commander of Fiume's police force simultaneously reported to the Italian National Council that nationality information on his men was unavailable for "the simple reason that employees in general refuse to express their own nationality."[95] Even for those who proudly celebrated their dedication to all things Italian, convictions could prove murky. Frustrated with the efforts of Fiume's provisional government to promote the impression of an all-Italian Fiume, the local Croatian-language newspaper, *Primorske novine* (Coastal news), began printing a regular column titled "The Newest Italianissimi," which told of how, until the war's end, many members of Fiume's Italian National Council had pushed to aid Austria-Hungary in its war against Italy, in part because of self-interest but also in part because of their own non-Italian ethnic and cultural backgrounds.[96]

As one anonymous note sent to the provisional government pointed out, many members of Fiume's Italian National Council were seen as "today Italian, tomorrow Croatian, once great Hungarians."[97]

So if Fiumians were not all united by nationalist feeling, what kept them together during their government's push to be joined to Italy? How was large-scale violence averted in a multiethnic city with a government determined to promote a nationalist agenda? How was revolution warded off when trade was at a standstill, inflation rising, unemployment spiraling, and food and heating supplies ever scarcer? Giuseppe Parlato, one of the best historians of twentieth-century Fiume, puts it this way: "One can legitimately ask how the Fiumians, who had known a period of flourishing progress in the decades before the outbreak of war, could be at ease in a city where, between March 1920 and the 'Christmas of Blood' you had to survive with 300 grams of bread per person per day, 300 grams of flour and sugar a month, a kilo of potatoes a week and 2.5 liters of [cooking] oil a month. And yet there was not even one insurrection . . . against D'Annunzio who, in the final analysis, was the one really responsible for the situation."[98] Parlato reasons that the only possible answer is that "the myths of the nation" kept the Fiumians going when there were not enough calories to do so. But if we consider the fact that Fiume was not as nationally unified as the press made it out to be, is the "myths of the nation" answer sufficient?

These are the issues the more commonly told Fiume stories have hidden. And these are concerns that an on-the-ground history of Fiume can help address. A good first step in tracing how Fiume's postwar history embodies the post-imperial world's struggle to survive is to look at a commodity everyone yearned for after the hungry years of war: money.

2

Follow the Money

The Currency Debacle

In the fall of 1919, the 17-year-old runaway legionnaire Giuseppe Maranini spent a lot of his time in Fiume writing to his 16-year-old fiancée, Elda, back in Bologna. His letters were ones of reassurance, anxious to convince her that his mission was worth the pain of their separation. "Fiume! It's a city, a word, two syllables, but it is the most beautiful dream that I've ever lived!" Maranini exclaimed.[1] What made it so dreamy? He wanted a national adventure, and that was exactly what he got. Fiume itself "isn't big," he admitted, "but it is beautiful and rich." The "infinite number of Habsburg eagles" on trams and palaces reminded Maranini of the stories he had grown up with of Garibaldi and the Risorgimento, of Italians redeeming former Habsburg lands to make Italy. Entering Fiume in 1919, after the dissolution of Austria-Hungary, felt like what it must have been like to enter Venice just fifty years earlier, after Italy had wrested it away from the Austrians. But this time, there was nothing left to fear from the Habsburgs. The "last relics of the defunct monarchy," he wrote, were "the crowns, paper banknotes . . . bills as big as our twenty-five francs, and they're worth almost nothing!" Next to the ridiculous Habsburg money, there was also proof that what Woodrow Wilson and the rest of the Paris delegates had been spouting was just hot air. Fiume was no mixed city, Maranini assured Elda. Instead, "here everyone, or almost [everyone], speaks Italian, and everything is genuinely Italian."[2] As far as Maranini was concerned, Gabriele D'Annunzio's hypnotic balcony speeches described Fiume perfectly: "The patria is felt here, with a sense of purity and passion, so great. For this alone I am happy to have come."[3] Yes, the stories Elda had read about the legionnaires were on the whole true—"Everyone here is having fun, and spending money, and making love with the Fiume girls, who are famed for being pretty and easy."[4] But that's not why he loved Fiume, he hastened to add. It was the zeal he felt here that touched his heart: "What enthusiasm there is in this city! You have to come here to know what true patriotism is."[5]

If Elda had jumped on a train to meet her sweetheart, would she have seen what Maranini described? Was Fiume really all about Italian "patriotism"? Sure, the hearts of people like Maranini swelled when they saw local Fiumians roll out Italian flags, chant Italian nationalist songs, and cheer D'Annunzio when he stepped out on his balcony. We know for a fact, however, that much of what Maranini and his fellow Italian activists described was not true. It was, as he put it, "a dream." Not everyone in Fiume was "genuinely Italian." Over half of those living in the city and its environs learned to speak in other languages and identified with cultural worlds very different from those permeating Italian cities and countrysides.[6] We also know that after four years of war, Fiume's wealth—visible in its beautiful palaces and modern port-rail infrastructures—spoke more of prewar times than postwar realities. As in the wartime and immediate postwar Vienna described so eloquently by Maureen Healy, Fiume's trade had been at an almost complete standstill for five years. Fuel and food were scarce; jobs disappeared; families worried.[7] Before the troops arrived, Fiume's sexual mores were not noticeably different from those of any other early twentieth-century European urban landscape. The famed "pretty and easy" Fiume girls were the result of having soldiers stationed in a war-struck town. More than one Fiume resident lamented the changes caused by Italian soldiers, who, with money in hand, "came to Fiume to ruin women and corrupt them."[8] The ration cards, the long lines at the welfare and unemployment offices, the spike in petty crime, the expansion of whorehouses (both formal and informal), and the seemingly endless demand for emigration papers were just some of the indicators that Maranini and much of the literature dedicated to the "National Question" of Fiume overlooked.

Turning away from the dream of Fiume's "pure patriotism" and focusing instead on something Maranini himself noted as a peculiarity of the Fiume experience—"the last relic of the defunct monarchy," the Austro-Hungarian crown—offers insights into life in of-this-world Fiume. Let us look at the history of one of Europe's most contested successor states not through the eyes of legionnaires or nationalist dreamers but through what went on in people's wallets.

The Last Relic of the Defunct Monarchy

What Maranini saw when he looked in his wallet was not what a Fiume resident would have seen. What he saw was that sitting among his familiar Italian lire were "big" colored bills, covered with double-headed Habsburg eagles, portraits of regal-looking women, and multiple languages interspersed between the dominant German and Hungarian large-type print. From Maranini's perspective, upon arriving in Fiume, he had entered a world that used a "relic" currency of a dissolved adversary.[9] Fiume residents, however, would have seen not only lire and crowns but usually at least four different currencies crinkling in their wallets at any time.

Thumbing one's way through the Fiume police reports gives a sense of this currency diversity. When the 20-year-old student Borislavo Gjurić was arrested in one of Fiume's main whorehouses, police noted that his wallet contained Italian lire, French francs, Serb dinars, Serb-Croat-Slovene crowns, and Fiume crowns.[10] His friend, the unemployed 29-year-old veteran Nicolò Kuprešanin, had an even larger array of currencies in his wallet: "6,621 crowns, 50 lire, some silver coins, and small change in French, Serb, and Greek [currencies]."[11] The 52-year-old foreman of the Fiume Railway Warehouse, Giorgio Roosz, reported being robbed by a woman he was trying to court, and declared that his "used, small, yellow leather wallet contained circa 300 crowns in banknotes of different denominations, with Fiume and Yugoslav stamps

A fifty Austro-Hungarian crown note with a "Città di Fiume" stamp, upper left. The two sides of the bill represented the two halves of the Habsburg Empire. Shown is the Austrian side, with the German language foregrounded, and on the left the main official languages used in the lands ruled by Vienna. The Hungarian side of the bill is only in Hungarian.

[on them], as well as some change in Italian [lire]."[12] When 46-year-old businessman Gabriele Stejčić had his wallet stolen (also in a whorehouse), he declared it contained "2,130 [Serb] dinars, 2 1000-crown pieces in Austrian money as well as one piece of 50 crowns and several pieces of 20 crowns."[13] After being robbed by their maid, the Neumann merchant family declared that their missing wallet contained "circa 700 crowns with the Yugoslav stamp."[14] Though the Kingdom of Serbs, Croats, and Slovenes was not called Yugoslavia until 1929, in daily parlance throughout Fiume, "Yugoslav" was a short-cut denominator many used to describe the crown stamped by the Serb-Croat-Slovene state. Another shortcut was using just "Serb," as the Belgrade ministries determined the value and number of crowns to be stamped. Many of Fiume's bureaucracies employed acronyms like SHS (from the Croatian "Srpski-Hrvatski-Slovenski") or SCS (from the Italian "Serbo-Croato-Sloveno") before writing "crown." The confusion about what to call dif-

ferent monies added to the complexities of what living in a multicurrency world meant.

Maranini was right to assume that the average Fiume wallet held lire
and crowns, but he was wrong to end the story there. A crown in the
average Fiume wallet was usually one of three different currencies: the
"relic" unstamped crown Maranini described, the Fiume-stamped
crown, and the Serb-Croat-Slovene-stamped crown. How did these different crowns make their way into a Fiume wallet? The answer lies
with the dicta of state and market. When the Habsburg Empire was
dissolved in November 1918, all lands of Austria-Hungary made use of
the same unstamped crowns. By February 1919, the provisional governments in two successor states, Czechoslovakia and the Kingdom of
Serbs, Croats, and Slovenes, required inhabitants to bring their crowns
in to be stamped. The logic behind this move was to begin separating
out the financial responsibility of the successor states vis-à-vis war rep-
arations and the dissolved empire's debt. Czechoslovakia and the
Kingdom of Serbs, Croats, and Slovenes hoped that their share in rationing out responsibility for Habsburg finances could be limited to the
relative number of Habsburg crowns circulating in their lands. The practice of stamping crowns was also inspired by the prospect that this would
encourage business and trade to circulate nationally (within the boundaries of the new provisional states) instead of cross-regionally, as prior
Habsburg infrastructures intended. Separating out the money seemed
like one of the first tasks necessary to secure national sovereignty, the
ability to govern and administer a "national" territory independently.

Fiume was the last successor state to stamp its crowns, for reasons
related to how its wealth was built before the war and how its government thought it could re-create a fiscally secure trajectory in the future.
On January 15, 1919, the Italian National Council discussed a recent article in the Croatian newspaper *Narodne novine* (People's times),
which outlined how the Kingdom of Serbs, Croats, and Slovenes planned
to put overlay stamps on all the Austro-Hungarian crowns in its territory. Since most of the lands to the north and the east of Fiume were
already incorporated into the Kingdom of Serbs, Croats, and Slovenes,
the Italian National Council felt it necessary to discuss the ramifications

of this move. This issue was important not just because a neighboring state was changing its currency policies; these lands also supplied most of the city's food, and almost all its transit structures passed through them. In short, money between Fiume and the Kingdom of Serbs, Croats, and Slovenes inevitably would flow back and forth and currency transformations mattered. After discussion, the Italian National Council decided to take no measures, "as this will not cause us any harm." Like the convinced liberals they were, they believed currency should flow according to the market, but orders were given that "the state treasury not accept any paper money with Yugoslav stamping."[15] Austro-Hungarian crowns (unstamped) and lire were welcomed into the state coffers. Stamped Serb-Croat-Slovene crowns could be used where applicable. The only thing not allowed was for Fiume's state treasury to fill with the currency of the neighbor who, in Paris diplomatic halls and throughout the media, the Fiume government was opposing.

Only five days later, the Italian National Council realized that the ramifications of the Kingdom of Serbs, Croats, and Slovenes' currency stamping would affect Fiume sooner and more profoundly than they had imagined. On January 20, 1919, Fiume's mayor informed the Italian National Council that "people in the suburbs, incited by the Croatian papers, have begun today to withdraw deposits in mass amounts . . . so as to have the banknotes stamped by the Yugoslav authorities." When asked whether this meant that the Fiume government should do something to limit this currency flow, council members stated, oddly enough, "It's in the general interest that cash money be exported from the city," and so money should continue to be paid out "whatever the amount."[16]

How could a city-state behave so nonchalantly about a shift in the monetary policy of the country surrounding it—with which it shared the same currency, from whom almost all of its food reserves came, and through which most of its transport networks passed? And why was it "in the general interest" to have cash leave the city? The answer to these questions was simple, at least according to the council members: annexation to Italy meant that Rome would oversee monetary policies, and, so, the council should not act prematurely. Further, Fiume's officials, focused as they were on imminent annexation, thought that the more "cash money" they had, the bigger and more costly a task the Italian state would have transforming the Austro-Hungarian crowns into lire. As the Austro-Hungarian crown markets began to spin more and more out of control, Fiume officials became increasingly desperate for Rome to step in, wipe out their multicurrency crown chaos, and install a monocurrency lira culture. This attitude shaped all large-scale infrastructure discussions. In scrutinizing the railway budget, the postal budget, the pension and subsidies budget, and especially monetary policy, the Italian National Council consistently focused on ways to try to force the Italian state to step in quickly. As Fiume's mayor said after a particularly grim discussion of how to cover costs for the postal network, "This whole budget is the best proof that Fiume as a state in and of itself cannot exist."[17]

The Italian National Council's pessimism regarding Fiume's ability to become a "state in and of itself" and its reluctance to confront the brewing currency debacle underscores the way the semiautonomous Fiume city-state had boomed over the last forty years. From the late 1860s until the war, Fiume's economy and population grew because Hungary invested to make it grow. Its expanded ports, state-of-the-art railway network, oil refinery, chemical plant, horse depot, wood terminal, ship-building factory, tram system, sewage system, aqueduct, modern hospital, electrical network, and the hundreds of stately buildings Maranini so admired were the product of either direct Hungarian subsidy or Budapest-based private investments in local entrepreneurs.[18] The Hungarian Kingdom was determined to turn Fiume into a commercial hub from which to sell its flour, sugar, and wood and get the wine, rice, rope, and tobacco its heartland gobbled up.[19] The Budapest government (with local Fiumian oversight) made the infrastructure, then opened up the city's license office to absorb the private investment opportunities that followed. Reassured by the stable prewar Austro-Hungarian currency, Hungarian, Croatian, British, Austrian, Czech, German, Italian, and French businessmen took the bait. To sweeten the deal, Hungary also reduced tariffs and discounted transportation rates. Fiume welcomed ships from all over the world at cheaper prices than elsewhere, encouraging an influx of "colonial" goods from the Ottoman

and British Empires and an outflux of poor European emigrants eager
to get to the New World. Factories (almost all benefiting from some
sort of state subsidy) mushroomed in Fiume's outskirts, processing
what arrived in its ports and employing thousands of workers (many
of them women) who had recently arrived in Fiume. A state-of-the-art
emigration station was built to house the thirty thousand emigrants
the Hungarian state contracted to provide the British-owned Cunard
shipping line annually for transport to New York City. In 1913, imports
into Fiume were twenty-one times higher than in 1867, exports nineteen
times higher. As James Callaway eloquently puts it in his forthcoming
book, "To Budapest, any trade that traveled through Fiume was good
trade," and so Fiume grew thanks to a metropole that nurtured the
macrostructures of its rise.[20]

With the war and the accompanying maritime blockades, most of this
trade had come to a standstill. Fiume businessmen still had their networks; sailors and dockmen still took pride in their ability to harness
the sea; workers (both male and female) were still eager for employment; and most of the city's factories were still intact, waiting to churn
out products for sale. But with the communication interruptions of the
war, the dissolution of the kingdom that oversaw its networks, and the
bordering up of Europe, the port was inactive and its provisional government bled funds to keep its inhabitants afloat until things looked
up. Regulating the currency chaos was just one more thing Fiumians
considered above their pay grades. All the members of the Italian
National Council agreed that the "Government in Rome" needed to
"minister to the economic difficulties of the city (for example, either
by equalizing the crown to the lira or by lowering the prices for food)."[21]
Their prewar Hungarian experience had taught them well: this was the
kind of thing kingdoms solved, not free cities.

The Italian National Council wanted to continue enjoying the privileges of being an autonomous city under the infrastructural umbrella
of a kingdom, but Rome was adamant that it would not provide permanent, structural economic and monetary help until the diplomatic
crisis centered on Fiume was resolved.[22] In the meantime, Fiume was
left to fend for itself, with just enough Italian loans and negotiated food

shipments to ensure that the city's population did not starve. A little more than a week after the beginning of the Serb-Croat-Slovene stamping campaign, Italy also started stamping the crowns held within the ex-Habsburg lands that the Italian military had occupied after the war (to the west of Fiume). A week after that, the Italian National Council was informed that Fiume's "banks are accumulating ever greater quantities of Yugoslav banknotes, that the non-stamped notes are being taken to [Italian-occupied] Trieste to be exchanged into lire, so that soon we will find ourselves in the difficult position of not having our own [unstamped] banknotes."[23] A few days later, on February 15, 1919, the head of the Inter-Allied forces met with the Italian National Council, warning that unless the currency debacle was addressed, banknotes in Fiume "whose value today is relative if not imaginary" would be replaced with a barter system between Fiume's Serb-Croat-Slovene hinterland and the city, leading to almost complete economic dependence on "the Croatians."[24]

At this point, few options seemed to remain. Fiume could stop the inflow of Serb-Croat-Slovene crowns by stamping their own crowns and making it the legal currency, it could declare the Italian lira Fiume's only legal currency, or it could accept that the Serb-Croat-Slovene currency was underwriting the city's economy. The third option was rejected out of hand. The provisional government's entire political platform was dedicated to securing Fiume's annexation to Italy. For them, as repeated ad nauseam in council meetings and pleas to the Italian government, Fiume's economic problem was its political problem, and no economic solution that undermined their political goals could or should be considered.[25] Though never mentioned overtly, it is very likely many Fiumians also discounted having the Serb-Croat-Slovene crown act as their legal tender because these crowns were pegged at an official exchange rate almost half that of those stamped in the Italian-occupied territories. Though among contemporaries in the United Kingdom, France, Germany, and the United States, Italy appeared "backwards," in comparison to the newly forming Kingdom of Serbs, Croats, and Slovenes, it was light-years ahead in capital investment potential, and Fiume elites knew it.[26]

Many in the Italian National Council wanted to simply declare the Italian lira the official currency. What easier "preparatory measure for the definitive conversion into Italian lire" could there be?[27] Unfortunately for the Italian National Council, that proved pragmatically impossible. The biggest obstacle was getting enough lire into Fiume's economy. Fiume banks, whether state or private, held mostly crowns, not lire, and most of the few inflows of capital that Fiume still could count on were with former Habsburg networks, also still using crowns instead of lire. Salaries and pensions still paid for by the Hungarian state were dispersed in crowns.[28] The Italian state refused to allow unlimited conversion of crowns into lire at the beneficial rate provided in the Italian-occupied territories. "Not being able to mathematically cover" what would be required to anoint itself as a lira currency regime, in March 1919 the Italian National Council finally conceded that the only option left was to join the rest of the Habsburg successor states in stamping crowns. And so, in April 1919, the provisional government begrudgingly and nervously fiumanized its money.[29]

With Fiume added to the mix, by spring 1919 all the provisional governments of the ex-Habsburg lands were stamping the crowns within their territories. Soon crowns with different stamps had different values. Determined by the Zurich stock exchange, those values depended on the number of crowns stamped in each country, the import-export trade of the provisional state, and the amount of debt accumulated in the first months of state formation.[30] The successor states required residents to use only crowns stamped by their own state. But personal and financial networks still crossed borders, leading ex-Habsburg subjects to collect an assortment of crowns. Given the fluctuation in relative value, many ex-Habsburg subjects began playing the exchange market game, spending or saving a particular stamped crown in hopes of making money off their money.[31]

On the whole, Fiume's experience negotiating a world of stamped and unstamped crowns was akin to that of most ex-Habsburg trading hubs.[32] As we saw by peeking in their wallets, Fiumians did not limit their economic transactions to the stamped crowns of their provisional government. Most carried at least Fiume- and Serb-Croat-Slovene-stamped crowns. Partly this was because the relative values of the two currencies fluctuated enormously. For example, between October 1919 and December 1919 the difference in value of Fiume crowns over Serb-Croat-Slovene crowns rose from 10 percent to 60 percent, meaning that in October you had to pay 110 Serb-Croat-Slovene-stamped crowns for 100 Fiume-stamped crowns, while in December those same 100 Fiume-stamped crowns would cost you 160 Serb-Croat-Slovene-stamped crowns.[33] Given the choice, Fiumians disposed of their Serb-Croat-Slovene crowns whenever they could, for fear that their value would decrease even more.

Serb-Croat-Slovene crowns didn't just circulate heavily because they represented "cheap" money. They also embodied the lifeline of trade to the north and east of the city-state. If you wanted to buy fish from Dalmatia, you needed Serb-Croat-Slovene crowns, as 25-year-old fishmonger Ernesto Bianco explained to a judge during a counterfeiting trial in 1920.[34] If you joined 49-year-old housewife Maria Tisma at the nearby port town Bakar for her daylong shopping trip to buy meat and sugar, which were hard to find in Fiume, the trip would be worthless without Serb-Croat-Slovene crowns in your purse.[35] Some trudged to Bakar with Serb-Croat-Slovene-stamped crowns even for things available in Fiume because, as Lucia Bozenich, an illiterate 40-year-old housewife from Zadar, Dalmatia, explained, "there you could find more and for cheaper than in the Fiume marketplace."[36] In the city itself, Serb-Croat-Slovene crowns were a must at market, as shown in a court trial involving a judge seen exchanging currencies. In the trial it was stated as common knowledge that "civil servants were paid in Fiume-stamped crowns and were therefore forced to change them into Yugoslav-stamped crowns to make purchases in Fiume."[37]

At the same time, Serb-Croat-Slovene crowns were impractical in official transactions in Fiume. If you needed to pay a fine, then you would do well to bring Fiume-stamped crowns. If you owed money to a bank, owed rent, needed to pay for postage or administrative fees, or wanted to buy a tram ticket, crown notes with a "Città di Fiume" insignia did the job. Each crown had its usages, and any practical person tried to have a supply of both.

The marketplace was where Serb-Croat-Slovene crowns dominated in Fiume, because the majority of goods on sale came from the surrounding Serb-Croat-Slovene hinterlands. It was here, too, that an enormous amount of the city's illicit money exchange took place, with holders of all the different crowns using purchases to shift the ratio of currencies in their wallets.

What made Fiume's experience different from that of the other successor states was not the diversity of currencies that filled local wallets but rather the relationship of those crowns to the currency Maranini was most familiar with: the Italian lira. Provisional governments in Poland, Czechoslovakia, Hungary, Romania, Austria, and the Kingdom of Serbs, Croats, and Slovenes stamped their crowns to fence off "national" trade from greater Habsburg markets, to control the value of their own currency, and to curtail liability for Habsburg debt. In Fiume, the provisional government stamped crowns for all these reasons *and* to regularize currency conversion with the Kingdom of Italy. As discussed earlier, the Italian National Council only started stamping crowns to forestall possible incorporation into the Kingdom of Serbs, Croats, and Slovenes and to secure an easy absorption into the Kingdom of Italy. However, from the start, the city's stamping campaign did not put a stop to the enormous influx of Habsburg crowns, in part because Fiume's location made it a particularly enticing site for currency speculation. Monies moved in and out of Fiume thanks to its port-railway infrastructure and the dollars, pounds, francs, and lire flowing first from the Inter-Allied forces who occupied the city from November 1918 to September 1919 and then from D'Annunzio's lire-carrying legionnaires from September 1919 to January 1921.

Efforts to control the flow of crowns into Fiume throughout 1919–1921 resembled the control today's states try to exert to block drug trafficking, with about as much success. Police—either city police or soldiers of the Inter-Allied regime or soldiers under D'Annunzio—manned the major thoroughfares, checked the trains, and inspected the few incoming ships, all on the hunt for crowns. As more and more crowns continued to sprout up within Fiume coffers, under mattresses, and between hands in its marketplace, the searches by Fiume's armed services went into overdrive. Body searches were initiated in mid-1920, and officials got an earful from women "of status" about the intolerable humiliations suffered when they were forced to "take off their jacket, hat, shoes, socks, skirt, underclothes and remained in shirt and underwear . . . [only then to be] ordered to take off the underwear . . . for a body search." An affront to the norms of the time, no doubt. No one enjoyed the body searches, though some complaining matrons asserted that "coquettes" intentionally used the opportunity of being patted down in front of the police and male passengers "to show off their silk underwear and underclothes." Whatever the truth to these stories, officials filed the ladies' complaints but continued in their brusque ways. If they were going to "impede the clandestine importation of a.h. [Austro-Hungarian] paper currency," physical searches were one of the only means available to them.[38]

For locals like Paolo Rukavina—who lived in Sušak and had daily business in Fiume proper—these initiatives were more exasperating than effective. He explained why to the Italian National Council: Rukavina had been stopped on the Sušak bridge on his way to Fiume. A policeman asked him whether he was carrying any crowns with him, and Rukavina showed the 840 crowns he had declared. The policeman

Two women crossing the Fiumara bridge into Fiume are stopped by a legionnaire so that he can inspect their papers and purses.

then proceeded to sequester 540 crowns in accordance with a new law
changing the crown limits to 300 crowns in place of the prior 1,000-
crown law. Rukavina exploded, saying "he had not even stepped foot
in Fiume and he could have easily just returned home and left there
the crowns sequestered from [him]."[39] He had a point; since he crossed
in and out of Fiume daily, he did not need to bring in the full 840
crowns. Rukavina could instead have left a chunk of the hunted currency at home, stayed within the law, and crossed the bridge over the
next few days with the remaining crowns he kept legally in his apartment. The extreme body searches show how dangerous the state found
unchecked crown circulation to be. But the challenges of hindering the
movement of money into a city that was at the heart of an entire regional and extraregional network of food, merchandise, and medical
care showcases how futile a mission that was.

Crowns poured into Fiume in part because of the natural money
flows of a market and service center. But the state instituted the body
searches because Fiume was where ex-subjects of the Habsburg Monarchy living within the Adriatic territories newly occupied by Italians

hoped to either have their crowns stamped "Fiume" or exchange them "off the books" for the currency they all expected would become their official one: the lira. Crowns streamed into Fiume because lire were a speculative commodity, and Fiume was one of the only places not under direct Italian military control where lire were available. Exchanging crowns for lire outside Italian state supervision was attractive because Italian state-supervised stamping and exchange procedures were usually more expensive and included research into the provenance of the crowns. The Italian military regime set fines and exchange limits for those suspected of war profiteering, illicit money exchanging, or any other form of "new capitalism" that put suspiciously large amounts of crowns into people's bank accounts. Exchanging crowns for lire in Fiume bypassed these "inconveniences" and fed the hope for a clean-money, all-lira slate.

Physically trying to stop crowns from flooding into Fiume was one rather clumsy and ineffective technique. Stamping was the other method that the Italian National Council used to curb "the clandestine speculation of Italian lire . . . and the [resulting] importation to Fiume . . . of the currency of the ex-Austro-Hungarian Monarchy." When stamping was first introduced in April 1919, the Italian National Council declared that only its stamped crowns would function as the city's legal tender.[40] Unstamped crowns could no longer be used for trade. Initially residents were told that the exchange rate of Fiume crowns to Italian lire would be set at 1 to 1 *once* Fiume was annexed to the Kingdom of Italy.[41] Later, those promises shifted to 2.5 to 1—not great, but better than the 4.5 to 1 Fiumians regularly experienced in the local marketplace and the 4-to-1 exchange rate enforced in the Kingdom of Serbs, Croats, and Slovenes between Serb-Croat-Slovene-stamped crowns and their Serb dinar equivalents. In the meantime, the Fiume government tried to set the daily exchange rate at 1.3 Fiume crown to every Italian lira, though throughout 1919–1921 it fluctuated between 1.3 and 1.6. The Fiume crown thus functioned at two different values. On a day-to-day level it represented devalued currency, anywhere from 30 to 60 percent less valuable than Habsburg crowns had been before World War I. But if the Italian National Council succeeded in annexing the city-state to

Detail from a photograph of one of Fiume's most important banks. The
German sign WECHSELSTUBE (Currency Exchange Booth) is covered with
an Italian sign saying VOGLIAMO L'ANNESSIONE (We want annexation).

Italy, then Fiume crowns would—it was hoped—function as an equivalent to the Italian lira, or maybe a discounted Italian lira, but certainly
a brighter future than the monetary penury they were experiencing. In
short, annexation to Italy, with its currency conversions, promised to
bring holders of Fiume crowns closer to their prewar wealth.

A monocurrency law did not make a monocurrency culture. Taking
a fixed number of Habsburg crowns, stamping "Città di Fiume" on
them, and calling them quasi lire created a situation ripe for turmoil.
There was an immediate run on Fiume-stamped crowns, as not enough
had been stamped. The Fiume stamp was supposed to represent a first
step toward leaving behind a degraded Habsburg-crown reality for a
lire-filled Kingdom of Italy future. The pledge that Fiume-stamped
crowns would exchange at a rate of 1 to 1, or even 2.5 to 1, offered Fiumians of all languages and backgrounds an incentive to support the pro-
Italy government. But in the day-to-day, the government's deflationary

policies that tried to keep the value of Fiume crowns relatively in line with the lire hurt most of its populace. As an industrial port town whose population had boomed by 60 percent over the past thirty years, Fiume was filled with businesses, factories, sailors, workers, unemployed, widows, elderly, children, and the rainbow of others who depended on money being available daily. The Fiume government's anti-inflationary measure might have been good for nationalist politics and for people with savings to protect, but for the tens of thousands of Fiumians living on the edge, a currency shortage proved disastrous.

The costs of this disaster also explain why the contents of Fiume wallets did not reflect the monocurrency culture the state had hoped to establish. More money was needed to fill the gaps the deflationary Fiume crown measures had created. In July 1919, just three months after Fiume's first round of stamping began, the city's rations office informed the government that they were "seriously embarrassed because of the absolute lack of bills stamped Città di Fiume and in general all businesses have fallen behind with their payments."[42] Two weeks later, the rations office again warned the government about the dangers of not allowing Serb-Croat-Slovene crowns to be accepted as legal tender, "especially because of the complete lack of Città di Fiume bills among the lowest strata of the population, who nonetheless must use the rations market for the purchase of foodstuffs."[43] In response, the government permitted Serb-Croat-Slovene crowns to be used at market and to pay salaries. After numerous complaints from businesses throughout the city indicating they did not have enough currency to pay their employees or their taxes, in November 1919 the state began stamping more crowns.[44] But the Italian National Council had miscalculated again: not enough money was stamped. In February 1920, Fiume's Borsa Mercantile (Mercantile Stock Exchange) wrote the government to denounce "the very grave inconvenience caused by the total lack of currency in small denominations, an inconvenience that makes every commercial and industrial undertaking impossible."[45] That same month, three local factories warned the government that they would have to fire all their workers because the small-denomination Fiume crown notes "necessary to pay the workers and to cover daily expenses" were unavailable.[46] Similar complaints were made by all the major employers in the city.

If businesses complained, workers complained more. In November 1919, D'Annunzio's forces intercepted communications from the city's shipbuilding offices: workers were angry about being paid in Serb-Croat-Slovene currency while their costs were calculated in Fiume crowns. "Mutinies amongst the workers have already begun," one foreman reported to his higher-ups. To resolve the situation, managers decided they "would try to pay half the salary in Yugoslav bills and half in Città di Fiume." The fate of those "who refused to accept the Yugoslav bills" was clear: "They must be fired."[47] Three months later, in February 1920, a group of workers from Fiume's factories met with municipal representatives to explain their untenable situation. Their laments were summarized this way: "With the recent ordinance . . . requiring that the payment of rents needed to be made in Città di Fiume bills, workers see themselves as harmed beyond what is reasonable, as they receive their salaries <u>exclusively</u> in Yugoslav bills."[48] Two months after that, in April 1920, there was a general strike, with workers pushing to be paid in Italian lire and demanding lower prices at the rations market. Eventually, workers accepted being paid in other currencies if lire were not available, but only if their pay was pegged to the daily exchange rate with the lira.

To many, the government's efforts to push through a deflationary Fiume crown monocurrency culture reflected decades of liberal politicians' heartless disinterest in the struggles of the less fortunate. And to some degree this was correct: the Italian National Council cared more about its plans for annexation and protecting investments than it did about protecting the fates of those who survived on their daily earnings. But fear of revolt did force the government to install a plan B, a multicurrency system allowing Serb-Croat-Slovene crowns into its economy to neutralize rancor among the populations hit hardest by this strategy. And so, Fiume's multicurrency wallets were as much a result of the market as of a state trying to push annexation forward while simultaneously keeping insurrection at bay.

The Fiume Italian National Council might have created a multicurrency system to stem revolt, but the multiple fluctuating currencies proved ruinous for many of its other constituents. First, businesses contracted to pay or be paid in more than one currency often had to eat the loss caused by differences in currencies' fluctuating values. The owner of the Prima Lavanderia Fiumana a Vapore (First Fiumian Dry Cleaner), 31-year-old Vio Zoris, tried to explain the problem to one of the military hospitals servicing D'Annunzio's troops. According to Zoris, the hospital had agreed to pay his business in lire because the Italian National Council had ordered that the "carbon and gasoline [needed for steam dry-cleaning] be paid for in lire." However, D'Annunzio's military command insisted that it would pay "its bills in Yugoslav crowns at a rate of 8.60 Yugoslav crown [to the lira]." Zoris was outraged, mainly because the going rate for lire was higher than the official rate. According to Zoris, the "rate today is 9.70," 12 percent higher than the 8.60 the military command offered to pay. Zoris sized up this situation clearly: "You must understand that it is impossible to work this way. The military authorities can play the currency game, but a small business can't do it, especially since we work at a loss. The currency we use to pay for combustibles is the currency in which we must have our accounts [paid]."[49] When Zoris received no answer, he offered another solution. Since his business could not afford to be paid in Serb-Croat-Slovene crowns while simultaneously paying for energy in Italian lire, he suggested that the military command supply him with "10 tons of carbon and 660 kg of gasoline." In return he would wash "5,000 pieces of laundry, whether small or large, without any exchange of money."[50] In essence, Zoris suggested that Fiume retreat from money, since he (and by extension many of his fellow Fiumians) couldn't afford "to play the currency game."[51] Until the government could realize the favorable annexation currency solution it promised, barter seemed the most propitious strategy for the immediate future.

It wasn't just businesses that wanted to opt out of money. Civil servants, too, believed they couldn't afford to be paid until the currency situation was regularized. Clemente Marassich, a 26-year-old veteran and former prisoner of war in Russia, asked the Fiume school board *not* to reinstate him as a full-time teacher "at least until the currency is regulated and salaries are definitively systematized." Until then, Marassich preferred to work as a freelance journalist, especially as "within days [he would] have to sustain great and extra costs for the pregnancy of [his] wife."[52] The teacher and grieving widower, Giuseppe Stefan, petitioned the school board requesting that, "in view of the precarious conditions of the city, the payment of [his] pension be deferred until the regulation of salaries and the return of normal conditions."[53] Pension deferment was a common request, especially for those living outside Fiume. Retired schoolteachers 61-year-old Enrico Bombig and his wife Elena Molnár had moved to Gorizia during the war. When fighting erupted there, they were transferred as refugees to Milan, even though their only income was the pension they received from Fiume. The Bombig family wrote regularly to the Fiume civic magistrate "warmly praying . . . to defer sending [pension monies] . . . until the equalizing of the crown with the lira." Otherwise, given the current exchange rate, they "would be forced to lose 60%" of their pensions' value.[54] For the Bombig family, the Stefan family, the Marassich family, and the thousands of others whose salary, pensions, and insurance were set by contract on the Austro-Hungarian crown, the unstable currency of the city appeared dire enough that they pleaded to be paid when "improvement of the financial situation would render less disastrous the conditions of [currency] exchange."[55] Until then, it was better to go without money than to be paid less than the state owed them.

Obviously, most people could not "go without money" while they waited for the Fiume government to realize its currency-beneficial annexation to Italy. And for this reason, perhaps the most astounding proposal to bypass money was made by those who could afford it the least: unemployed laborers. When workers' representatives met with the municipal council in February 1920, they did not just make the case that they needed to be paid in the same currency with which they paid their rents; they also suggested the government not offset rising costs by increasing unemployment subsidies, as it had been doing since the end of the war. Instead, the workers proposed that the government give to the "unemployed workers who are truly in need . . . a ration card authorizing the <u>withdrawal without payment of foodstuffs from the rations market</u>."[56] For those with too much to lose and for those with nothing to lose, leaving money behind seemed the best option until "the question of Fiume could be resolved favorably and for the conversion of the currency to follow."[57] By "favorably" they meant the realization of the government's plan to annex Fiume to Italy and thereby successfully substitute lire for crowns.

Fiume civil servants, pensioners, and the unemployed who wished to leave the world of money temporarily behind did so because they believed (or at least hoped, or had no other option but to hope) that this "favorable" annexation to Italy would come. And these hopes were not without basis. Italy, institutions affiliated with Italy, and even Italian private citizens had been sending money to Fiume since the dissolution of the Habsburg Monarchy. In December 1918, the Italian military took over the Italian National Council's four-hundred-thousand-crown deficit in maintaining a nearby hospital.[58] In 1919, Italy donated one million lire worth of postal stamps to the Fiume state to ease communications.[59] And from 1919 until at least 1921, the Italian Red Cross, thanks in great part to indirect support from the Italian government, supplied necessary food and heating supplies to keep the city fed when it did not have the means to feed itself.[60]

On a more symbolic, quotidian level, Italian "help" for Fiumians was widely visible and publicized. For example, in December 1918, the Italian army gave half a loaf of military bread to each student wearing the red, white, and green cockades signifying commitment to the Italian national cause.[61] A few days before Christmas, the Royal Italian Army gave every student who attended school "½ kg. marmalade and ½ kg dried prunes."[62] On February 20, 1919, the Queen of Italy sent shawls, shoes, and sandals to be distributed to Fiume's needy children.[63] In March 1919, the crew of the Italian naval ship *San Giorgio* donated three hundred lire to help Fiume's poor.[64] In April 1920, Italian nobles from Emilia-Romagna and Tuscany visited Fiume schools, giving out one thousand lire and telling of Italy's deeply felt "humane and patriotic" loyalty to Fiume.[65] In July 1920, a nationalist association in Padua donated ten thousand lire to "help Fiume."[66] For every one of these, there were ten more in which Italian organizations and private citizens sent money and supplies to aid Fiume. Both official and unofficial Italy seemed determined to help, so why not forgo devalued money now and wait to prosper later?

It was not just Fiume locals or Italian nationalists who believed Italy would enact a highly favorable Fiume crown conversion rate upon annexation. The 38-year-old Hungarian investor and businessman Károly Fischbein—a man who did not speak Italian and had only arrived in Fiume from Budapest in August 1918—testified that he began collecting Fiume crowns in late November 1919 "to have a margin in Fiume bills, for the eventuality of their conversion into Lire."[67] All in all, crowns in Fiume wallets were far from simply relics of a defunct monarchy. They were constantly changing, ambiguous commodities. For some they represented "a currency game" too rich for most Fiumians' blood. For others they promised an entrée into a new (Italian) monarchy that was far from defunct.

Counterfeiting Crowns

Most Fiumians did not put all their eggs in the annexation-to-Italy basket, however. Like the aforementioned Hungarian businessman Károly Fischbein, they hedged their bets. Fischbein set aside "a margin in Fiume bills, for the eventuality of their conversion into Lire."[68] But he did not pay the roughly 70–80 percent difference in value it would have cost him to obtain those Fiume bills. Instead, he paid to have his crowns stamped "off the books" at a rate of 45 percent, securing himself a profit of at least 18 percent, but as much as 486 percent if the promised currency parity conversion to lire came through. This off-the-books method, otherwise known as counterfeiting, was widespread. Figures as low on the social totem pole as the 27-year-old unemployed naval mechanic and veteran Vladimiro Masovcević and as high up as the 27-year-old aviator and Italian war hero Eugenio Casagrande were taken with the possibilities of a "wonderful speculation: you buy unstamped crowns, you stamp them, and then you make three times more."[69]

Crowns were counterfeited throughout the ex-Habsburg lands. In February 1919, Serb-Croat-Slovene officials reported that of the thirty-seven billion crowns circulating in their territories, at least seven billion were considered counterfeit.[70] In Czechoslovakia, it was estimated that between February and November 1919 at least one billion fraudulently stamped notes were introduced.[71] An Austrian weekly in 1920 tried to make light of how powerless successor states were at thwarting forgers by saying,

> Our only hope—however absurd it may sound—is that the Hungarian and Polish crowns will soon rise higher than the Austrian crowns, and that the Hungarian and Polish stamps can be counterfeited just as easily as the Austrian stamp, so that it will become again more profitable for the forgers to counterfeit them (just as was formerly the case with the Yugoslavian and Czechoslovakian stamps) and that we no longer be the victims of their favor.[72]

In Hungary, Poland, Austria, and the Kingdom of Serbs, Croats, and Slovenes, counterfeiting was considered such a profitable business that unstamped crown notes (the raw materials required for stamped-crown counterfeiting) sometimes traded at higher values than locally stamped bills.[73]

Counterfeiting was tempting not just because it was a quick way to make a lot of money; it was also ridiculously easy.[74] Modern currency counterfeiters usually have to replicate industrially produced, specialized paper covered with intricate, multicolored patterns. But since the counterfeit successor-state crowns had all been created by the Habsburg imperial state, the feel of the paper, its size, and most of the banknotes' visuals had already been officiated. On the whole, counterfeit stamped crowns and genuine stamped crowns felt and looked the same. The only indicator of whether money was counterfeit or genuine was the irregularly placed, dimly inked, small overlay stamp added on top.[75] And since the design of these stamps was often rudimentary, replicating them was easy sport for many.

Few stamped crowns were as overvalued and easily forged as the Fiume crown. The first stamp, issued in April 1919, was an indistinct imprint of the Italian royal crest whose lines of engraving were crudely fashioned and indistinct. It did not specifically mention Fiume. The second stamp, introduced in October 1919, was an improvement: the "Città di Fiume" insignia was made up of clear lines, but it was so simplistic that within days forgers were making convincing replicas. The Fiume authorities realized their mistake and added a third stamp to the mix a few weeks later. With a clear and ornate design, "Città di Fiume," and this time even the emblem of the Istituto di Credito del Consiglio Nazionale (the administrative body that controlled Fiume's currency), this stamp was much more difficult to copy, though it was initially only applied to Fiume crown notes in denominations of one hundred crowns and higher.[76] Even so, within a few weeks, some of the more expert counterfeiters could replicate it, making Fiume famous domestically and abroad as "the promised land for counterfeited money."[77] The *New York Times* offered its readers the spectacle of prominent Fiume bankers complaining, "Our currency has been counterfeited to such an extent that now we do not know any values. There are all kinds of crowns in circulation—Fiume, Jugoslav, Polish, Hungarian, Czechoslovak and Austrian. Then there is the lira. All of them in circulation, stamped, defaced and counterfeited."[78]

Fiume officialdom was at a loss as to how to control the counterfeiting. To keep in check the circulation of counterfeited crowns from other Habsburg lands, it tried to bolster the monocurrency policies discussed earlier. But as we saw, fencing off trade and bubbling up Fiume into a self-sustaining economic unit was impossible. Given the unavoidable multicurrency system of immediate postwar Fiume, the inflow of counterfeited crowns from the Kingdom of Serbs, Croats, and Slovenes; Austria; Hungary; Czechoslovakia; and even Poland was inevitable. The situation improved a bit in late 1920, when Fiume's neighboring successor states had either decommissioned their stamped crowns completely or excessive counterfeiting had made their market value minimal.

The Hungarian side of a fifty Austro-Hungarian crown note, with forged Fiume overlay stamps. The handwriting on the right reads, "Timbro falsificato" (Forged stamp). Here one can see versions of the second "Città di Fiume" insignia used from October 1919 and the much more complicated third "Città di Fiume—Istituto di Credito del Consiglio Nazionale" stamp.

The forging of Fiume-stamped crowns, however, was another matter. Counterfeiting rings in Fiume did not just threaten faith in the money supply per se; they directly challenged the government's deflationary initiatives intended to ease eventual conversion with the Italian lira. As such, though the circulation of counterfeited "foreign" crowns was treated as a necessary evil, the government focused most of its energy on bringing counterfeiters of Fiume crowns in line. To limit the number of people who would be interested in forging Fiume stamps, in October 1919, the Italian National Council announced that Fiume crowns could not be converted outside city territory.[79] Then the Fiume police cracked down on forgers within the city itself.

The crackdown was effective to an extent, especially considering the conditions in which it began. In October and November 1919, when the Italian National Council instituted a recall of Fiume crowns to replace the first stamp with the second and third, circa 60 percent of the Fiume crowns circulating in the city were found to be marked with forged stamps. In September 1921, when Fiume crowns were again recalled, only 10 percent were marked with forged stamps.[80] A 10 percent counterfeiting rate is definitely better than 60 percent, but a world where one out of every ten bills in your pocket is probably forged underscores the point made by the anonymous Fiume banker in the 1920 *New York Times* article mentioned earlier: when "currency has been counterfeited to such an extent . . . we do not know any values."[81]

After his men apprehended several gangs of counterfeiters responsible for almost a million falsified Fiume crowns, the head of Fiume's police force described the forgery as an assault on both Fiume's economy and its annexation hopes: "If we had not tracked down the forgers and if we had not stopped the trafficking of the forged money, mistrust in Fiume bills would not just have resulted in its high depreciation, but it would have permanently undermined the conversion into lire, which would have been equivalent to complete economic ruin."[82] For the government, counterfeiting Fiume crowns equaled blocking annexation and the much-anticipated replacement of lire for crowns.

State and business communities might have viewed counterfeiting as a dangerous menace, but Fiumians ate up the counterfeited money, absorbing it into their economies with a combination of prudence and pragmatism. Not only did they not spend and make money along the monocurrency structure their government devised, they did not value their money along any nationalist or state-initiated lines. Ironically, it was the sites of the counterfeiting crackdown—the trials of those in the counterfeiting rings—that shone a light on these contradictions.

A case in point was the biggest counterfeiting trial to be held in Fiume from 1919 to 1921: the Del Bello-Smoquina-Zustovich-Velcich-Fischbein trial of late January 1920. The defendants were accused of introducing circa 450,000 forged Fiume crowns into the money supply between November and December 1919.[83] The head forger, Benvenuto Del Bello, a 25-year-old mechanic, veteran, and driver for the Fiume public services administration, admitted to having successfully replicated all three of the stamps produced by the Fiume state. The other four defendants were accused of knowingly circulating counterfeit money.[84]

During the trial, much was revealed that undercut the "single-minded desire to unite with Italy" that both D'Annunzio's military regime and the Italian National Council were trying to project. For example, the head forger, Del Bello, was not "a Jew," "a Slav," or a "Hungarian" eager to undermine Italian wealth, as articles in the Fiume nationalist newspaper *La vedetta d'Italia* had intimated throughout the fall of 1919.[85] He was an Istrian-born, native Italian speaker who worked for the Fiume government. The vision of Fiume as a city cut off from the rest of the ex-Habsburg lands, just waiting to be embraced by the Italian motherland, also suffered as testimony was given. The forgery of the third stamp—the tricky Istituto di Credito del Consiglio Nazionale insignia—was produced in Vienna, where Del Bello had traveled in November 1919 to align himself with other forgers there. The majority of the unstamped bills used to forge the Fiume crowns were supplied by Austrians and Hungarians passing through the city: Hungarian financier Károly Fischbein (also on trial) and Austrian nurse Daniela Bürger, with whom Del Bello had had a long-standing affair.[86] The idea—often repeated in both the diplomatic chambers of Paris and most newspapers throughout the world—that Italian Fiumians and Croatians hated each other was also weakened by trial testimony. Police explained that they missed apprehending the sixth prime suspect, Fiume-born, native Italian speaker Dante Stiglich, because he had heard of his impending arrest and had escaped to Zagreb just hours before the police arrived. As a showcase of efforts to "crack down" on counterfeit circulation, the trial put into public purview and print the broad multilingual and multinational Habsburg networks that still existed within and beyond the Fiume city-state.

But the contradiction between the ways that Fiume's provisional government and Fiumians themselves valued money was clearest in the testimonies of the thirty-seven Fiumians questioned for possessing or aiding in the circulation of counterfeit Fiume crowns. Spanning the divides of gender, class, ethnicity, age, primary language use, and neighborhood affiliation, witnesses were asked to explain how and why they had access to counterfeit money. Brought to the stand were figures as high in the Fiume administration as the 38-year-old director of the tax

office, Felice Derenzin, and the 50-year-old merchant and banking
agent Ferdinando Cretich, a leading member of the chamber of commerce. The trial was also populated with testimonies of less exalted
Fiume residents such as 42-year-old unemployed waiter and veteran
Antonio Bauk, 22-year-old housewife and ex-waitress Maria Ladisch,
36-year-old butcher Antonio Badjak, 27-year-old tobacco kiosk atten-
dant Mario Smojver, and 22-year-old fishmonger and veteran Narciso
Scalembra. Unsurprisingly, if in every wallet at least one bill out of ten
was counterfeit, the tendrils of a counterfeiting ring touched all levels
of Fiume society.

When asked how they had access to counterfeited bills, witnesses
tended to have the same answer: they bought or sold Fiume crowns
because that's what the situation demanded. Clothing-store owner and
seamstress Elvira Gattinoni explained that her friend, 47-year-old unemployed barber Adolfo Martini, had "come to her store one day and
while [they] were talking offered to sell [her] banknotes with the 'Città
di Fiume' stamp." She continued, "Since I wanted to exchange Yugoslav banknotes at any cost, I very happily accepted his offer and exchanged with Martini at a rate of 65%."[87] The 58-year-old businessman
and large landholder Giorgio Rora told of acting as a middleman for a
friend who "wanted to sell 26,000 crowns with the Fiume stamp." Rora
said, "He asked me to find him a buyer, adding that the money was
the property of two fishermen who were looking for a 74% exchange
rate."[88] The 24-year-old unemployed bank cashier and veteran Simeone
Radovich stated, "Being in need of 'Città di Fiume' banknotes I asked
Smoquina [a defendant], who I ran into by accident, if he could get
me said banknotes."[89] The 42-year-old unemployed waiter Antonio
Bauk said, "A certain [man with the surname] Linda, upon entering
the Caffè Marittimo, told me that he needed 'Città di Fiume' banknotes
and asked me if I could get him some."[90] The 35-year-old unemployed
clerk and veteran Cosimo Domancich testified that his former employer,
the 29-year-old textile merchant Giovanni Abramovich, "charged [me]
to procure for him 'Città di Fiume' banknotes." Domancich said, "Three
days later [while I was] in the main square I ran into Zustovich [an-
other defendant], who upon hearing that I was looking to obtain Fiume

currency, offered to sell me 10,000 crowns."[91] These and similar testimonies in other counterfeiting investigations sent a clear message: Fiumians circulated counterfeit money because they continually needed to convert currencies, and Fiume crowns were a hot commodity. It was as simple as that. Their testimonies evoked little response from the court and the public because everyone knew that informal currency exchange was not an illicit activity. It was a Fiume way of life.

Since most witnesses testified that they converted currencies informally, outside the structures of state-licensed currency exchange booths or banks, police and the court asked them how they evaluated the Fiume crowns they were exchanging. Most witnesses maintained their innocence by showing they paid relatively high rates of exchange in line with official prices, meaning they paid good money for what they thought was good money. The 32-year-old merchant and veteran Annone Erbisti revealed he had had no idea he was purchasing forged money by underscoring that for the six thousand Fiume crowns he purchased, he "paid [Clemente] Bacchia a rate of 80%."[92] The 21-year-old accountant and veteran Renato Skarso cleared his name of any suspicion by assuring the police he "paid a 100% premium to purchase" the fifty thousand forged Fiume crowns held within his company's account.[93] The aforementioned clothing-store owner and seamstress Elvira Gattinoni insisted she was innocent in another currency conversion exchange she conducted with her 23-year-old brother Giuliano Teck, an unemployed smelter, by stating, "I didn't doubt in the least the validity of the banknotes offered me . . . , so much so that I paid a rate of 66%."[94] As none of these informal currency exchanges included receipts or other forms of documentation to certify their legality, witnesses counted on the viability of the exchanges they claimed to have made to prove their innocence. Innocence and currency validity thus both depended on the same foundation: going market value and a court's cognizance of it.

Surprisingly enough, the most troublesome testimonies for Fiume authorities were those made by witnesses who traded Fiume crowns *below* market value. The aforementioned Simeone Radovich asserted that he had purchased twelve thousand Fiume crowns from one of the

defendants at a rate of 50 percent. This should have put him in difficult circumstances with the police and court, as paying well below
market value suggested he probably knew they were counterfeit. But
this is where things got complicated. Radovich, too, doubted the validity of Fiume crowns traded so low and therefore required the de-
fendant Smoquina to accompany him to the Fiume Italian National
Council's Credit Institute with the seven thousand Fiume crowns he
intended to purchase. Once there, he "showed the banknotes to the cashier, who found them to be good. The next day [the accused] Smoquina brought . . . another 5,000 crowns, which were also determined
to be good by the cashier of said Institute."[95] The institute to which
Radovich brought his Fiume crowns to be verified was the same institute that had supposedly stamped the money in the first place, whose
emblem served as the third stamp, the one Fiume authorities hoped
would nip counterfeiting activities in the bud. How could private citizens of Fiume be held accountable for circulating counterfeit money if
the office in control of the money supply could not tell the difference?
Radovich was quickly dismissed as another victim of currency fraud,
but his statement pointed to a much bigger problem. Informally determined market value was a safer indicator of currency validity than
state authority. When Radovich judged the money on its rate of exchange, he found it suspicious. It was the state that had led him astray.

Throughout the counterfeiting trial, there were indications that the
Fiume provisional government was unable to manage the money situation. Ferdinando Cretich, the aforementioned banker and leading
member of Fiume's chamber of commerce, testified that the seventy-
eight thousand forged Fiume crowns found in his bank account had
been purchased from a licensed currency exchange booth and verified
by the Fiume Credit Institute.[96] If the incompetence (or internal corruption) of state authorities was not clear enough, the director of the
tax office, Felice Derenzin, testified, "I personally certified the deposits
made by [the defendant] Fischbein. I had absolutely no suspicions concerning the authenticity of the banknotes deposited by him."[97] Though
the Hungarian investor Károly Fischbein was eventually arrested for
currency fraud, many officials had certified his counterfeited Fiume

crowns before they were finally judged fraudulent. If the informal Fiume currency market had had a say in the validity of Fischbein's bills, however, they would never have passed muster. The 45 percent exchange rate Fischbein paid for the Fiume crowns was proof enough that something fishy was going on. What Fiume's counterfeiting trials made obvious was that the city as a whole was "continually buying and selling banknotes," and not out of patriotic impulses, nationalist convictions, or any sense of security that their state held the authority to secure their fortunes.[98] Fiumians worked around the hollow infrastructures as best they could, hedging their bets, minimizing their losses, buying and selling currencies because that's what was required, and looking for whatever opportunities might arise out of the chaos surrounding them.

Postwar Crowns: A History of Imperial Conversions and Balancing Acts

It is hard to imagine what Lieutenant Carlo Trevisani Scoppa—a 31-year-old legionnaire, born outside Naples, and Italian war veteran—thought when he wrote D'Annunzio a four-page typed letter titled "Reserved-Personal." Nothing in the letter was very personal. No information was given about Trevisani Scoppa or D'Annunzio specifically. Trevisani Scoppa labeled it that way to limit the damage its contents—an assertion of fiscal corruption—could do. In the letter he accused one of D'Annunzio's closest associates, Lieutenant Ulisse Igliori—a 24-year-old Italian war hero, Florence native, and one of the masterminds behind D'Annunzio's arrival in Fiume—of exchanging an enormous amount of money illegally to benefit the D'Annunzio command's coffers at the expense of both Italy and Fiume. The letter described the financial exchanges Trevisani Scoppa found suspicious: to help cover the costs of feeding Fiume's hungry during its upcoming winter, the Kingdom of Italy offered to purchase circa 7 million Fiume crowns at an exchange rate of 0.40 lire to 1 Fiume crown. This sale would give D'Annunzio's regime the lire necessary to purchase food and energy reserves from Italian suppliers who refused to accept crowns. Things

started to look suspicious to Trevisani Scoppa, however, when he realized that the Fiume crowns Igliori sold to the Italian state were purchased illicitly from a local Fiume bank at a rate of 0.28 lire to 1 Fiume
crown instead of the 0.40 lire to 1 Fiume crown negotiated with the
Kingdom of Italy. The discrepancy of the two exchange rates left an
extra 840,000 lire in D'Annunzio's accounts' favor. To make matters
even worse, Trevisani Scoppa revealed that Igliori had also contracted
simultaneously with the same bank to pay off D'Annunzio's command's
debts of 7 million Serb-Croat-Slovene crowns by fixing an exchange
rate of 5.75 Serb-Croat-Slovene crowns to 1 Italian lira, instead of the
going rate of 7.50 Serb-Croat-Slovene crowns to 1 Italian lira. This exchange rate discrepancy saved D'Annunzio's treasury office 933,000
Italian lire. Trevisani Scoppa took four pages to trace the complicated
maneuvers that allowed Igliori to skim nearly 1.7 million lire for
D'Annunzio's command's benefit. Toward the end of the letter, Trevisani Scoppa spoke plainly: it was hard not to see this as anything other
than "fiscal bartering . . . given the exchange rates do not correspond . . .
to the average exchange rate."[99] Sometimes numbers don't lie, and the
exchange rates Igliori had negotiated followed the logic of a black
market, not a legal one.

Trevisani Scoppa hoped Igliori had acted alone and that D'Annunzio
was ignorant of the entire operation and would stop it immediately. Unfortunately, his hope was misplaced. D'Annunzio knew precisely what
was going on, as other members of his treasury office had told him days
before about the illegal dealings, emphasizing that if annexation to Italy
were realized, Igliori's contracts would prove even more costly to "the
Italian treasury that one day will have to make the conversion at a rate
much higher than the sale."[100] Even worse, the treasury office's files still
contain D'Annunzio's signed orders supporting Igliori in his negotiations. And indeed, the money-scheming Igliori rose higher in D'Annunzio's
favor, while traces of the anxious Trevisani Scoppa within the history of
D'Annunzio's Fiume escapade remain faint at best.

The details of Trevisani Scoppa's naive effort are revelatory not
because they show D'Annunzio knowingly participating in corrupt financial dealings: before and after Fiume, D'Annunzio had bamboozled

banks and manipulated states to support his flagrant lifestyle. Why should this time be different? But there was something different here: instead of defaulting on loans or fleeing abroad to avoid moneylenders, D'Annunzio and his Italian-born followers joined local Fiumians in finding ways—often short of legality—to survive and even thrive in the city's multicurrency environment. Like everyone else, D'Annunzio's crew gambled on what the teenage legionnaire Maranini had described as the "last relic of the defunct monarchy, the crown."[101] Their entire operation was funded with Habsburg money, and communications with ex-Habsburg money agents from Vienna and Budapest abound in D'Annunzio's archives, along with negotiations with Croatian merchants and counterfeiting schemes with other post-Habsburg rings. As in the rest of Fiume, neither ethnic identifications nor nationalist convictions determined which currency would be used. Sometimes D'Annunzio's command used Fiume crowns, sometimes Italian lire, and more often than not they pushed forward their "Italy or death" campaign while carrying Serb-Croat-Slovene currency in their wallets. Even in moments when illicit activities came to the fore, someone like Trevisani Scoppa—who had grown up under the shadow of Mount Vesuvius instead of along the shores of the northern Adriatic—reasoned in the same way the Fiume fishmongers did: the simplest way to tell whether money was "legal" was its trading rate, not what officials declared. Though they had all just fought in World War I to bring the Habsburg Empire to its knees, by coming to Fiume, D'Annunzio and his legionnaires had become post-imperial actors themselves.

Money has always been and will always be a promiscuous commodity, and highlighting that legionnaires in Fiume had "gone native," "gone post-imperial," and used Serb-Croat-Slovene money while simultaneously arguing, as did the young Maranini, "that everything [in Fiume] is genuinely Italian" in no way indicates that they were not deeply committed to their nationalist convictions.[102] What following the money shows is that we need to put aside the dream narrative that the Fiume Crisis was driven purely by the energies and politics of nationalism. Even the most fervent nationalists, which D'Annunzio's legionnaires undoubtedly were, were affected by the context in which they lived.

And the tens of thousands living in Fiume, often less zealous for the nation than D'Annunzio's legionnaires, were even more affected.

This ambiguity is important to remember because most histories of postwar east central Europe follow the storyline presented by the diplomatic historian Zara Steiner: the history of east central Europe is characterized by "the primacy of nationalism," while that of western Europe was guided by "the primacy of economics."[103] Thanks to D'Annunzio's theatrics and later Italian Fascists' ritualized insistence that Fiume was the seed of Benito Mussolini's "revolution," the history of postwar Fiume has seen more of this "primacy of nationalism" argument than most ex-Habsburg lands. But as we have seen, national sentiment did not primarily or necessarily serve as the compass for how Fiumians, and even D'Annunzio's legionnaires, lived out their lives. Despite what the publicists wrote, Fiume was not populated solely by Italians or Italian nationalists. Fiumians did not push aside Habsburg networks of communication and trade to promote their Italianness above all else. They did not empty their wallets of money stamped with the insignia of other nations or states to prove how Italian they were. Forging or converting nationalist seals and stamps did not give them pause, not if it meant they could make money or just lose a little less. The only body willing to try all these strategies was the provisional government. And the inability of the government to enact these initiatives and still keep Fiume's populace fed and paid convinced many to work around the state.

It is true that many historians of east central Europe have emphasized the importance of economics in determining the challenges the Habsburg successor states faced.[104] But few have linked the economic chaos and hardships of the post-imperial moment to the greater difficulties these states confronted in winning over the populations they attempted to govern. One of the few was the Oxford-educated eminent historian L. B. Namier. In the immediate years after World War I, Namier spent much of his intellectual energy writing about the plight of his native Galicia—today split between Ukraine and Poland, at the time part of Poland, and before the war controlled by the Habsburgs. In his 1922 article titled "Currencies and Exchanges in an East Galician

Village," Namier argued that all the currency shifts since the beginning of the Habsburg Empire's demise had taught the average Galician peasant, no matter how rural or remote that individual's home was, to distrust the state and take control of his or her fragile economic life by playing the world currency market.[105] Fiume was no isolated village, of course, but the same phenomenon emerged. With the value of money unclear, Fiumians determined it on their own in a way they had never done before, no matter what their state said about it or what the stirrings of nationalism might seem to dictate.

But with Fiumians and legionnaires working around the state, how was anarchy or revolution avoided? One of the only explanations for this strange balance lay in the hopes expressed throughout the mountain of paperwork contained within the Fiume archives: if the provisional government (with the help of D'Annunzio) could succeed in realizing annexation to Italy, Fiumians' money could perhaps double in value. The "primacy of nationalism" and the "primacy of economics" were wholly interlocked in Fiume's day-to-day, as they doubtless were for all the successor states.[106] The government worked to achieve its promised nationalist-oriented annexation; locals put up with government initiatives as long as they were livable. Some of the ways the government tried to keep this balance going were the clumsy handlings of the Habsburg crown and the concessions to a multicurrency culture discussed here. But the Italian National Council finessed other remnants of the former Habsburg state to avert revolution and instill order. And the legacy that they proved much more adept at manipulating was the law system inherited from the Austro-Hungarian Monarchy.

3
Legal Ins and Outs

Crafting Local Sovereignty

"Please work" was probably echoing in Vladimiro Masovcević's head on January 7, 1920, as he scrubbed away at a forged overlay stamp on a twenty-crown bill. Much was riding on his efforts. If he successfully wiped clean traces of the stamp, he would be found not guilty of counterfeiting. If he failed, prison and extremely high fines awaited him. Masovcević faced this test because Fiume police had seized stamp molds from his apartment for counterfeiting currency, along with ink, gasoline, 840 crowns in denominations of 20, 740 of which were covered with forged overlay stamps and 100 of which had been "washed." Masovcević—a 27-year-old unemployed naval mechanic and veteran—testified to having purchased all of the seized materials from a stranger he had met on the train from Trieste. He went on to say that he subsequently decided to wash some of the forged notes as he judged their overlay stamps too deficient to pass muster. An expert currency witness for the prosecution, the 44-year-old high school chemistry teacher Umberto Ricotti, challenged Masovcević's testimony by stating that money could only be washed within seven hours of being stamped, thereby suggesting that Masovcević had stamped the money himself, then washed it when he found his work unsatisfactory. Masovcević refuted Ricotti's allegations and asked the three judges sitting on his case "that [he] be given some gasoline, so that [he] can prove that the erasure [of overlay stamps from crown notes] is possible, even today."[1] The three judges—Zoltán Halász, Otmaro Gregorich, and

Carlo Bonetta-Zotti—acceded, and the whole courtroom watched as
Masovcević tried to scrub away the overlay. He failed. As the chemistry teacher had testified, the forged overlay stamp was unwashable.
Masovcević was asked to step down to await sentencing. Immediately
thereafter, the prosecution requested Masovcević be found guilty of
counterfeiting, under "article 7 of the November 2, 1919 notification issued by the Command of the City of Fiume."[2]

Here is where Masovcević's trial moved from being a case about the
validity of a man's word to one about the validity of a state and its law.
Masovcević's defense lawyer responded to the prosecution's request by
asking for an acquittal, arguing that the November 2, 1919, notification the prosecution had referenced had no juridical basis because "the
Command of the City" was not a legislative organ. "Only the Italian
penal code could be applied," Masovcević's lawyer insisted, and Italian
law had no legal provisions against forging overlay stamps on money.
No law meant no crime, which meant that Masovcević should be released. The prosecution responded that "the commission that issued
the notification was invested, via delegation, with legislative powers."
Masovcević's defense replied that "the delegation of sovereign powers
to a subaltern authority was not admissible."[3] Though no record remains of the judges' deliberations about Masovcević, their deliberations
in another counterfeiting trial just two weeks later reveal the reasoning
behind their verdicts on both Masovcević's guilt and Fiume's sovereignty: "The notification was published and . . . the public therefore
considered it law."[4] Masovcević's sentence and Fiume's sovereignty
were judged valid because Fiume's public considered them so.

Masovcević's trial reflected the inescapable tensions around law and
sovereignty that permeated life in postwar Fiume. The courthouse
where it was held flaunted all the Habsburg architectural niceties that
had so impressed the teenage legionnaire Giuseppe Maranini: large, impressive, and modern, it was typical of Austro-Hungarian administrative centers built in the late nineteenth and early twentieth centuries.
Carved into the stone of this functional palace were Hungarian symbols
and an "infinite number of Habsburg eagles," in case anyone wondered
which grand state was responsible for the building.[5] Furling in the

wind at the front of the building and draped above the judges' seats
were new post-1918 additions, most notably multiple Italian monarchical flags. Court procedures were held in the name of "His Majesty
the King of Italy Vittorio Emmanuele III," even though Fiume was not
officially part of Italy. Most of the personnel in the courtroom while
Masovcević desperately rubbed gasoline on his forged stamp had been
raised, educated, and trained in the same Austro-Hungarian state that
had originally printed Masovcević's crowns. Fiume's judges, lawyers,
and clerks knew the Hungarian penal code backward and forward;
most were still learning the ins and outs of the Italian legal code that
was trickling in piecemeal. Fiumians lived not just in a multicurrency
culture but also in a multi-law culture, where numerous trials ended
with a defense attorney calling for acquittal because of the questionable juridical status of the laws its citizens were to follow. Questions of
sovereignty and the validity of law came up regularly in day-to-day
life before, during, and after Gabriele D'Annunzio's escapade. But
whereas in the currency chaos everyone hedged their bets to survive as
best they could, it appears that when facing the cacophony of legal possibilities, Fiumians responded with remarkable élan. Mixing and
choosing between legal traditions cemented a culture of "Fiumian self-
determination" that directly challenged the pronouncements from the
Paris Peace Conference that cities did not self-determine, Great Power
nations did.

Old Hands at Multi-sovereignty

While Fiume's multicurrency system was the result of the dissolution
of the Austro-Hungarian state after World War I, Fiumians had negotiated a multi-legal system all their lives. For Fiume was not just any
city in any state before 1918. It was a corpus separatum—a Free City—
within a kingdom (Hungary) headed by a monarch living in Vienna
who was simultaneously Emperor of Austria and King of Hungary. This
meant that Fiumians lived their lives within the contours of a sovereignty mosaic, a world of "layered sovereignty," as current historians
and social scientists characterize such imperial legal systems.[6]

This multiform quality of authority was not hidden; people living in Fiume were required to acknowledge it and be proud of it. Anyone employed by the state in Fiume had to sign a loyalty oath attesting to a layering of authority. In June 1915, for example, 41-year-old accountant Antonio Allazetta was named head accountant of the civic tax office and swore "loyalty to the King, obedience to the laws of the Kingdom, [and] to the Statute of Fiume."[7] This tripartite authority structure referenced the Austro-Hungarian Monarchy (loyalty to the king), Budapest (laws of the kingdom), and Fiume itself (Statute of Fiume). When Allazetta was promoted to tax office director two years later in 1917, his loyalty oath repeated exactly this same tripartite authority structure.[8] As late as January 1918, 27-year-old Gemina Benussi swore "loyalty to the King, obedience to the Laws of the Kingdom, [and] to the Statute of Fiume" upon accepting a position as an elementary school teacher.[9] When accepting a job, applying for a license, or giving testimony, Fiumians acknowledged these three layers of power. This tripartite sovereignty system did not mean that Fiumians were the disenfranchised subjects of three masters. Instead, it framed a genealogy of available rights, for Austria-Hungary had been a constitutional parliamentary state since 1867, and Hungary boasted its own rights-oriented legal code.

Fiumians' rights were protected by the laws of Hungary and the Statute of Fiume. The imperial authority of the Austro-Hungarian Monarchy oversaw the umbrella infrastructures of foreign relations, defense, and cross-imperial finance that, ideally, allowed the parliamentary Hungarian and city administrations to work unencumbered. As the mayor of Fiume explained when announcing municipal elections in July 1915, it was the "loyal and generous act of the Royal Government, that maintains firm our ancestral prerogatives, culminating in our city autonomy."[10] Hungary's protective role in maintaining Fiume's rights and prerogatives was regularly described as that of the *madrepatria*. Translated today as "motherland" or "native country," within the imperial rhetoric of Fiume, madrepatria meant something different. In a 1901 pamphlet analyzing Fiume's status within the empire, Nicolò Gelletich—61-year-old city representative and businessman—explained that Hungary's relationship to Fiume was that of "a mother to daughter," and thus "in our city it [Hungary] is called the madre-patria."[11] Put simply, madrepatria meant "metropole," with Hungary acting as the mother (*madre*) of the homeland, Fiume (*patria*).[12] Expectations that Hungary's sovereignty over Fiume consisted in protecting and nurturing the city's autonomy and economy continued, and Fiume's mayor ended his July 1915 speech by summarizing the city's relationship to Hungary as "centuries-old bonds which united it [Fiume] to the great Hungarian madrepatria."[13]

As in most mother-daughter relationships, these "bonds" between Hungary and Fiume were not equal, and they were distressingly unstable. This meant that Fiumians focused much of their political energy before and during the war on guarding, defending, and expanding their autonomy, especially as political elites in Budapest worked tirelessly to centralize and homogenize the administration of the lands within their kingdom. From the mid-1870s until World War I, Fiume's elites challenged Budapest's dictates about how much juridical sovereignty the Fiume corpus separatum wielded. By the beginning of the twentieth century, this defensive strategy among Fiumians against increased Hungarian centralism resulted in the creation of a political party, the Autonomism Party, which dominated local elections throughout the entire period leading up to the dissolution of Austria-Hungary.[14] According to the Fiume Statute and rulings by the Austro-Hungarian king Franz Josef, Hungarian legal codes did not automatically extend to Fiume. Instead the Fiume municipal government had the right to consult on the application of Hungarian laws to Fiume's "special circumstances." Fiume political activists fought hard to stave off the full-scale introduction of "foreign [Hungarian] laws," but after years of Hungarian pressure, Budapest succeeded in forcing Fiume to relent. By 1900 Fiume had incorporated the Hungarian penal and civil codes en masse.[15] With every passing year, more paperwork in Fiume was translated into Hungarian so it could be authorized, confirmed, or at least acknowledged by Budapest-based offices.[16] Fiume's chamber of commerce regularly increased its budget for telegraph, telephone, and travel expenses, noting that this was partly because of increased costs (especially during the war) and partly because communications with the metropole were "intense."[17]

This "intense" communication between metropole and corpus separatum meant that Fiume's administrators, civil servants, law practitioners, and political activists were highly skilled at working within a layered sovereignty system. That intensity went both ways: Fiume elites regularly demanded increased, or at least continued, autonomy from Budapest. Occasionally, the corpus separatum tried to set itself as a model for how the whole kingdom should be run. For example, in response to a letter from the Hungarian Commerce Ministry asking Fiume officials whether wine should be sold by both weight and container, the chamber of commerce replied that Fiume already had a wine-per-liter pricing system and that it supported Hungarian wine growers' efforts to enact a law that matched the one that had "already been in practice in Fiume for thirty years now."[18] Similarly, in 1917, when proposing a new city initiative for a tax on entertainments to aid war widows and orphans, Fiume municipal representatives invited "all the Cities, all the Municipalities of the Kingdom . . . [to follow] the example of Fiume."[19] Undoubtedly, pride and a bit of smugness laced these missives to Budapest-based offices, suggesting that the daughterland might outrank the motherland.

But Fiume elites also learned from what other parts of the Hungarian and Austrian Kingdoms did to promote local interests. In proposing pension increases for employees during the inflationary war years, for instance, the Fiume chamber of commerce recommended that pensions be doubled after "collecting authentic information on the acts of Sister Cities [*Consorelle*] of the Kingdom. . . . 16 Hungarian Chambers were queried, as well as those of Zagreb and Sarajevo."[20] It took research to determine which were the most advantageous policies acceptable within Hungary's layered sovereignty system. Collecting such information helped ensure that Fiume chose its battles with the madrepatria wisely, avoiding initiatives that had proved unsuccessful elsewhere. Even private lawsuits cited judgments made in Austria and Hungary to show

precedent for how Fiume courts should or could rule, as in 43-year-old
Mario Rossi's lawsuit against his dry cleaner for not providing damages
when his clothing was stolen during a break-in. Rossi's lawyer argued
that the dry cleaner should repay the cost of the clothing just as dry
cleaners in similar Austrian cases had done.[21]

So even before the dissolution of Austria-Hungary, Fiume political
elites, legal professionals, and many of its residents were well practiced
in navigating a multi-authority state system and defending their interests through the manipulation of foreign precedents and legal loopholes.
That's what the protectionist metropole-madrepatria system offered,
and Fiumians were adept at trying to get as much as they could within
the Austro-Hungarian-Fiumian sovereignty triangle.

From Layered to Colliding Sovereignties

When Austria-Hungary was dissolved at the end of October 1918, two
legs of Fiume's tripartite sovereignty system suddenly disappeared, with
only the corpus separatum remaining. But this did not mean that a
multi-sovereignty system was curtailed. Quite the contrary. Just as the
varieties of currency used in Fiume multiplied after 1918, so did the different authorities ascribed to ruling the city. A glance at letters between Americans and postwar Fiume gives an idea of the conundrum
Fiume presented for postal workers and the world at large. In December 1918, the president of Fiume's Italian National Council sent a
letter to the US secretary of state listing its address as "Fiume, ~~Hun-
gary~~ Quarnero."[22] Two days later Woodrow Wilson's private secretary,
Gilbert F. Close, addressed a letter with just "National Council of Fiume,
Fiume."[23] In March 1919 the New York–based company Press Illustrating Service posted a letter to the "Fiume National Council, Fiume,
Croatia."[24] And in May 1919 the New York–based Federation of Italo-
American Irredentist Societies sent a letter addressed to the "Mayor of
the City 'Fiume,' Italy."[25] The differences in address did not reflect re-
gime changes or border repositionings. "Fiume, ~~Hungary~~ Quarnero,"
"Fiume, Fiume," "Fiume, Croatia," and "the City 'Fiume,' Italy," were
just a few of the many designations used to place the port city on the

map or in a state.[26] With a scratched-out "~~Hungary~~," Fiume was outside systems, and its post-imperial mailboxes were filled with a dizzying array of sovereignty monikers.

As we have seen, most looked to the diplomatic hallways of Paris to resolve the Fiume enigma. Inter-Allied troops were sent to the city to ensure the decision was not foreclosed by a fait accompli occupation. D'Annunzio's arrival pushed international relations closer to the brink, and Fiume remained an unresolved legal-diplomatic issue for twenty-six months after Austria-Hungary dissolved. For all involved, the Fiume Crisis, as it quickly became known, was a reminder that international diplomacy was not necessarily the best agent for resolving questions of sovereignty.

As Natasha Wheatley has rightly noted, "There was no international handbook for unmaking imperial sovereignty."[27] But there were hints of what the Great Powers had in mind and Fiumians jumped to play the cards they had to win at the game they saw set before them. The watchwords for postwar political reorganization were clearly "national self-determination." Vladimir Lenin's new Soviet Russia had announced in October 1917 that every nation, large or small, should be "given the right to determine the form of its state life."[28] In January 1918, Lloyd George proclaimed that Britain and its allies were fighting for peace, which was only possible if "a territorial settlement . . . be secured, based on the right of self-determination."[29] Wilson's January 1918 Fourteen Points declared that "the peoples of Austria-Hungary, whose place among the nations we wish to see safeguarded and assured, should be accorded the freest opportunity of autonomous development."[30] What more needed to be said? With Austria-Hungary gone, the gaps in Fiume's layered sovereignty documents were emancipatory. Fiume was a corpus separatum no longer. It was now a *corpus liberatorum*, "freed" and independent. With its long history of autonomy politicking, Fiume was ready to determine its own place among the nations. And while Paris diplomats haggled over where Fiume should sit on a map and Inter-Allied troops worked to keep the city up for grabs, the Italian National Council assumed for itself the role of "sovereign" administrator of "Fiume, Fiume" and demanded that the world at large recognize it as "Fiume, Italy."[31]

Members of the Italian National Council, with its well-bearded, elderly president, Antonio Grossich, at the center.

Little had changed and much had changed. Before November 1918, the municipal government of Fiume negotiated within a tripartite layered sovereignty system to maintain and broaden its autonomy. After November 1918, the municipal government (with the newly created umbrella "state" government of the Italian National Council filling in the space of the Hungarian Kingdom) wrangled with two other entities: Great Power diplomacy in Paris and Inter-Allied troops on the ground. This tug-of-war continued for almost a year until D'Annunzio's entry in September 1919 added a new player into the mix. As the mayor of Fiume told the head of Inter-Allied forces in January 1919, Fiume was where "an indefinite number of authorities collide."[32] Not only did they collide, they joined forces to "disauthorize" the Italian National Council as the city's provisional government.[33]

To fight the disauthorization by Paris diplomats and occupying troops, Fiume elites updated their old layered-sovereignty tactics. Before 1918, they had resisted challenges to their municipal authority by citing historical precedent and pointing to the imperial patents that protected their corpus separatum status. After 1918, they anchored their sovereignty in their ability to legislate, something they had not been able to do freely before.[34] Like the judges in the Masovcević trial, Fiume's provisional government exercised authority because "the public . . . considered" what it proclaimed to be "law."[35] Diplomatic authority lay in Paris, where Great Power politicians worked on making treaties that would determine the new borders of Europe. Military authority lay first with the Inter-Allied command and then with D'Annunzio's command, both of which barracked troops in Fiume to keep the city in play for political negotiations. Fiume elites claimed their post-Habsburg sovereignty by focusing on the law; they offset diplomatic and military authority by jealously retaining administrative authority over day-to-day life.[36]

Scratch That: Useful Shortcuts for Unlayering Sovereignty

As mentioned earlier, 41-year-old Antonio Allazetta and other state employees under Austria-Hungary swore "loyalty to the King, obedience to the laws of the Kingdom, [and] to the Statute of Fiume."[37] When he was promoted two years later, as the war neared its close, he took the same oath. Two years after that, on May 9, 1919, he signed a new loyalty oath for the new Fiume state he served: "I, Antonio Allazetta, promise on my word of honor to scrupulously observe the laws and ordinances in force and to fulfill conscientiously and with zeal and integrity my post as permanent director of the Civic Tax office."[38] Allazetta's new oath wasn't specific to his high office. Elementary school teachers like the 39-year-old Elisa Sirola also vowed "to scrupulously observe the laws and ordinances in force."[39] What is remarkable about this new post-Habsburg oath is that the source of authority for these laws and ordinances went unnamed. Allazetta, Sirola, and all their fellow Fiumians vowed to observe laws as they were enacted, regardless of where these laws originated or what they contained. This is the essence of how Fiume's municipal wranglers retained some form of authority within the city: they redefined their sovereignty as stemming not from diplomatic recognition (Paris) or military might (Inter-Allied or D'Annunzio troops) but from the ever-evolving practices of legislation. In short, the population living in Fiume swore loyalty to the laws issued—and those who issued them.

To leave the source and substance of legislation unqualified might seem like a precarious foundation for sovereignty, for how binding was a loyalty oath when no one knew what they were swearing to uphold? How much obedience could a state expect from its populace when all the rules could and did change? Fiume's provisional government handled these questions by indicating that, except for the fact that Hungary was out of the equation, everything would stay the same as before. For example, on January 22, 1919, the Italian National Council proclaimed that the new Fiume-based court would rule over "all civil, penal, disciplinary, and administrative issues that once were under the domain of the Budapest court."[40] On January 25, 1919, the provisional government clarified, adding that the law code administered within these new Fiume-based courts "would be regulated by the ordinances of the Hungarian Minister of Justice given on July 25, 1878."[41] What this meant was that Fiume's laws would remain the same, but now the Fiume courts would be the supreme judicial bodies instead of the former Budapest ones. In another law issued immediately thereafter, the Italian National Council stressed that lawyers and judges would only be reconfirmed if they could exhibit work experience within the city of Fiume, passed an exam on the "Hungarian Minister of Justice's ordinances from July 1878," and, like Allazetta and Sirola, pledged "to scrupulously observe the laws and ordinances in force."[42] On March 16, 1919, Fiumians read in the official state bulletin that all properties of the Hungarian state currently located within Fiume (including the railways and the tobacco factory) were now the property of the City of Fiume.[43] Laws regulating the rights and responsibilities of citizens and foreigners were updated in a similar manner. On April 2, 1919, the provisional government announced that "from now on wherever [a law] indicates 'Hungarian citizen' the expression 'pertinent of the Comune of Fiume' should be substituted."[44] With a few strokes, Austria-Hungary was scratched off the surface of the city's daily administration, replaced by the city of Fiume.

Keeping the laws the same as they had been under the dissolved Hungarian Kingdom served many purposes, mostly pragmatic. Life did not restart when Austria-Hungary fell, and changing the rules of the game midway through is the definition of lawlessness. Crime—especially black-market employment, money scams, slander, corruption, theft, and violence—may have increased in Fiume after October 1918, but the definition of what constituted a crime remained the same. Though the Italian National Council could not suppress the booming illegal activities that permeated postwar life, it sustained the same Hungarian legal system that adjudicated what was acceptable and legitimate behavior.

A telling example of how useful it was to keep Hungarian legal codes in force after the kingdom had disappeared can be seen in a civil dispute between two merchants, first brought to court in November 1918 and continuing on through appeal until March 1920. At issue were the contractual obligations of the 56-year-old inn owner and agricultural supplier Ivan Rošić, who lived in a Croatian village (Škrljevo) fifteen kilometers east of Fiume. On October 23, 1918, the 35-year-old Fiume resident and "trader in comestibles" Slavko Ivančić paid a four-thousand-crown deposit to Rošić to have three wagons of cabbage delivered the next day to the Fiume port. Between October 23 and 24, 1918, however, the Hungarian forces overseeing the area departed. On October 24 Rošić sent an envoy to Fiume to return Ivančić his deposit and inform him that, in light of political events, he could not deliver the cabbage, as Croatian authorities had just "banned the export" of food to Fiume. In his testimony, Rošić maintained he should not be held responsible for shirking his contractual obligations as "this was a matter of a force majeure."[45] Rošić's lawyer argued that not only should his client be excused from paying the fine for failing to make good on his contract, his legal fees should be covered by Ivančić because Ivančić had brought such a frivolous suit.

If Fiume authorities had discontinued Hungarian legal procedures with the fall of the kingdom, the matter would probably have ended there. Few would argue that train lines, communication networks, and cabbage shipments were not interrupted in the days after Austria-Hungary dissolved. But with the January 1919 laws indicating that the new Fiume-based court would rule over "all civil, penal, disciplinary, and administrative issues that once were under the domain of the Budapest court" and that these rulings would follow the same Hungarian ordinances already in place, the Ivančić-Rošić case went on as it would have before the war.[46] Testimonies were given by the two merchants, the envoy Rošić employed, parties in the Croatian depot where the cabbage had stalled, and in the Croatian village where Rošić lived. In the end, it was the notarized, written statement of the stationmaster in Bakar, Croatia, that determined the verdict. His statement revealed that Rošić's cabbage was not stalled because of a Croatian ban on exporting food to Fiume but because Rošić had failed to apply for the proper Croatian certificates to export perishables, certificates required well before the dissolution of Austria-Hungary. Imperial downfall had nothing to do with the missing cabbage shipment: it was Rošić's failure to follow existing legal norms that had blocked the transaction. Ivančić won his lawsuit, proving to the satisfaction of a renamed judicial system that Rošić had skirted bureaucratic requirements, been caught, and used the excuse of the fall of his kingdom to cover it up.

This strategy of taking "Hungary" and replacing it with "Fiume" was not just pragmatic; it had a conservative purpose as well. As one subcommittee of the provisional government put it,

> With the city of Fiume no longer being a part of the Kingdom of Hungary and therefore standing independently . . . there can be dispensations from the Hungarian laws currently in force. In fact, there would be no obstacle even in introducing new laws to substitute those in force. . . . Above all, however, one has to avoid every impulsive reform and . . . to proceed with the greatest caution.[47]

Fiume elites understood that with the dissolution of empire, they could make a fresh start and enjoy the heady freedom of a tabula rasa, so to speak. But instead of embracing utopia, the infrastructures of the city proceeded "with the greatest caution," and snubbed those intent on disauthorizing the provisional government.[48] The city's law codes, properties, and fiscal infrastructure replicated much of the imperial ordinances of the metropole-madrepatria from which they had been released. It was this that made it possible to catch a sneaky cabbage seller like Rošić. Another reason to be conservative about changes was the radical movements like Bolshevism catching fire throughout Europe.[49] The fear that Fiume's uncertain geopolitical designation could be an opportunity for bureaucratic scoundrels or radicals with "subversive and Bolshevik ideas" convinced many that it was better to keep the laws they had in force, in the hope of forestalling movements for excessive change.[50]

Pragmatism and conservatism explain why the Hungarian legal system was maintained, but not why state employees pledged loyalty to the "laws in force" instead of the "laws of Fiume." It is here that the Fiume experience diverges from a relatively simple story of navigating regime change while upholding law and order. For the Fiume Italian National Council did not just assert the right to self-rule when its umbrella empire disappeared. It claimed the right to national self-determination as well. The council did not turn the semiautonomous municipal government into a state government. Instead it formed a *provisional* state government to replace the Hungarian government, while also retaining the municipal branch of self-administration it had so jealously protected before the war. This explains how and why Fiume had a president and a mayor simultaneously. This system allowed for a local government (the Italian National Council) to remain in charge only until Fiume was annexed to its chosen new madrepatria, Italy, all without altering the city's own autonomous regime.[51] Thus the loyalty oaths were not empty phrases but rather vows to support the Italian National Council's diplomatic and political objective, repeated endlessly between 1918 and 1921, to join Italy. Pledging to uphold the ordinances and laws in force was the same as pledging to follow the provisional government's course as expressed in the January 1919 decree delineating its sovereignty:

Freed from Hungarian dominion, on October 29, 1918, strong in their rights employed over the course of centuries as a Free City, the people of Fiume assumed public authority—via the National Council constituted to supplant the Hungarian authorities—, declaring the Fiume city, port and district an independent State, and proclaimed on the 30th of the same month unification of Fiume to Italy, making use of the right to self-determination recognized by special laws and conventions and today solemnly affirmed by the universal democracy.[52]

As noted earlier, Fiume's self-proclaimed unification with Italy was not recognized by either the Kingdom of Italy or by the Kingdom of Serbs, Croats, and Slovenes. It was definitely not recognized by the Paris Peace Conference or the Inter-Allied troops. But in the day-to-day life of Fiumians, the provisional government's determination that it would be so was easy to see. State currency policies and exchange rates were organized to ease eventual incorporation into Italy; so were the laws.

Take the Ivančić-Rošić cabbage case mentioned earlier. Though the legal system used to pursue the case between 1918 and 1920 was Hungarian in content and origin, in name it was something quite different. When the case began in November 1918, it was under the jurisdiction of the "Court in Fiume," just as it would have been during the Hungarian administration. In April 1919, when further testimony was collected, it was held in the "royal [reg.] Court of Fiume," with "royal" referring to the Italian monarchical state. When a first verdict was reached in July 1919, court documents had the heading "royal Court of Fiume" crossed out and substituted with "royal civil and penal Court of Fiume." Below this heading was written, "In the Name of His Majesty the King! Vittorio Emmanuele III, for grace of God and the will of the Nation King of Italy!"[53]

Loyalty oaths to "laws in force" were, by extension, loyalty oaths to support the transitions needed to bring about "the definitive unification of Fiume to Italy."[54] In March 1919, laws were passed to replace the symbolic sovereignty of Hungary with that of Italy. Hungarian flags, stamps, insignia, and emblems were divested of "any signification or representative character" and "the Italian national banner" was declared the official banner of the Fiume state.[55] Failure to respect Fiume's new state-mandated Italian face could lead to a sentence of six months prison and a fine of one thousand crowns. There could be no clearer decree: with government sovereignty anchored to legislation, allegiance to laws in force meant obedience to all the steps involved in transforming the "Court in Fiume" into the "royal Court of Fiume" and then to anything declared "In the Name of Vittorio Emmanuele III."

It was the open-endedness of "in force" that provided such fluidity. And this laws-in-force strategy was something Fiumians understood quite well. In fact, when lawyers were required to take the oath so they could practice in the city, a group opposed to unification with Italy tried to demonstrate against the provision and were quickly put down by Fiume police.[56] There was nothing vague or empty about laws-in-force oaths to someone on the ground in 1918–1921 Fiume. The oaths recognized the authority of the city government and acted as a passive endorsement of its plan to make the King of Italy the King of Fiume.

Add That: Returning to Layered Sovereignty with a New Madrepatria

On April 24, 1919, newspapers throughout the world published Woodrow Wilson's Paris assessment of the Fiume Crisis, in which he made clear that Fiume should not be united with Italy, that its geopolitical future lay to the east, and that Italian sovereignty in the city would "inevitably seem foreign, not domestic."[57] In response, the Italian National Council met with the commander of the Inter-Allied forces, General Francesco Grazioli. With "brief and emotional words," the president of the Italian National Council "explained how Fiume, which since October 30th last year has solemnly proclaimed its immoveable self-determination to be annexed to the Kingdom of Italy, today, in the face of Paris events, offers to the Italian General . . . the Government of the city in order to secure that its [Fiume's] free and sovereign expression of will is actualized." The general thanked the council but said that "the transfer of powers will only be enforced when the Italian Government declares the annexation of Fiume to Italy." Not vice versa. In the meantime, Grazioli "begged the Council itself to remain in office."[58] In short, Grazioli demonstrated what Paris diplomats and the Italian and Serb-Croat-Slovene governments had said all along: a city cannot annex itself to a nation-state. Nation-states (especially the big ones) decide where cities belong.

But Fiume's provisional government had no intention of letting things end there. In a statement issued the same day, the Italian National Council "solemnly swore, that however events unfold, the people of Fiume will know how to make their inviolable will to be united to Italy respected."[59] Beginning in April 1919, Fiume government officials intensified their initiatives to make clear that Italian sovereignty in the city was domestic, not "inevitably . . . foreign."[60] Was there a way for a city to annex itself to a kingdom, no matter what an American said in far-off Paris or an Italian general pronounced in Fiume? Could a city act as a state and force another state to take over its sovereignty? These questions boggle the twenty-first-century mind. But Fiume elites thought they had a way. They took their prewar imperial expertise in layered sovereignty and set about constructing a new layered sovereignty regime. With little to no influence in the diplomatic, military, or economic sphere, they focused their efforts on domestic legislation. Little by little, decree by decree, Fiume's provisional government embedded itself into Italy's legal tapestry. Through legislative bricolage, Fiume fashioned a de facto unification with Italy. Before April 1919, Fiume's provisional government had declared the city Italian in name, flags, and all the other trappings of symbolic sovereignty; after April 1919, it worked to make Fiume Italian in practice.

The provisional government had been working since March 1919 to Italianize the content of Fiume's laws in force. When legislation was enacted replacing the symbolic authority of Hungary with that of Italy, a government commission indicated that it was "urgently necessary that similar provisions of a juridical nature be made with the task to reform and adapt administration of local justice to the exigencies of the material and formal laws of Italy."[61] The Italianization of Fiume's legal

culture was conceived as a process, not a coup. The commission recommended that the government proceed piecemeal, beginning with the
penal code and leaving the civil, tax, and commercial codes for later.
Commission minutes indicated that the Italianization of the penal code
was to be initiated in July 1919, but after Wilson's April 1919 pronouncement and Italy's refusal to recognize Fiume's self-proclaimed annexation, the process was expedited. Two weeks after Wilson declared that
Italian sovereignty in the city would "inevitably seem foreign, not
domestic," Fiumians were informed that the "penal Code . . . and all
other penal laws, decrees, ordinances, patents and dispositions actually in force in the territorial jurisdiction of the city of Fiume would
be abrogated" and replaced with the "penal code in force in the Kingdom
of Italy."[62]

The provisional government declared that these Italianizing reforms
were necessary because the Hungarian laws they were replacing were
"a product of a foreign mentality, very different from our own, and an-
tiquated."[63] However, the transition from the Hungarian to the Italian
penal code reveals that Fiume's government also knew that the Italian
system being introduced was itself foreign. The government explicitly
worked to make the Italian system seem more appealing to win Fiumians over to the new laws. All crimes committed before the introduction of the Italian system were tried under the Hungarian penal code.
However, during sentencing, defense attorneys were invited to request
an appeal or clemency if the Italian legal code defined the crime dif-
ferently or punished it less severely. In short, if the Hungarian code was
tougher on the accused than the Italian code, lawyers were encouraged
to request leniency.

The provisional government wanted its populace and its lawyers to
look to the Italian code as a means either to be freed "from any penal
legal action" or to receive "a more mild punishment than that contem-
plated by the abrogated legislation."[64] In hundreds of cases brought to
Fiume courts, defense lawyers attempted to take advantage of such
transitional initiatives. And though the use of Italian law to procure a
lightened sentence was available only through judicial discretion, it undoubtedly made an impression on Fiumians, whether they were on the

stand or just watching the proceedings. In many ways, as has happened in so many other historical cases when states worked to soften the effects of transitioning law regimes, these initiatives taught Fiumians that Italian justice was more equitable than its Hungarian precursor.

The characterization of the provisional government's legal initiatives as a return to layered sovereignty is not based solely on the fact that the city used its sovereignty to join up with another state entity. The government's decision not to ratify Italian legal norms in toto was a layered-sovereignty tactic. No matter how foreign official pronouncements made Hungarian legal culture out to be, Fiume officials did not just throw out their Hungarian past and wholeheartedly adopt their desired Italian future. Instead, they studied their options, selected the best of both systems, and made a piecemeal marriage of the two. Much like the pre-1918 commissions that collected "authentic information on the acts of Sister Cities of the [Hungarian] Kingdom," when determining tax law, commissions were formed to study Italian protocols.[65] An example of this can be seen in the Italian National Council's copy of a pamphlet on taxes placed on "entertainments" within the province of Venezia-Giulia, a region of former Habsburg lands (including neighboring Istria) now incorporated into the Kingdom of Italy.[66] Fiume officials dissected the laws, using red ink for what they found important, black ink for what they questioned, and pencil when translating values for imports from the Italian lira used in Venezia-Giulia to the Fiume crown. When new taxes on entertainments were issued in the months following this analysis, most Italian precedents were followed, but there were also exceptions considered necessary to promote local businesses.

Sometimes Fiume's layering of Hungarian and Italian codes created a more enticing version of Italy than that actually on offer in Rome. For example, Fiume legislators did not set aside Hungarian laws permitting divorce. Divorce was legal in Hungary as early as 1895; as Eszter Herger and Robert Nemes have shown, state initiatives to centralize and nationalize the Hungarian Kingdom resulted in marriage being secularized, which meant civil marriages could be terminated. This was unimaginable in neighboring Catholic countries like Italy or even the other half of the Habsburg Empire, Austria.[67] Under Hungarian law, unhappy spouses, both men and women, could request fault-based or relative-based divorces. Fault-based divorces, the most commonly awarded, had grounds such as adultery, fornication, bigamy, willful desertion without just cause, infliction of willful or grievous bodily harm, or an attempt on the spouse's life. Relative-based grounds, which were much harder to establish, let judges award a divorce if, "having thoroughly considered the personalities and living conditions of the spouse, he [the judge] satisfied himself that the maintenance of the bond is unbearable for the party seeking dissolution."[68] Like any other subjects of the Hungarian Kingdom, Fiumians before, during, and after the war could sever their marriages as they would any other contract: before the courts, with testimony and a legal code outlining how they could proceed.

Divorce was not common in Fiume: before 1914 the average number of divorces awarded was 37.5 per year in a population of circa 50,000.[69] But the option was there, and Fiume residents, both men and women, took advantage of it. From the richest to the poorest, divorcees cited one or all of the accepted grounds to sever their disappointing unions. Members of Fiume's financial elite like the Incognito-Barbieri family usually cited adultery or willful abandonment. Someone as low on the Fiume social pole as the 38-year-old railway brakeman Giuseppe Német (who lived with his wife in a one-room apartment without a kitchen) sued for divorce because, as he said, "My wife constantly mistreats me and I can no longer live with her."[70] And among the middle class, people like the 35-year-old white-collar railway administrator Emerico Koós took no chances that a judge would deny him a divorce; Koós pleaded almost all possible grounds, stating that his wife "ignored her conjugal duties," "regularly abandoned him," "tried to strangle his son," and corrupted his food "with filthinesses, for example blood, [and] dirt from fingernails."[71] So standardized was divorce in the legal Fiume mindset that when 25-year-old Giuseppina Kunzarich née Sluga was informed her husband was suing her for divorce with charges of adultery and willful abandonment, she sent a letter to the Fiume courts indicating that she was "happy to sign our divorce, and delighted [*contentissima*] that these things get done, by the book, without my presence."[72]

Picture of Giuseppina Kunzarich née Sluga submitted to the courts by
her husband, Antonio, to prove his wife's long-standing adulterous
ways; Antonio is not the man in the portrait, though it was taken after
their marriage. Giuseppina did not deny the claim and impatiently
urged the Fiume courts to grant her husband a divorce so she could
marry the father of her new child, with whom she had moved to
Trieste.

The idea that someone could legally seek divorce, let alone for causes
such as "mistreatment" or filthy cooking, was unthinkable within the
Kingdom of Italy. As Mark Seymour has illustrated, debates over introducing divorce law had plagued the Italian parliamentary system
since the country's founding in the 1860s.[73] Though many Catholics
fought tooth and nail to keep divorce out of the Italian legal code, others
wanted it incorporated. The issue was so contested that before 1914, parliament dissolved six times over the issue. And while divorce remained
illegal, newspapers regularly featured articles about "divorce Italian

style," in which husbands and wives resorted to homicide to free themselves of their unwanted spouses. Seymour notes that though only the
most shocking cases made the news, court files show that 699 cases of
spousal murder were reported in Italy from 1866 to 1880: apparently
about once a week an Italian citizen looked to murder to obtain the
divorce Italian courts refused to grant.[74]

The decision of Fiume's provisional government to keep divorce even
while Italianizing its legal codes is one of the clearest examples of how
the provisional government believed its self-annexation to an Italian
madrepatria could and would provide enough layered sovereignty to
allow for fairly substantial differences in legal culture. While determined to Italianize, Fiume was not interested in losing its claims to
prerogatives more attractive than those available under the direct sovereignty of the Italian king Vittorio Emanuele III.

Layered sovereignty in Fiume went beyond picking and choosing
from among the most attractive Italian and Hungarian laws on offer.
It also incorporated new laws formulated in situ. Such was the case with
suffrage. In September 1919, the Fiume provisional government announced that the city would abrogate Hungarian voting laws, but not
in favor of Italian ones. Instead, it declared universal suffrage for pertinents over the age of 20.[75] Italy did not grant universal suffrage until
after 1945; Hungary did briefly during its revolutionary republic, but
quickly rescinded it, not to reinstate it until after World War II. Fiume
beat both its former and hoped-for madrepatrias to the punch by a
quarter of a century. This initiative served two purposes, one domestic
and one international. Domestically, including women in the electorate
upped the number of people voting in Fiume, adding a little more
weight to the relatively minuscule "Fiume state." Internationally, the
initiative was promoted to show the world, especially Italians, how
Fiume promised "modernity[,] . . . a young Italy, renewed, representing
the Italy of the people, the Italy that has made and knows how to make
the true miracles of history."[76] This language reflects the decision Fiume
officials made when the Italian Kingdom refused to recognize Fiume's
self-annexation; their city-state represented not just an Italian Fiume
but a better future Italy overall. When D'Annunzio arrived a few days

after the universal suffrage law was enacted, this rhetoric of Fiume as a better Italy expanded exponentially. Through their mixing, melding, and tweaking of Fiume's legal code, the provisional government and D'Annunzio's command celebrated the idea that Fiume's Italian-oriented autonomy served not only its populace of 50,000 but also the 36.5 million Italians in the kingdom to which they were attempting to annex themselves.

It is difficult to appraise what living in a laws-in-force, layered-sovereignty state felt like on the ground. The bureaucratic files of the many different branches of the Fiume administration reveal moments when locals seem uncertain about what legally appropriate behavior looked like. A particularly absurd example can be found in the Fiume school archives. On November 25, 1920, the teaching body of the Leonardo da Vinci Technical Institute was called in for a special meeting to discuss the expulsion of a troublesome and violent student. All agreed the student should be expelled. The problem was that the teachers didn't know whether they had the right to do so. Italian law said that students could only be expelled if the testimony taken in the expulsion procedures was cosigned by all the teachers present. But under Hungarian law, only the school principal needed to countersign the testimony. When testimonies were taken for the case under review, only the principal had countersigned. The school board informed the Leonardo da Vinci Technical School that "the National Council had decreed that all Hungarian laws not abrogated or modified remained in force" and thus the student could be expelled.[77] Two teachers objected to this announcement and left the meeting, with one stating that though he censured the student, he considered "only Italian laws legitimate and he would not submit himself to foreign laws." In the end, the remaining teachers agreed "to obey the directives legally constituted by the government," and the student's expulsion was pronounced binding. The teachers, however, also agreed to petition the school board to ask "that this anarchy in scholastic legislation be brought to an end."[78] Fiumians—lawyers, civil servants, counterfeiters, parents, students, and members of all levels of society in between—were aware of the difficulties and opportunities involved in Fiume's multi-legal administration. Many of them debated which sovereignty should order day-to-day life. More often than not, as seen in the Masovcević trial, the student's expulsion procedure, and many other moments in which multiple laws collided, Fiumians did what their provisional state directed them to do.

The most surprising consequence of postwar Fiume's layered-sovereignty strategy, however, can be found in the ledgers that tracked divorce cases after 1918. As mentioned, before the war, an average of 37–38 divorces were awarded annually to Fiumians. During Fiume's years before its 1924 incorporation into the Kingdom of Italy, however, the number increased exponentially. In 1918, 14 divorces were issued. In 1919, 66. In 1920, 122. In 1921, 229. In 1922, 466.[79] This divorce boom did not reflect a shift in gender expectations, family stability, or sexual mores among Fiume's residents. The increase in divorces came from an influx of Italian citizens—including Guglielmo Marconi, the Noble Prize–winning inventor of the radio—who moved to Fiume to take advantage of its divorce code. Just as US citizens took advantage of quickie divorces available in Las Vegas, Mexico, and the Dominican Republic, Italian citizens traveled to Fiume from 1919 to 1924 to benefit from the legacy of its Hungarian legal code and the stubborn attempts of its provisional government to imbed itself in the Italian legal framework, partially but not fully.[80]

Shortly and Perpetually United with the Great Communal Madrepatria—Why Not?

In April 1919, while Paris diplomats were haggling about where Fiume's sovereignty should lie, Fiume's provisional government received hundreds of letters and telegrams from Italy, South America, the United States, and some European countries, all supporting the city-state's efforts to determine its future. Among the missives was a telegram from the Republic of San Marino, a centuries-old microstate located in the middle of Italy. The telegram was short but sweet:

> The new electorate of the republic's supreme magistrate we send our ardent salute to the noble city of fiume fervidly hoping that shortly and for always it will be united to the great communal *madre patria*.[81]

The president of the Italian National Council instructed the local newspaper to publish the message. He also responded to the telegram, thanking the leaders of the microstate for their "message of greeting" and hailing the Republic of San Marino as a place where "perpetual liberty is enjoyed."[82] This exchange with a microstate that, despite being located in the middle of the Kingdom of Italy, was recognized as sovereign, with its own civil code, suffrage laws, constitution, and currency, while its population (only half that of Fiume) enjoyed the protection of the Kingdom of Italy madrepatria, leads one to wonder whether Fiume elites believed they could wrangle a similar deal. Didn't Italy already have a layered-sovereignty arrangement with San Marino, one similar in some aspects to what Fiumians had enjoyed under Hungary? And what about all the new imperial-colonial territories Italy was working to add to its state tapestry, like the Dodecanese islands of Greece? Why would joining the Italian Kingdom be different from what Fiume's past had been and what San Marino's present was? Italians moving to Fiume appreciated the corpus separatum's legal differences. Surely there was a way for Fiume to keep them and become Italian?

Of course, the answer to this turned out to be no. Vittorio Emmanuele III's kingdom never accepted Fiume's self-annexation. And by September 1920, Gabriele D'Annunzio had appropriated the administration of the city, renaming its government the Regency of Carnaro, a supposed direct democracy led by a supreme leader, the duce, D'Annunzio himself. D'Annunzio also issued a constitution that proclaimed its continued intention to bring about the forced annexation of Fiume to Italy, but now with a completely different infrastructure than that of either Fiume or the Italian state, one created ex nihilo. No Fiumians were involved in drafting the constitution, which was never put into force.[83] According to one of Fiume's most famous sons, Leo Valiani—a socialist resistance fighter, Italian senator, and renowned historian of the dissolution of the Habsburg Monarchy—"The population [of Fiume] could make little sense out of the Dannunzian proclamation of the Carnaro Regency, no one wanting to be in conflict with the Italian government."[84] According to Valiani and consistent with how Fiumians organized their life before, during, and after D'Annunzio, the

Carnaro constitution was not a product of Fiume. Joining a madrepatria based on its rights of autonomy, self-determination, and special
prerogatives, however, was a Fiume initiative that it appears many residents understood and with which they complied.

What can we understand about Fiume by seeing it through the lens
of its multi-law culture? First and foremost, the mere fact that even
after World War I a city-state thought it could stand proud and loud
on the map of Europe and use legislation to anchor its sovereignty despite the dictates of international diplomacy reveals that the mindset
of layered sovereignty and its infrastructures did not die when Europe's
continental empires disappeared. Second, the ease with which Fiume's
elites challenged the diplomatic and legal structures of the wider world
into which they were thrown, as well as the relative success they had
at harnessing the narrower world in which they lived, reveals just how
well subjects of empire had learned to negotiate layered sovereignty.
They were so skilled at it, they even pushed to continue a similar setup
through their own layering. Despite the power differential, a city-state
believed it could remake the nation-state monarchy it was trying to
push itself into. Finally, Fiume's strange post-WWI legal history reveals
something that is often overlooked: imperial sovereignty structures were
not just extra-European experiences, hashed out far away from the
powerful metropoles of London, Paris, Berlin, Amsterdam, Madrid, and
Rome. They were also intra-European experiences that half the continent's population lived with, and the legacies of imperial layered sovereignty shaped the futures of Europeans who had been ruled by the
Russian, Habsburg, German, and Ottoman Empires. So much, in fact,
that some of these former imperial subjects did not understand why
the Italian Kingdom could not be brought into the layered-sovereignty
fold, with San Marino and Fiume as exemplary substates of an Italian
metropole-madrepatria model. For this all to work, of course, defining
who was and wasn't part of this "laws in force" substate would prove
vitally important.

4

Between City and State

The Contradictions of Citizenship

Around eleven o'clock on the evening of March 20, 1919, a group of French and Italian soldiers began arguing in a crowded café in Fiume's city center. Apparently French soldiers had made hand gestures to their Italian counterparts to let them know just how little they thought of Italians' (and the Italian state's) potency. Undoubtedly, the Italian soldiers responded with equally vulgar remarks and gestures. Finally, in order to prevent angry words from becoming angry punches, a British captain of the Inter-Allied command ordered everyone out and back to their quarters. Several civilians had joined the fracas, most siding with the Italians. One, however, sided with the French, and when he left the fray to return home, a few of his angry fellow Fiumians decided to teach him a lesson.

The civilian was 20-year-old Francesco Pospek, a Fiume-born clerk who had served in the war, returned unharmed, and now worked for a local merchant. Minutes after leaving the café, Pospek was assaulted by two other Fiume natives, 22-year-old clerk Oscarre Nossan and 22-year-old barber Roberto Pellegrini. When Giuseppe Castellicchio, a 37-year-old local police officer, arrived on the scene a few minutes later, the beating ended. But when Castellicchio asked to see personal documents, it was not the assailants' papers he requested, but Pospek's. Castellicchio recognized Pospek as the man who had just been supporting the French and, therefore, he considered Pospek, not the two men providing the beating, the real troublemaker.

At the police station the following day, the belligerents gave statements about what had happened after Castellicchio examined Pospek's documents. According to Nossan, Castellicchio exclaimed, "How [is this], you live here, you are pertinent here, you work here, and [yet] you speak against Italy?"[1] Nossan said that Pospek replied by saying, "Fiume was never and never will be Italian." Pellegrini provided an almost identical account. Pospek's version was slightly different. According to Pospek, on seeing his documents, Castellicchio asked, "How can you be Slav, as you were born and are registered in this city?" Pospek testified that he had responded, "My father was Slovene, I attended school in Sušak, and Fiume during the war and before was not Italian."[2]

For his part, Castellicchio did not mention any exchange about Pospek's documents, stating in his report simply that Pospek had

incited the French soldiers against the Italian soldiers by yelling out "Fiume was always Croatian and never Italian," thereby provoking the resentment of numerous citizens who were at the café and its environs. . . . Pospek is a fanatical Croatian petty politician, who is known as such by the citizenry.[3]

To document Castellicchio's claim, two of Pospek's identity papers were included within the report: his Fiume residency card and his membership card in the Serb-Croat-Slovene National Council, which had acted as the provisional government for ten days before the Italian National Council took control in November 1918.

Apparently, little else needed to be shown. Pospek was arrested and charged with "inciting hatred among the nationalities."[4] Nossan and Pellegrini were not charged for assaulting Pospek, as their victim had incited them. Castellicchio continued to perform his police duties.[5]

To the modern-day reader, what may appear most astounding about this case is the way the immediate postwar Fiume establishment used laws against "inciting hatred among nationalities." The thousands of flyers, posters, chants, parades, and demonstrations sponsored by Fiume's provisional government declaring Fiume "Italian" were all fine and good, even though those signs undoubtedly made Fiumians who didn't identify as Italian uncomfortable. And the fact that Pospek was considered a criminal for saying "Fiume was always Croatian" or "Fiume was never and never will be Italian" reveals the degree to which the provisional government and its supporters were determined to Italianize the face of Fiume. All agreed that Pospek's evocation of a hated image of Fiume was intolerable, reminding people that the city they lived in had been Habsburg, contained just as many people who were not Italian as those who were, and had never been part of the Kingdom of Italy. Charging Pospek with "inciting hatred among the nationalities" was just one way to teach people that emphasizing Fiume's multinational Habsburg past was anathema; the goal now was annexation to Italy, and for that to work, Fiume's Italianness was the only thing anyone should be shouting about.

But on closer examination, this case also points to the contradictions that surrounded the idea of who belonged in Fiume in the immediate postwar years. Nossan, Pellegrini, and Pospek agreed that Castellicchio became truculent when confronted with the fact that Pospek was a registered member of Fiume's body politic and yet still spoke against Italy.[6] In essence, according to Nossan and Pellegrini, Castellicchio did not ask, "How could *you* be from Fiume?" Instead he demanded to know how a *Fiumian* could be against Italy. Even Pospek's version of the exchange points to an assumption that living in Fiume equaled agreeing with an Italian nationalist agenda. According to Pospek, Castellicchio did not ask, "How could a Slav be a legal member of the Fiume body politic?" Instead, he asked, "How could you identify yourself as a Slav after being born here and registered here?" Pospek did not answer this question by defending his right to call himself Fiumian. As his documents showed, that was a given. Instead, he emphasized all the influences that made him oppose an Italian agenda for Fiume: his non-Italian father had raised him in Fiume; he had gone to school in Sušak's Croatian-run secondary schools. None of this was surprising: Fiume was filled with thousands of locals with just such trajectories. The issue was that Castellicchio and Pospek held conflicting visions of how Fiumians should characterize their city. Castellicchio thought that Fiumians should speak well of Italy, whereas Pospek did not see support for Italian Fiume as a default Fiumian position.

Castellicchio's and Pospek's opposing visions of the responsibilities enmeshed in Fiume belonging and nationality were the direct result of the fact that, in immediate postwar Fiume, nationality was not a marker of legal, full membership in the Fiume body politic. Instead it was that seemingly strange concept "pertinent" that entitled a local to benefit from all the rights and privileges that living in the city-state entailed. Pertinency (*pertinenza* in Italian, *Heimatrecht* in German, *zavičajnost* in Croatian, and *községi illetőség* in Hungarian) was a prewar legal category omnipresent throughout all the lands of Austria-Hungary before 1918, which actually increased in importance after the Habsburg Monarchy dissolved. Castellicchio's confusion about Pospek's status—his pertinency—was probably compounded because the personal documents Pospek presented showed that his rights as a member of Fiume's body politic were not based on some prewar certificates commissioned under the Habsburg regime. If Castellicchio had seen those older papers, he would have seen that Pospek—though still listed as born, raised, living, and working in Fiume—was not registered as "pertinent" to the port city, but instead to the Styrian town Celje (in today's Slovenia), where Pospek's father had been born.[7] Instead, Castellicchio saw newer documents, documents produced while the Italian National Council administered the city. And these documents pointed to the fact that Pospek, a man who identified nationally as Slav, belonged in Fiume.

That this could happen is a sign of how complicated Fiumians' experiences of belonging and exclusion were in the immediate postwar period. This chapter investigates the various ways in which the questions of who could and could not benefit from membership in the Fiume body politic were addressed. Here we see how issues of citizenship, localism, and nationality were navigated in a way that could extend new rights to non-Italian Fiumians even as the state criminalized locals for challenging its Italian nationalist claims.[8]

Imperial Fiume: A Rainbow of Pertinencies, Citizenships, and Nationalities

Four years before World War I began, bureaucrats across Austria-Hungary collected the data required for the next round of censuses. Conducted every ten years, these censuses were to determine the population density of towns, villages, and countrysides; make draft lists for the military; and set tax rates for municipalities and counties. The censuses helped determine what languages should be used in local schools and what religious organizations represented the interests of local populations. They measured the economic successes and hardships of different Austrian and Hungarian regions in terms of production and export, and served as indicators of the general health, welfare, and life expectancy of a subject of the Habsburg king.

In the mid-nineteenth century, Habsburg census takers counted and analyzed households. In the late nineteenth and early twentieth centuries, they counted individuals. Over this period, census takers for the Hungarian-held semiautonomous city of Fiume noted astounding transformations taking place. In 1890, they had reported 29,494 individuals living in Fiume. In 1900, with 38,944 inhabitants, the city's population had grown by 32 percent. The trend continued in 1910: with 49,806 souls calling Fiume home, the city was 27 percent bigger than ten years before and 68 percent bigger than twenty years earlier. Not even war stunted Fiume's growth: in January 1915, Fiume city officials reported that 52,379 people were registered in the port city in January 1914, as opposed to 54,750 in December 1914, just eleven months later.[9]

The increase was not the result of ambitious baby-making, but of immigration triggered by the employment opportunities offered by Fiume's growing industrial port. And, as is usually the case in growing port cities, the influx came from different lands, language groups, and religions. In 1910, 49 percent of city dwellers declared their mother tongue Italian, 26 percent Croatian, 13 percent Hungarian, 5 percent Slovene, 5 percent German, and 2 percent an amalgamation of other tongues. These data on language speakers did not indicate exclusive language use. As Ivan Jeličić has brilliantly shown, the 1910 census offers deeper insights into Fiume's linguistic culture.[10] People were not just asked what language they felt most comfortable speaking (their mother tongue); they were asked what other languages they knew. Putting all those numbers together lets us see a city whose population overlapped and intersected. While 49 percent identified as mother-tongue Italian speakers, 73 percent of those living in Fiume could communicate in Italian. Twenty-six percent cited Croatian as the language they spoke most freely, but almost twice that number (53.5 percent) could speak Croatian. For Hungarian, the figures are astounding in the opposite way: along with Italian, Hungarian was the city's official language, but a mere 13 percent declared Hungarian their mother tongue, and only 23 percent of city residents claimed to know it. The baseline takeaway of this is that most residents in Fiume and its immediate suburbs were multilingual, with most capable of using Fiume's official language, Italian, and over half able to communicate in the language of its hinterland, Croatian.

Religiously, the city was much less mixed. Of the population, 92 percent was baptized Catholic; 3 percent paid dues to the city's Jewish houses of worship; 2 percent followed the doctrines of Calvin or Luther; and nearly 2 percent followed the rites of Greek or Serbian Orthodoxy.[11]

Different language capabilities and religious beliefs did not indicate or determine rights, however. The majority of the nearly 50,000 souls who called Fiume home and were questioned for the 1910 census were not full members of its body politic. This is not to say that they were living in Fiume illegally, but rather that only around 34 percent of the population had a right to the city's poor relief and could not be expelled if they proved to be a burden on the community.[12] And of that 34 percent, only male adults over the age of 25 with significant economic stature could vote in or stand for local elections. In essence, this meant that before 1918, in a city of circa 50,000 people, only about 17,000 had the right to live in the city regardless of what befell them, and only a little over 2,300 had active, local political rights.

The 34 percent with access if needed to the city's poor relief and immunity from expulsion were categorized as Fiume pertinents. How pertinency was obtained varied across Austria-Hungary, but by the beginning of the 1900s it had increasingly become something you obtained almost automatically based on how long you lived somewhere and whether you paid municipal taxes (with how long and how much varying according to the where and when).[13] Because of Fiume's special status of corpus separatum, however, these "easings" for obtaining pertinency did not apply, mostly because Fiume's elite wanted to keep its political power consolidated and its economic responsibilities toward the poor and unwanted limited. While in most of the Habsburg Monarchy, pertinency began looking more and more like long-time residency, in Fiume it did not. And so, only 34 percent of the city had it.[14]

Before 1918, only three things guaranteed Fiume pertinency. It was automatically yours if you were the legal offspring of a Fiume pertinent, an abandoned infant found within Fiume proper, or a woman who married a man holding Fiume pertinency. It was also yours if you worked in an official and stable capacity for the Hungarian state bureaucracy, the noncombatant officer corps of the Habsburg military, the Fiume city bureaucracy, or a state-recognized religious establishment. Nothing was automatic. If you had any of these qualifications, once you applied your pertinency was assured. However, you had to apply to receive it.[15] Everyone else who wanted it had to invest time and money to apply.

For the tens of thousands of immigrants who moved to Fiume and did not fit into the "guaranteed" categories, obtaining Fiume pertinency was a question of social class and power. Until 1908, applicants for Fiume pertinency had to

1) prove legal and financial independence,
2) have no criminal record,

and

3) live at least one year uninterruptedly within the city while simultaneously
    a) proving adequate means,
    b) owning property within Fiume city limits,
    c) owning long-distance ships,

    or

d) conducting one of the following professions: independent merchant, independent commercial agent, long-distance ship captain, long-distance ship lieutenant, university graduate, lawyer, notary, engineer, architect, teacher, surgeon, pharmacist, or any other profession considered valuable by city authorities.

As immigrant influx into Fiume grew, the pertinency laws tightened even more. In 1908 the requirements were increased: applicants were now required to prove that they had had a stable domicile in Fiume for at least five years before applying or, if they had considerable economic means or practiced a profession listed above, they could show that they had two years of stable domicile within the city instead of just one.[16]

Though pertinency laws helped keep the thousands of immigrants to Fiume from accessing local suffrage rights, becoming a burden on local budgets, and securing the right to remain, pertinency was not a Fiume invention and, thus, if you did not have it, you probably had it somewhere else even though you lived in Fiume. Again, before 1918, almost every citizen within Austria and Hungary was assigned a pertinency.[17] Pertinency was determined by family ties, while residency (*Aufenthalt* in German) was determined by where one lived. For example, in his application for Fiume pertinency, Giorgio Bayer, the 46-year-old head warehouseman of a local beer factory, stated that he had lived in Fiume with his family for over three decades. All that time, however, he had been a pertinent of German-held Ziębice (in today's Poland) because he was born there and his father held pertinency there. Thus, though Bayer's wife and two sons had never been to Ziębice, all of the Bayer family living in Fiume held their pertinency in this far-off Silesian burg rather than Fiume, where they had lived legally and quite successfully most of their lives.[18] Bayer petitioned for Fiume pertinency to cement his family's rights in the town they called home. Had he not petitioned, it would not matter how many generations the Bayer family lived in Fiume; they would be Fiume residents with Ziębice pertinency.

Women's pertinency was almost always determined by family ties rather than geographic or biographic senses of "home." Upon marriage, every woman in Austria-Hungary was automatically assigned her husband's pertinency, whether she desired it or not. Any woman who had pertinency in her hometown before marriage lost it upon marrying someone without such pertinency. Consider the illiterate housewife Nemesia Haller. Born in Fiume in 1858 to a Fiume-pertinent father, she lost her pertinency when she married her second husband, the Pula-pertinent Antonio Gambel, even though she continued to live in Fiume. Upon Gambel's death, she was still registered on the Fiume population rolls as an *estranea* (outsider), and at the age of 61 the widow Gambel née Haller applied to be reinstated as a pertinent of Fiume, declaring she did so because she held "good feelings towards the city where she was born."[19]

Being a pertinent of prewar Fiume had nothing to do with religion, language use, or ethnicity. When the 37-year-old policeman Giovanni Krmpotić applied for Fiume pertinency for himself; his wife, Giuliana née Medic; and his underage children, Giovanni, Caterina, Irene, and Germano, he presented only his personal documents attesting that he was born in a Croatian village over 150 kilometers away, was financially independent, had no criminal record, had lived uninterruptedly in Fiume for nine years, and had been steadily employed as an officer within Fiume's security forces.[20] As was true of all pertinency petitions before 1918, no mention was made of his linguistic abilities, ethnic identity, or religious beliefs. Nor did his petition serve as an indicator of his fluency in Italian, as it had been prepared by a local Fiume lawyer. Well-placed Jewish applicants who had Hungarian citizenship and participated in the city's economic and civic spheres received pertinency just as quickly and easily as the Catholic Croatian Krmpotić did.[21] Just as Sylvia Hahn has shown in the Austrian lands, applications exhibiting economic stability and good "moral-political" behavior were what made a successful bid for pertinency in pre-1918 Fiume.[22]

For circa 40 percent of the people living in Fiume, the greatest impediment in applying for Fiume pertinency was citizenship.[23] Only Hungarian citizens could be Fiume pertinents, so applicants had to prove Hungarian citizenship.[24] For someone like the policeman Giovanni Krmpotić, this was no great impediment, as his prior pertinency was in a Croatian village, making him a Hungarian citizen.[25] For someone with Austrian, Italian, Serbian, Ottoman, German, Greek, British, or French citizenship, things were much more complicated.

Consider the case of 33-year-old grocer Francesco Bavec.[26] In 1916, Bavec petitioned the Fiume magistrate for Fiume pertinency, providing a wealth of documentation. He included the record of his marriage to his 28-year-old wife, Fiume-born Giovanna Versoni, as well as the birth certificate of their recently Fiume-born daughter, Pia. He provided a police certificate attesting that he had no criminal record, had a good moral-political reputation, and had lived in Fiume since infancy. He documented that he had legally owned his own grocery store since 1905 and was licensed to run it. The only problem with his application was that he held pertinency in the Carniolan village of Mačkovec, today located in Slovenia, and at the time part of the Austrian half of the empire. With Austrian instead of the required Hungarian citizenship, Bavec ended his petition with this plea:

> Since for over 22 years I have lived uninterruptedly in this city, where I have formed my family and where all of my interests are held, for this reason I plead of this illustrious Civic Magistrate . . . to assure for myself, my wife Giovanna Bavec née Versoni, and my daughter Pia acceptance into this town under the condition of obtaining Hungarian citizenship on the part of the Royal Hungarian Minister of the Interior.[27]

Bavec's request was granted, and he was given official assurance that if he obtained Hungarian citizenship within one year's time, his Fiume pertinency would be confirmed. The fact that the Fiume magistrate gave Bavec a year to obtain Hungarian citizenship indicates how intricate citizenship transfer was in the early twentieth century, even between two states ruled in conjunction like Austria-Hungary. Unfortunately for Bavec, perhaps because of the war, one year was not long enough. At the end of 1917, he applied for (and was granted) an extension of his Fiume pertinency petition, but when the Austro-Hungarian Kingdom was dissolved in November 1918 and Fiume was set loose as a contested city-state outside the strictures of any country, Bavec had still not received Hungarian citizenship. His family was still listed as pertinent to a Carniolan village that his wife and daughter had never seen and of which he likely held but childhood memories. Nonetheless, the rights and protections Fiume pertinency entailed remained out of reach.

Citizenship and Fiume pertinency were difficult bedfellows. For those born in the lands of Hungary (which included Croatia-Slavonia), Fiume pertinency was an internally administered affair. But a significant number of new arrivals did not hold Hungarian citizenship papers, and for the many from the Kingdom of Italy, Bosnia and Herzegovina, or the Austrian half of the empire (Trieste, Istria, Dalmatia, Vorarlberg, Styria, Tyrol, Lower and Upper Austria, Carniola, Carinthia, Bohemia, Moravia, Galicia, Bukovina, Silesia, and Salzburg), applying for Fiume pertinency required months if not years of legal and bureaucratic paperwork in their respective capitals and Budapest. The meager number of citizenship petitions held in the Fiume archives and the relatively small percentage of Fiume residents who held pertinency suggest that few possessed Francesco Bavec's patience or determination.

Thus, before Austria-Hungary was dissolved, ever-growing, multi-lingual, semiautonomous Fiume had almost fifty thousand legal residents, 67 percent of whom held pertinencies or citizenships outside their place of residence. Many of them had lived their entire adult lives in Fiume: they married, raised their children, formed their opinions, and suffered their heartaches there. As non-pertinents but legal residents, they paid taxes, owned property, sent their children to city schools, and had their illnesses treated in city hospitals. Not having pertinency affected the overwhelming majority of Fiume residents very little. You only "felt" pertinency if you were well off (and wanted to participate in local politics) or very poor (and needed the city to help feed, house, or heal you) or were a political opponent of the status quo (socialists and anarchists often were expelled if they did not hold pertinency). Many in fact did not even know they did not hold pertinency, because in the lands where many came from, longtime residency and tax payments automatically triggered pertinency status and so they did not think to check. In a paradox they lived daily, non-pertinents in the city were both legal outsiders and ordinary Fiumians.

Kingdom Dissolved: New Counting, New Citizenship?

On March 15, 1919, the 29-year-old Fiume-born secretary to the Italian National Council, Salvatore Bellasich, excitedly sent a telegram to the Italian delegates at the Paris Peace Conference: "After the plebiscite of the living comes the plebiscite of the dead stop." But Bellasich didn't "stop" after his melodramatic first line. Instead, he spent several costly telegrammed pages outlining how an "imposing voice of the deceased has joined with the unanimous chorus of the living stop." What was he talking about? He wired Paris delegates to share statistical findings collected by "some youths from the Alessandro Manzoni Circle" to prove that "the further you go back in time the more evident the Italian character of Fiume appears" and that "Croatian immigration is of recent times." One feels almost sorry for Bellasich's attempts to back the Italian National Council's claims of Fiume's Italianness with hard "statistical data." Did he really think Wilson and his Inquiry specialists could be swayed by the knowledge that "of 2,853 epigraphs on tombs in the last 100 years 2,304 that is more than 80 percent are in Italian"? Did he really think that Lloyd George and Clemenceau would change their minds if they knew that "in the churches out of 93 epigraphs from the sixteenth to the nineteenth centuries 83 were in Latin 7 Italian 2 German and only one in Croatian"? Were these really the "crushing figures" that would "undo childish assertions of Croatian newspapers that Fiume was Italianized in recent times by the Hungarians"? Apparently he did, because after information on the cemeteries, he listed censuses of boats, ships, and local Fiume politicians' names over the last centuries.[28] Line after ridiculous line, Bellasich's tone remained the same: heady, cocksure, impatient. The message remained the same as well: No matter how you counted it, Fiume was Italian. Its dead were Italian. Its living were Italian. Its ships were Italian. Its distinguished forebearers were Italian. Its graves were Italian. Why did Woodrow Wilson and his diplomat cronies in Paris continue to heed the "childish assertions of Croatian newspapers"? Bellasich sent his costly telegram in the hope that this data would awaken the Great Powers to what he saw as the indisputable truth of Fiume's Italianness. He also sent it to the ten most widely distributed newspapers in Italy. If no one in Paris would listen to Fiume's government, perhaps someone in Italy would.

On the same day Bellasich sent his telegram, Paris Peace Conference delegates from the Kingdom of Serbs, Croats, and Slovenes published their pamphlet on the national character of Fiume (which they called "Rijeka"). They, too, sent extracts to major newspapers throughout Europe and the Americas. Though it was not as frantic or morbid as Bellasich's, in essence the argument was the same: Fiume's national character should be determined by names and numbers, just not the ones Bellasich used. In the Serb-Croat-Slovene pamphlets, the 1910 Habsburg census was used to show that the Italian national presence was limited to the Fiume city center. After insinuating that the 1910 Habsburg figures were "fixed" by Hungarian realpolitikers eager to downplay Croatian influence, the pamphlet insisted that

> as soon as one leaves the Fiume city center for its outskirts, let's say for example toward Sušak, which in and of itself is a small city center, one finds 11,705 Yugoslavs compared to 658 Italians. When one moves out into the "hinterland" or across the narrow canal that separates the mainland from the Island of Krk, one finds oneself in a completely Slavic territory. Not just the hinterland but all the outskirts of Fiume, everywhere that surrounds the city by land and sea, and in general everything that forms part of the organism of the city . . . everything is purely Yugoslav. . . . From an ethnic point of view, the Italian and Hungarian colonies in Fiume give the impression of being a wedge [*cuneo*], a body completely extraneous, embedded within the Slavic element.[29]

Like Bellasich and his Italian nationalist cohort, the Serb-Croat-Slovenes had a case to make. Fiume, they said, was "Croatian-Yugoslav" except for the extraneous Italo-Hungarian colonies nurtured in the heart of the city by recent immigration and Italianization campaigns by the "Italo-Hungarian interests of the ex-Monarchy."[30] Similar battles were occurring in most of the territories that the newly dissolved Romanov, Ottoman, and Habsburg empires had once reigned over, with census numbers being deployed to judge which national self-determination narrative was most valid for an ethnically mixed territory.[31] These numbers revealed individuals' national will, or so postwar political activists maintained, and the only way to get them was by census taking (sometimes of graveyards, usually of living inhabitants).[32]

The new provisional governments that rose when Europe's empires dissolved also set out to provide new numbers based on new censuses. In almost all cases, results supported the nationalist claims of whichever government had organized the counting. Fiume's Italian National Council was no exception. Habsburg censuses in 1910 had reported that Fiume's city dwellers were made up of

49 percent Italian speakers
26 percent Croatian speakers
13 percent Hungarian speakers
5 percent Slovene speakers
5 percent German speakers
2 percent other tongues.

However, the new December 1918 census conducted by the Italian National Council reported

62.5 percent Italians
19.6 percent Croatians
9.6 percent Hungarians
3.6 percent Slovenes
3.5 percent Germans
0.8 percent other.

The 1918 Fiume census, along with all the other immediate postwar population data of its kind, was generally disregarded by the diplomats in Paris, for obvious reasons. How were ethnic language groups determined? Were these censuses truly "plebiscites," with individuals asked to state the language they identified with? Or were the census takers instructed to determine for themselves each individual's language?

What assurances were there that individuals were not pressured to present themselves within the language group that served the government's political goals? Were protections in place to monitor the corruptibility of the data collected? Though scholars like Emil Brix have rightly pointed out the untrustworthy nature of prewar Habsburg census results (because of the tendency of bureaucratic language to overdetermine findings), in comparison with the many ways immediate postwar results could be discounted, the prewar censuses were the apex of trustworthy population data.[33] Few of the diplomats in Paris acknowledged the reported 13.5 percent increase of Italians and 6.4 percent decrease of Croats in the 1918 census organized by the Italian National Council. They ignored the new numbers and continued to regard Fiume as a mixed city, as Croatian-Slovene as it was Italian.

Fiume's December 1918 census was not a total act of nationalist contrivance, however. Though its numbers on the national divisions of its population might have been questionable, the census did take place. Not only that, it elicited almost full participation of its residents. Fiume politicians like Bellasich characterized this participation as a "plebiscite of the living," but actually, Fiumians stood in line outside the census offices in the cold December weather because they had no choice if they wanted to keep receiving the necessities for living.[34] The government's announcement of the census left no doubts about this: participation in the census was the only way to receive "an identification card in order to facilitate the enjoyment of food provisions."[35] For Fiumians, the census was about aid and nationality numbers. With little food available in Fiume's marketplaces, thousands of people out of work, and the winter months just starting, the importance of participating in the 1918 Fiume census was clear; access to food and government subsidies was at stake.

The Italian National Council might have proclaimed the need for a census primarily to organize aid relative to population size and unemployment numbers, but the 1918 census also introduced a new, more expansive interpretation of Fiume "belonging." The extent of the change can be gleaned from just one number in the many charts issued after the census. Before the war, only 34 percent of people living in Fiume held pertinency, but in the December 1918 census 86 percent of Fiume-born people aged 20 or older now possessed the once nearly unobtainable Fiume-rights status.[36] This sea change was not triggered by a mass exodus of Fiume residents without pertinency rights (population records indicate only a 10 percent population drop at war's end). It was because when issuing identification papers in December 1918, the Italian National Council opened up the right to apply for pertinency to anyone with five years of stable residency, no criminal record, and the willingness to renounce any other citizenship.

The length of the required period of prior residency was the same as the 1908 pertinency requirements, as was the requirement that applicants not have a criminal record. But the abolition of the Hungarian citizenship requirement was a significant change. It meant that long-term residents of Fiume who were Italian or Austrian citizens could now become pertinents. The greatest effect of this was on the thousands of locals registered in the nearby Austrian-held regions of Dalmatia, Istria, Carniola, Styria, and Trieste (regions that are now located in today's Croatia, Slovenia, Austria, and Italy and consisted of large Italian-, Croatian-, and Slovene-speaking populations). Pertinency was not just opened up because of this change in citizenship laws; it was also closed down. The new provision excluded anyone from applying for or *retaining* pertinency who could or would receive aid through another state, meaning that where once Hungarian state connections could help you obtain Fiume pertinency, now they precluded you from it. For everyone, however, pertinency no longer functioned as a distinction shaped by family origins, social class, economic might, or Hungarian citizenship qualifications: a new spectrum of rights eligibility was available to prewar locals. In perhaps one of the strangest paradoxes in Fiume's paradoxical postwar story, the counting of people to fuel a nationalist Italian agenda was one of the key mechanisms in opening up real membership in the Fiume body politic. Before the war, pertinency was limited mostly to those tied into social and political power; after the war, someone as low down on the totem pole as 20-year-old Fiumian-born, Styrian-pertinent clerk Francesco Pospek was eligible, even if he would soon be arrested for "inciting hatred among the nationalities."[37]

Pertinents above All Else

Before 1918, Fiume pertinency granted the right to vote (for eligible men), hold public office (for eligible men), receive poor relief, and live in the city regardless of economic, social, criminal, or political status. After 1918, what Fiume pertinency granted expanded dramatically, partially because times were much tougher and more protections were needed. This was doubly the case for the many in Fiume who saw the state in which they held their citizenship (whether Habsburg Hungary or Austria) dissolve overnight. Before the war 66 percent of Fiume's inhabitants could get along quite nicely without Fiume pertinency by relying on the rights and privileges of Austrian, Hungarian, Italian, or some other citizenship; after November 1918 Fiume pertinency became imperative for survival for most in the city-state.

Just as Fiume's provisional government stamped over Austro-Hungarian currency and co-opted Hungarian legal practices, it adopted Habsburg Hungary's pertinency regime—with modifications. Though functioning as an independent state, postwar Fiume did not proclaim its body politic "citizens" of Fiume. Instead, the Italian National Council continued using the category of imperial pertinency, perhaps hoping it would ease inclusion into an Italian citizenship regime after annexation. As the Council announced in April 1919, rights to any state services or employment were obligated by "Fiume pertinency in place of Hungarian citizenship."[38] This did not mean that all Hungarian citizens in Fiume were automatically transformed into Fiume pertinents: the Council later amended post-1918 pertinency laws to give itself the right to exclude Hungarian civil servants who had received Fiume pertinency before 1918 because of their state service *if* the Italian National Council opted not to reconfirm their positions. As we have seen, the new Fiume pertinency regulations had nothing to do with prior citizenships and everything to do with length of Fiume residency and local rights. In short, the postwar recasting of pertinency worked to shift the rights and duties away from a broader royal (Hungarian) citizenship in favor of a homed-in Fiume (city) localdom.

The impact of the conversion of Hungarian citizenship to Fiume pertinency on Fiumians' daily life was significant. For example, in March 1919 the Italian National Council announced that subsidies for the families of Hungary's war veterans would only be disbursed "provided that they are Fiume pertinents."[39] Everyone else had to find another state to support them. At the end of May 1919, the Italian National Council requested that the Inter-Allied command uphold its state initiatives to offer employment to industrial workers "appurtenant to the Town of Fiume."[40] In February 1920, pension increases for state employees, teachers, and veterans were available only to "pertinents of the Town of Fiume."[41] In March 1920, railway employees, railway pensioners, and widows and orphans of railway workers were provided cost-of-living indemnity payments "providing that they are pertinents of the Town of Fiume."[42] And finally, in July 1920, the Fiume provisional government announced that payments for disabled soldiers or the families of fallen soldiers would only be available upon "verification of pertinency to the Town of Fiume."[43] Before 1918, veterans would have received their payments, industrial workers their special employment opportunities, pensioners their cost-of-living increases, railway workers their indemnities, and widows their war provisions thanks to claims on Austrian or Hungarian citizenship. After 1918, only those with Fiume pertinency could count on automatic state support. With Fiume's currency situation out of control, unemployment skyrocketing, and the cost of food and coal increasing by leaps and bounds, these sorts of pertinent-only initiatives to ease the pains of the postwar crisis rendered Fiume pertinency a must-have for any individual trying to keep his or her head above water.

Not having Fiume pertinency was not just costly—it could be life altering. As early as February 1919, city dwellers considered "dangerous," "disruptive," or "non-law-abiding" were either threatened with expulsion or forcibly banished. In July 1919, for example, the Italian National Council announced that store and restaurant owners had to make their prices publicly available or face heavy fines, temporary revocation of commercial licensing, and, if "having to do with persons not holding Fiume pertinency, banishment from the city."[44] In

February 1920, threat of expulsion was expanded: by law, "for reasons of order, security, or morality the Police can expel from Fiume anyone not pertinent to this town, either for a predetermined amount of time or definitively."[45]

These were not just empty threats; they were applied. Reasons for expulsion ran the gamut from pre-1918 grudges to high-state intrigue, anti-Slavic nationalism, anti-socialism, petty crimes, and a desire to ensure that the poor (especially poor women suspected of illicit prostitution) would not burden Fiume and its annexationist mission. The following is a short list of people without pertinency who received expulsion orders: 41-year-old Hungarian citizen Arturo Gerő—who owned a profitable clothing store in the Fiume city center and was pertinent to Vel'ký Meder (in today's Slovakia)—was "evicted from this city because he worked as a spy for the defunct Austrian government to the detriment of Fiume citizens."[46] Carniolan-born 25-year-old unemployed mechanic Giuseppe Smerdel was expelled because he was considered "of extreme tendencies dangerous to public order," evidenced by his leadership role in organizing a workers' strike.[47] Lošinj-born 33-year-old Giovanni Camalich received expulsion orders because "he was without stable domicile and he worked clandestinely in the sale of fabrics."[48] Menotti Silotti, 30 years old, got kicked out more because of his wife than for anything he did. Apparently his "Croatian wife, Anna Raicich, Italophobe, once arrived in Fiume . . . began speaking against Italians and said that if she had known that here one died of hunger she would not have left Yugoslavia."[49] Maria Svat, a 25-year-old maid and Hungarian citizen pertinent to the small village Felsőmocsolád, was banished because her employer denounced her to the police for taking his wallet while cleaning.[50]

Expulsion orders were clearly triggered by the fear of sharing ever more limited resources with those seen as outsiders. Hungarian laws surrounding pertinency had also been used to expel indigent or politically unwanted elements. However, from the moment the Italian National Council took over, Fiume armed forces also issued expulsion orders to neutralize socialist and anti-Italian annexation activists. These motivations were also deeply enmeshed with the desire to cook Fiume's census numbers to aid diplomatically oriented Italian annexation initiatives. We see this often in the Italian National Council and D'Annunzio archives: In November 1920, after the largest round of expulsion orders were given by D'Annunzio's command, 33-year-old Fiume-born Edoardo Susmel—former teacher, professional propagandist, and one of the main protagonists in organizing D'Annunzio's entry into Fiume— spoke as the Secretary General of D'Annunzio's newly founded Regency of Carnaro. Susmel advocated holding a new census "for the highest of political reasons, being that if the 1918 census organized by the [Italian] National Council gave the result of an absolute majority of Italians (62 percent), then that majority will undoubtedly result considerably greater thanks to the recent depuration of many hostile and foreign elements from the city."[51] To depurate is to free from impurities. As was the case throughout post-Habsburg Europe, expulsions of those lacking pertinency papers was seen by many of the more extreme nationalist activists as a way to "cleanse" the community of national "others." In Fiume's case, as Susmel happily noted, this meant that non-pertinent Croatian and Slovene speakers who refused to identify themselves as Italian were often targeted for expulsion.

The total number of non-pertinent, long-term residents who suffered expulsion from Fiume is still unknown; figures range from at least 500 (far too low) to well over 6,000 (perhaps too high, perhaps too low). If we include the waves of recent arrivals during or immediately after the war, the number is much, much higher. For example, in an August 1919 police report, officials stated that 1,220 people had been expelled from the city between January and August 1919, noting that most of these cases were on grounds of poverty, some because of missing documents, and 2 percent "for political reasons."[52] A March 1920 police report stated that between November 1918 and March 1920, fifteen thousand non-pertinents entered the city, but 80 percent of them just passed through. With increasing pressure to push newly arrived non-pertinents out of Fiume as quickly as possible, the police estimated that over three thousand of these new arrivals would warrant expulsion. From the summer of 1920 until the Christmas of Blood, D'Annunzio's command initiated a new round of expulsions of non-pertinents and Fiumian pertinents whom it considered "hostile to the cause." The Italian National Council, estimating that this would include well over four thousand people, strongly objected.[53] Out of fear of causing more internal dissent against D'Annunzio's command, most of the expulsion orders were repealed or not realized. Nonetheless, graffiti in late November 1920 demanded what many resenting the expulsion orders felt: "Out with the false liberators!"[54]

The reason why we cannot just add up all the expulsion orders to get a grand total of those expelled is because Fiume's police forces and D'Annunzio's command found it almost impossible to carry expulsions out. Internal resistance was one factor, but other, more pragmatic reasons dominated. First, many who were expelled never left the city at all, contesting their expulsions with city authorities, and thereby freezing procedures until well past 1921.[55] Second, Fiume's police and D'Annunzio's command had limited resources. Under the Hungarians, non-pertinents expelled from Fiume were forcibly escorted to their places of pertinency, making it very difficult for them to return. After 1918, Fiume's forces had no such resources or transportation possibilities, and so "expelled non-pertinents" were usually escorted across the Fiumara River, which they easily re-crossed.[56]

We might not know how many Fiumians were expelled, but we know that everyone in the city had a new awareness of how important it was to possess pertinency papers. The precarious situation of non-pertinents within post-imperial Fiume was so well known that Fiume pertinents even petitioned police to expel individuals who rendered their private lives difficult. An example is the 34-year-old guard and war veteran Matteo Biljanich. On February 9, 1919, Biljanich went to the police to have his neighbor Pasquale Lushinovich expelled, explaining,

> After having been absent from Fiume for 4 years, returned home
> I established that my wife was cheating on me with a certain

Pasquale Lushinovich, a dweller on the third floor of the same building. So as not to leave my two children without a mother, I forgave her on the condition she remain faithful to me.

Lushinovich, seeing the change in my wife Maria, began to harass me. . . . Considering that said individual is unemployed, not pertinent to Fiume, . . . he should be made to leave the city.[57]

It is not clear whether Biljanich was successful, but it is clear that the status of non-pertinents changed not just on the books but also on the ground. Before 1918, over 66 percent of the city did not hold Fiume pertinency, and having it or not made little difference except to the very rich, the political activists, and the very poor. After 1918, not holding Fiume pertinency was costly and perilous, and everyone knew it.

Fiume inhabitants responded quickly to this change. Already during the December 1918 census, residents were prosecuted for offering bribes to census officials to overlook missing papers required to apply for pertinency. On Christmas Eve 1918, 24-year-old Paula Peurača and her husband, Stanislao, headed to the local census office to request identity papers, which they wanted because Stanislao was pertinent to the Croatian town Karlovac, and neither spouse wanted to live there. According to Paula Peurača's statement to the police a few weeks later, it was only when they were at the census office that someone made it clear to them that her husband "could not obtain the identity papers being that he did not possess the right for pertinency in Fiume." In her testimony she insisted she had been assured that if you paid the policeman issuing identity cards ten crowns, the documents proving stable domicile required for pertinency could be "overlooked." According to Paula Peurača, they were so eager to obtain Fiume documents that they even offered to pay twice the going rate as long as the "affair got handled promptly."[58] It is difficult to gauge the prevalence of such corruption. It was rampant in many of Fiume's administrative offices, and Peurača's nonchalant tone and frank testimony suggest that pertinency papers could readily be bought. With expulsions and ration card limitations beginning in January 1919, it is very likely that many Fiume residents were willing to pay a pretty penny to obtain the needed documents.

After the April 1919 announcement by the Italian National Council that Fiume pertinency would replace Hungarian citizenship as the qualifier for rights and benefits, a new flood of pertinency requests made their way into the city's administrative offices. Their content and tone could not be more different from their pre-1918 equivalents. Before 1918, petitioners for pertinency documented their Fiume residency, financial and legal independence, criminal history, personal status, and citizenship. After 1918, pertinency requests either emphasized the absurdity of being pertinent to unknown, faraway lands or underscored Italian national attachments.

The first category of pertinency requests was typically filed in the months immediately following the April 1919 pertinency announcement. Some, like that made by 55-year-old Ignazio Levi on the part of himself and his wife, were relatively matter-of-fact. His petition read,

> We the undersigned Ignazio of Isacco Levi, born in Trieste January 17, 1864, living in Fiume since 1882, and Olga Levi née Heinrich, born in Karlovac March 1, 1868, living in Fiume since 1883, both of the Israelite religion, hitherto Ottoman subjects, pertinent to Istanbul, request with insistence that we be accorded pertinency to the city of Fiume.
>
> To the Ottoman consulate general in Budapest, within whose registers we are enrolled, we have communicated that we consider ourselves released from Ottoman subjecthood.[59]

Fiume officials diligently contacted the Ottoman consulate in Budapest, indicating that the Levi family would now be registered as Fiume pertinent. About a year later, the prefect of Istanbul contacted Fiume officials requesting precise details of where exactly the Levi family had lived in Istanbul, as no record of them could be found. In response, Fiume officials informed Istanbul, that since the Levi family had lived for a long time in Trieste, where the parents of the above mentioned were born, it is impossible to provide the information requested.[60] There was little more to say: the Ottoman Empire was in shambles. The Levi family fulfilled all the Fiume pertinency requirements, "considered itself released" from Ottoman citizenship, and requested "with insistence" Fiume pertinency as a result. Within a few weeks of the initial request, the Fiume government had processed the Levi petition. Despite the years it took the Istanbul offices to track down the Levi registers, on the Fiume side, the Levi family gained all the indispensable rights afforded by Fiume pertinency quickly and painlessly.

But most pertinency requests triggered by the dissolution of Europe's empires were less straightforward. More common were requests such as that made by the semiliterate 39-year-old Lorenzo Klevisser. Filled with spelling errors and written in an uncertain hand, Klevisser's petition explained how even though he and his deceased father held pertinency in a village outside Ljubljana, Fiume is where they were born and raised their families. In making his case for Fiume pertinency for himself and his three children, Klevisser emphasized he had "nothing in Comon [*sic*] with those Countries not having ever seen them, and knowing only Fiume [his] birth City and [his] Patria."[61] Perhaps owing to a lack of means, education, or the goodwill of the Fiume establishment, it took Klevisser years to provide the documentation needed to disentangle himself from his Ljubljana status and obtain Fiume pertinency. The same was true for other petitioners holding pertinencies in ex-Habsburg provinces that were now within the boundaries of the new Czechoslovak and Romanian lands.[62] When Fiume authorities wanted to supply acceptances quickly, it mattered little how complete the documentation severing applicants from their former citizenships was. When they had little or no interest in absorbing a new pertinency applicant into the body politic, the process could take months if not years.

Far more common among post-1918 pertinency petitions, however, was an emphasis on Italian national affiliation and cultural links to Fiume. Before 1918, no petitions mentioned linguistic, ethnic, religious, or national ties; after Austria-Hungary fell, most of them did. The petition of 39-year-old Filippo Lenassi epitomizes the newly Italocentric emphasis:

> I, undersigned Filippo Lenassi, [son] of deceased Filippo, humbly ask to be accepted within the Town of Fiume, together with my 25-year-old wife Alma née Springhetti, and our underage 9-year-old daughter Lidia, student.
>
> I was born in 1880 in Postojna [today's Slovenia] to a family of Italian origin and there I am also pertinent. As a boy I lived in Trieste from which I transferred to Fiume 15 or so years ago. I always socialized with Italian company and I grew attached to this elected patria of mine, where I plan to remain definitively. My wife is Fiumian from birth and has followed the same spirit of her family in educating our only daughter, who has always attended the city schools, distinguishing herself for diligence and achievement.
>
> I possess no fortune, but I have always made my living honestly through my work and I am sure that I will be able to support my family with dignity in the future, without being a burden on the City. Currently I am employed as a warehouse worker for the National Council's Office of Adriatic Affairs and my performance so far has not given any reason for complaint on the part of my superiors.[63]

Italian family origins, Italian friends, Fiume family connections, Fiume schooling, and a good relationship with the provisional government (his wife was related to a high official): these were the key criteria ticked off in one way or another in almost all quickly processed post-1918 applications for Fiume pertinency.[64]

The new focus on Italian national sentiment and Fiume local ties in pertinency petitions was not the result of eager applicants trying to give the authorities what they thought was required. This formula was precisely what *was* required. Consider the terse petition for Fiume pertinency submitted by the 35-year-old Fiume-born policeman Giovanni Liliak, pertinent to the Croatian town Gospić:

> I, the undersigned, having been born and raised here, courteously request of this Illustrious office to kindly grant me as well as my family pertinency to this town.[65]

Liliak's request was nothing more than a placeholder, and he was informed by the city administration that he would have to supply the necessary documentation. However, one of Liliak's superiors added this comment on the back of his petition:

> Having observed that the petitioner has always maintained uncensured political-moral conduct.
>
> Of Italian sentiment, he attended the national and Italian city schools, one of his daughters attends the Italian school in Melana.
>
> Throughout the period in which he has worked for the police department, he has never given reason to doubt that he held anything else but Italian sentiments.[66]

Again: Italian sentiment, local and Italian-oriented education of himself and his children, and a good relationship with city authorities— Liliak's superior supplied the information that Lenassi and hundreds of other successful petitioners knew was needed: successful applicants for Fiume pertinency were Italian oriented and Fiume bred.

In many respects the new emphasis within pertinency applications on being enmeshed in Fiume city culture was a response to the city's economic straits. As mentioned earlier, Fiume pertinency promised aid from the government in obtaining food, heating materials, employment opportunities, pensions, welfare payments, and indemnity subsidies. The provisional government went out of its way to protect its body politic, explicitly stating that job creation efforts for Fiume pertinents were under way for "obvious reasons concerning social politics and to reduce at least partially the considerable burden that the public Treasury must sustain."[67] Protecting locals was seen as a means of keeping the city calm. Ensuring that the city's body politic was limited as much as possible to "real locals" was another measure to decrease the "burdens" the government had to support. This political

A woman dressed in peasant garb has her identity papers checked in order to cross the Fiumara Bridge. Residents encountered such intimidating situations daily.

and fiscal reasoning was made more explicit in February 1920, when a law was decreed stating,

> Considering the extensive unemployment that has driven
>   thousands of Fiume workers into poverty;
> considering the precarious economic and alimentary conditions of
>   the city and its territory . . .
> All those who are not pertinent to Fiume but who have taken up
>   residence in Fiume after October 30, 1918 must abandon the
>   territory of Fiume by 8 P.M. March 8, 1920.[68]

Others agreed with the provisional government's goal of limiting pertinency rights to "real locals." On June 29, 1919, twenty-one of Fiume's most well-connected business leaders signed a petition demanding that "foreigners" be kicked out, as the city's welfare and charity programs could not afford to cover its own. "How is it acceptable," they asked, "that Fiumians are forced to submit to incredibly tough sacrifices to share their meager bread" with newly arrived Hungarians, Croatians, and all those others who "have landed here in the last months to take advantage of our unfortunate condition?"[69] The signers of this petition were not alone. Money was tight. Food and materials for braving the winter weather were scarce. Like others in the postwar world, Fiume's city government and many of its longtime residents wanted to limit city aid to those they considered their own.

Private initiatives to push the provisional government to weed out non-pertinents from the resource pool began almost as soon as the Habsburg Empire was dissolved. As mentioned earlier, the most likely candidates for exclusion were those seen not only as foreign but also as national outsiders or rivals. In December 1918, Fiume's chamber of commerce petitioned Fiume's mayor not to grant business licenses to three Hungarian businessmen who, the chamber claimed, had "no family or friendship bonds" to the city and were therefore untrustworthy.[70] In January 1919, thirteen employees of Fiume's tram system signed a petition demanding that "Yugoslav and mother tongue Croatian [tram] controllers and inspectors, most of whom are not pertinent to this town," be fired and replaced with "Fiumians or Italians from Istria or the Kingdom [of Italy]."[71] In April 1919, a note was sent to the police signed by "An Exceedingly Italian Fiume Citizen" stating that "in a bakery on via Fiumara N. 23 run by a certain Lagher (German Jew) you can hear people speak in German against Italians . . . against our politics, against the Italian occupation of Fiume, propaganda in favor of the Yugoslavs and against our interests. . . . Such dangerous people, such subjects are not worthy of being among us, they are not worthy of having industrial licenses."[72] Those who were most frequently identified as deserving exclusion from employment privileges and pertinency rights were Croatians, Hungarians, Slovenes, Germans, and Yugoslavs: the national affiliations of the prior hegemon (Austria-Hungary) or the unwanted future hegemon (Croatia-Yugoslavia). Jews, Romanians, Czechs, and Russians were targeted less often. Nationalism and chauvinism definitely came into play, but fears about Fiume's status in the geopolitical battles taking place were more common factors. Economic scarcity exacerbated ploys to limit access to jobs and services, while widespread poverty and unemployment rendered more people more vulnerable to these attempts at limitation.

As might be expected, the Italian National Council sometimes complied with requests for Croatian, Hungarian, Slovene, German, and Yugoslav "outsiders" to be denied pertinency or employment opportunities. In January 1919, for example, city authorities rejected Carlo Luppis's request to return to Fiume from the Italian-run refugee camp where he was stationed, saying that "the above mentioned is a person of terrible moral and political qualities. . . . He has always professed pro-Austrian sentiments."[73] In March 1919, the Italian National Council argued against allowing the Hungarian ex-policeman Vittorio Rosenberg back into Fiume, telling the Trieste prisoner-of-war camp where he was held that "his political and moral precedents are not at all good. He has always been against the Italianness of Fiume."[74] In the same month, Slavko Ivancić, Raffaelle Ban, and Giuseppina Udovičić, all applicants for industrial licenses in Fiume, testified that the secretary of Fiume's chamber of commerce told them that "we Croats would no longer receive industrial licenses in Fiume because those licenses from now on would be reserved purely for Fiumians."[75]

The provisional government did not always blindly discriminate against those seen as national outsiders. After the tram employees demanded that "Yugoslav and mother tongue Croatian [tram] controllers and inspectors" be fired, government officials investigated the case and rejected the petition, stating that the accusations were "baseless and unsubstantiated . . . with 9 of those [who signed the petition] having explicitly declared that they never observed in the inspector any partiality in treatment, and 6 deposed that they had signed the accusation purely out of solidarity for their colleagues."[76] Particularly noteworthy in the report was a suggestion about why the petition was originally made: the head of Fiume's public services department indicated, "It would behoove us to therefore think of the context of the current moment, one which a person could know to take advantage of and with these acts aim perhaps for a position which otherwise he could never obtain."[77] In other words, the government believed the petition was the brainchild of an ambitious, unqualified Fiumian of Italian ancestry who wanted his "Yugoslav and mother tongue Croatian" bosses fired to make room for him.

The government again demonstrated its awareness that these cases could be personal rather than political in its response to the anonymous note from the "Exceedingly Italian Fiume Citizen" mentioned earlier, who demanded that the baker "Lagher (German Jew)" be relieved of his store for promoting anti-Italian, pro-Yugoslav propaganda. Upon investigation, the police noted that

> Marco Lagher, son of the deceased Moisè and the deceased Dora Gabl, 54 years of age from Lviv [in today's Ukraine], living in via Manzoni n. 6, owner of a bakery on via Fiumara n. 23, residing in this city for over 6 years, is not involved in politics.
>
> Until a little while ago he produced bread for the Italian Army, the provision of which was quickly suspended because the bread was found to be badly produced.
>
> It is not true that Lagher expressed himself with offensive words against Italians or that he inveighed against the Italian occupation.
>
> Instead it has been verified that he fired all his workers who for their nationality were suspect of having spread Yugoslav propaganda.[78]

Within the precarious world of postwar Fiume, denouncing non-pertinent, non-Italian outsiders to the government did not guarantee moving up or removing unwanted competition. City inspectors were sent to corroborate statements and sometimes found that it was the "Italian elements" and not the "Hungarian," "German," "Jewish," or "Croatian" ones who were in the wrong. But non-pertinents were still vulnerable to such accusations. More than one non-pertinent probably followed Marco Lagher's example of firing workers solely because of their ethnicity, which made them suspect for spreading "Yugoslav propaganda." What easier way was there to prove dedication to Italian annexationist ambitions? Without pertinency, shorthand methods taken to prove that one was "worthy of being among us" were crucial, even though they often left others in the lurch.[79]

Locals above Italians

Croatian, Hungarian, German, Slovene, or Yugoslav national affiliations could block a Fiume resident from being given Fiume pertinency rights, but Italian national affiliations were not always rewarded. In fact, the applications most likely to be passed over were those submitted by Italian soldiers and D'Annunzio's legionnaires. For example, just ten days after D'Annunzio and his legionnaires entered Fiume, 20-year-old Camillo Lavini presented his pertinency petition:

> I undersigned Lavini Camillo son of Giuseppe and the deceased Croce Maria, born in Rome March 2, 1899 and there domiciled, now Ardito [Italian storm trooper] has the honor to request . . . citizenship to the Free City of Fiume.[80]

Newly arrived Lavini probably did not know the difference between "Fiume pertinency" and "citizenship to the Free City of Fiume," but the brevity of his application and the lack of any documentation suggests he probably did not fear being rejected for whatever Fiumians called "belonging" to their body politic. He was an Ardito, an Italian war hero. He had volunteered his life and livelihood to help Fiume join the Italian motherland. Was not adding his Italian self to the Fiume body politic just the next logical step to help make Fiume Italian? By joining D'Annunzio, he had disobeyed the Italian state's orders. At this point, why not double down by adding his Italian name and heritage to the city's rosters?[81]

Not just individual legionnaires like Lavini but entire D'Annunzio battalions reached the same conclusion: they could make Fiume more Italian by making themselves Fiumian.[82] Hundreds of equally laconic applications for pertinency were presented to the Fiume government in late autumn 1919, with some battalions even producing dittoed application forms for Italian soldiers to fill out. The Fiume government did not always reply to these petitions, but when it did, the response (often dittoed) was the same: no. Fiume pertinency was not available to those who were still registered "under the authority of their [the applicants'] patria," regardless of the fact that they were made by Italians.[83] By January 1920, Fiume functionaries had become so frustrated with these requests that they distributed a form letter telling applicants what they needed to apply for Fiume pertinency. The documentation necessary to obtain pertinency status included

birth certificate
domicile / pertinency certificate
good behavior certificate
family status certificate
proof of profession or means to sustain oneself and one's family
    economically
reasons / motives for applying for Fiume pertinency.[84]

By itself, Italian nationality did not come close to being enough. Applicants had to show that they would not be a drain on the city. And they needed reasons for thinking they should belong to Fiume that went beyond national feeling.

Pragmatic concerns trumped national arguments in part because many locals regarded newly arrived Italians either as potential competition for jobs or as a drain on the treasury. For one thing, immediately after the dissolution of Austria-Hungary, the precedence given to "outsider Italians" over locals for employment was undeniable, especially for positions in the security forces. In his April 1919 report summarizing how he had reformed Fiume's local police force, a member of the provisional Fiume government, Nicolò Biasi, noted that in hiring "a good corps of well disciplined and educated guards and agents," he looked abroad.[85] According to Biasi, "Not having been able to find enough good forces in Fiume, I looked for help from the Trieste and Trento [Italian irredentist organization]."[86] Fiumians who were worried about corruption also wanted police supervision manned by outsiders rather than locals. In a March 1920 note to the police complaining about contraband tobacco trade, an anonymous informant ended his note by stating, "Send good [police] agents not from Fiume but foreign, to assure a rigorous search."[87]

Generally, however, preferential hiring of nonlocal Italians over Fiumians was unpopular in the increasingly poverty-stricken port city. As Fiume's unemployment numbers kept growing, Italians from the Kingdom of Italy received curt rejections when applying for jobs. Francesco Pasculli, from outside Venice, was one of many school teachers told point-blank that Fiume jobs were for Fiumians, not Italians. In breaking the bad news to Pasculli, the Italian National Council wrote in June 1919,

> In response to your request of June 24 this year I have the honor to communicate to you that in the foreseeable future there will be no vacancies for an elementary school teacher in our town schools, which cannot be filled by a qualified Fiumian schoolmaster or schoolmistress to whom one must give preference.[88]

Though the state had undoubtedly given preference to Italians over Fiumians on occasion, this was not something for which the Italian National Council wanted to be known. Fiumians should come first.

Welfare was another area in which Italians from the Kingdom of Italy were pitted against locals. According to a memo from the president of the Italian National Council to the head of the Inter-Allied occupation forces in May 1919, family members of Italian soldiers living in Fiume had received "not even a cent of the subsidies due to them by law" from the Kingdom of Italy.[89] The result: families of Italian soldiers living in Fiume were in "dire circumstances" and "the number [of Italian families arriving] is increasing day by day."[90] The president of the Italian National Council warned that though the provisional government had tried to help the neediest, this could not continue, for "among many it is being insinuated the suspicion that the Fiume administrative bodies are making an odious distinction between [those] Italians [who were] formerly Austrian-Hungarian subjects and [those] Italians from the Kingdom of Italy [*regnicoli*]."[91] The 25-year-old Italian legionnaire Giuseppe Prosperi probably had no idea that his request for pertinency was hurt rather than helped by mentioning that he was "without wealth of [his] own" or that he had worked for the Florentine railway system and hoped "to enter into service for the Fiume railways, naturally after the question of Fiume was resolved."[92] Most likely, his request was pushed aside even faster than those of most of his fellow soldiers, as the last thing Fiume needed was an outsider without private fortune—of any nationality.

The reluctance to automatically adopt Italians as Fiume's own was perhaps made most explicit in February 1920 with the general banishment from the city of all non-pertinents except military personnel "who have taken up residence in Fiume after October 30, 1918."[93] October 30, 1918, was the date the Italian National Council declared itself Fiume's provisional state; shortly after that, families of Italian soldiers began pouring into Fiume, alongside Hungarian refugees and a hodgepodge of Italian, Slovene, Croat, Austrian, Romanian, Czech, Slovak, Bosnian, and Serb postwar migrants looking for work, home, and shelter. Hungarian refugees and postwar migrants were definitely unwelcome as things got worse in Fiume, but when the port city closed its doors to outsiders, it included Italians among the excluded.

There was yet another reason for Fiumians' negative response to Italians seeking pertinency: Italian soldiers' embrace of Fiume's female population. Italian soldiers and followers of D'Annunzio reveled in their good luck at arriving somewhere with such a "welcoming" female population, with seemingly few questioning whether it was their access to money and military rations that made them so attractive. Police were less blind to what having military men in town meant. Anxious reports poured in of "young girls, tender in age, [who] partake in public dances on holidays and Sundays and don't come home until late in the night."[94] The police doubted that the nights were spent just dancing, with the Fiume police commissioner summing up the situation thus: "The work of the police is notably blocked by the fact that every illegal prostitute has their protector and guarantor in the person of some military man."[95] Italian soldiers assigned to help the police proved perhaps worse than the average legionnaire, with some of them using their positions as defenders of public order to go to whorehouses and demand that prostitutes "cede to desires without being paid."[96]

As we have seen, legionnaires might have viewed their time in Fiume as one where "everyone here is having fun, and spending money, and making love with the Fiume girls, who are famed for being pretty and easy," but locals had a different view.[97] For example, 27-year-old Fiume-born Margherita Bydeskuty née Diracca testified in an August 1920 libel case that

> one night, in the spring of 1919, . . . I pointed out to them [her fiancé and her niece] a little girl apparently around 12-years-old who was entertaining a conversation with an elderly sailor, expressing thereby the negative impression this had upon me. . . . My fiancé added that it was truly sad how almost all of the Fiume women have allowed themselves to be corrupted.[98]

Bydeskuty's niece gave another version, stating that the fiancé had "spoken badly of the Italians, declaring that the Italians had come to Fiume to ruin its women and corrupt them."[99] In another court case, 36-year-old Fiume-born merchant Dante Grenier testified that his sister-in-law was incensed to hear that her 15-year-old daughter was said to have had relations with Italian soldiers. According to Grenier,

> The mother did not complain so much about the carnal relationship in and of itself, <u>as much as the fact that the relationship was had with foreign men,</u> staying only temporarily in Fiume, with whom there was no hope that there could be made a correction of the deed. She repeated continuously: "Damned the moment I decided to rent out the room, at least if she had had relations with a Fiumian . . . But with those rogues, those adventurers . . ."[100]

Over the weeks, months, and years that Italian soldiers were quartered in postwar Fiume, undoubtedly quite a few Fiume girls and women were "entertaining" the Italian soldiers. But those women were characterized less as "pretty" and more as "easy" or, worse, "corrupted" or,

One of hundreds of photographs showing the fun, sexy camaraderie between Italian men and Fiumian women. A Fiume local at the time, however, would probably have found this image less than entertaining.

even worse, "loose." In a town the size of Fiume, this branding could hurt. The 32-year-old war widow Anna Lenaz née Svat went to the police to complain that neighbors had heaped "scandalous epithets" on her 15-year-old daughter, including gems like, "Look at that whore and that daughter of a whore, you are the ass for all the Italians, you lost your honor at the age of 10."[101] For many Fiumians, the sexual politics connected to the arrival of the Italian soldiers definitely did not belong in the normative world of Fiume. And neither did the Italian soldiers.

Interestingly enough, the passing over of Italian soldiers' and legionnaires' pertinency petitions did not cause a scandal, a fact best explained by another lived reality: the soldiers' uniforms were badges much more powerful than Fiume identity cards. From the time of the dissolution of Austria-Hungary until D'Annunzio was chased out of Fiume, the uniformed men filling the city's streets were rarely held to the norms of the city. During the Inter-Allied occupation, reports of uniformed criminals were regularly made, but the Fiume police took no action. American soldiers sold stolen handkerchiefs with seemingly no consequences.[102] British soldiers smuggled stolen soap and reports were quickly filed away.[103] The French soldiers who robbed the homeless, the Serb soldiers who stole pepper shipments, and the Italian soldiers who tried to break into tobacco stores?[104] They kept right on. Once D'Annunzio arrived, the only people still wearing uniforms were the legionnaires, but uniformed crime continued, with, few if any, consequences.

It was easy for soldiers to take advantage of locals. For one thing, although they were often quartered within Fiume homes, socialized in civilian establishments, and sometimes ate at Fiume's dining-room tables, soldiers did not live like Fiumians. There was an enormous disparity in what was available to men in uniform compared with what civilians had access to. In March 1919, for example, three Italian soldiers agreed to pay the 61-year-old widow Ernesta Mersljak née Sucich to cook them dinner in her home. They provided the meat, beans, fish, salad, and wine they enjoyed at her table. Sometimes Mersljak procured the food, with the understanding that they would pay for it. However, when Mersljak demanded payment for groceries, the soldiers disappeared and the widow did not bring charges forward.[105] According to her nephew, Mersljak considered herself "cheated," but the story ended there.[106] What recourse did she have? After her untimely death, the manager of her apartment building testified that one of her neighbors had complained that she lived in fear: "According to her, drunks and soldiers entered the building all night long."[107] Most likely, Mersljak valued her safety above her savings and let the soldiers' malfeasance pass with little more than grumbles.

In December 1919 eight people robbed a shoe store in the middle of the city center. Witnesses indicated that four of the eight were Italian soldiers. According to 33-year-old Fiume-born industrialist Giuseppe Jerina, when the Fiume police arrived on the scene, they captured two of the thieves: a 16-year-old Fiume-born ne'er-do-well named Rai-

Checking papers and patting down the locals for weapons, uniformed men in Fiume were always the ones questioning, not the ones being questioned. This photograph was probably taken after December 1920, but represents well how uniformed men and civilians often interacted in Fiume since 1918.

mondo Scrobogna and an Italian sharpshooter with a tall, slender build and curly hair, called "Mussa" by his fellow thieves.[108] The witness Jerina registered surprise at the actions of the police on the scene, stating, "They arrested Scrobogna, while, I have no idea why, they let the sharpshooter go even though they were alerted to the fact that he, too, had participated in the theft."[109] Jerina's testimony on the sharpshooter Mussa was underlined in red within the Fiume police report, but nothing more came from the investigation. Eventually the other non-uniformed culprits were apprehended, but the uniformed thieves remained at large.

It was not just the police who looked the other way when they saw a uniformed Italian up to no good. Civilians, too, were meant to bow unquestioningly to authority in uniform. Some, however, like the 28-year-old

Fiume-born clerk Nicolò Rudan, complained to the Fiume police about
the mistreatment he had received at the hands of a soldier. According
to Rudan, on a late summer night in May 1919 he was stopped by an
Italian soldier "of tall build armed with a musket" while taking a stroll
with a female companion.[110] Rudan stated,

> [The Italian soldier] asked if I was armed and then invited me to
> present my documents: While I got my wallet and bifocals out of
> my bag, the soldier took these objects from my hand and left,
> telling me that he would deal with it. I followed him a few steps,
> but then the soldier threatened me, ordering me to step back or
> else he would shoot.[111]

Rudan never saw his wallet or bifocals again. The Fiume police sent
the report to the Italian military command, and the investigation stopped
there.

In truth, catching the uniformed man "of tall build armed with a
musket" would not have been easy for the Fiume or military authorities, for uniforms were not just worn by soldiers. Because of the power
they offered, soldiers' uniforms were a hot item on the city's black
market. Fiume policeman Francesco Kossich arrested 50-year-old Margherita Plesse for possessing "military clothing of suspect provenance."
Upon interrogation, Plesse confessed to having bought the military gear
from the 34-year-old widow and Fiume pertinent Maria Radetich née
Cerovac. When they searched Radetich's home, the police discovered
"3 Italian soldiers' jackets," as well as traveling papers for a woman
with another name.[112] Though, or perhaps because, uniforms could exonerate one from the law, these women were prosecuted for trying to
make money off them.

One of the most pitiful accounts of Fiume locals trying to profit
from trading in Italian uniforms was that of 42-year-old barber Nicolò
Serko, a war-veteran pertinent to the Hungarian village Zombor (in
today's Slovakia). Serko's barbershop was in the city center, and he
rented out a room in his home to an Italian colonel, the 59-year-old

Ferrara-born Ardito Vittorio Vitali. In March 1920, Vitali returned
home late to find his landlord, Serko, lying drunk and bleeding in his
bedroom, with Vitali's suitcase lying open and Vitali's uniform and
overcoat hidden in Serko's room. In Serko's police testimony the next
day, he stated,

> Last night I came home late and being completely drunk I wanted
> to commit a theft, being in need of money. . . . My drunkenness
> pushed me to the dishonest act . . . and mesmerized by the idea of
> stealing I took a suit and coat from the colonel into my room next
> door. I took his suitcase from the closet and searched inside it for
> money, when at that precise moment the colonel returned and
> caught me in the act. . . . I am turning over the suit and coat that
> were found in my room, admitting that it was me who took them
> from the colonel's room.[113]

At an earlier interrogation, Serko's story was a bit different, however.
He stated,

> I only remember confusedly what happened as I was completely
> drunk, so much so that when I returned to my room I fell and hurt
> my head. . . . I think I took that suit into my room because I no-
> ticed when I returned home that my son was drinking with friends
> of his in the kitchen and I was afraid one of them would take the
> suit for himself.[114]

In the end Vitali dropped the charges against his landlord, saying that
Serko was too drunk to be held accountable; perhaps he took pity on
him because Serko was not a Fiume pertinent and would have been
banished if found guilty of a criminal act. Regardless, the case reveals
how valuable an Italian uniform was thought to be: according to Serko's
full confession, "in need of money," he first stole the uniform and then
looked for cash. In the second version, he stole the uniform to protect
it from his son's friends, afraid of what would happen to such a trea-

sured possession with young boys around. Clearly the value of the uniform was known to all and sought by many.

That in an occupied town a uniform offered more power and rights than those bestowed by local identity papers is not a situation particular to immediate postwar Fiume. Countless histories of occupying forces living among civilian communities have trained us to expect nothing less. But what was different here was that many of these above-the-law uniformed men applied for legal status in the city they occupied, on the basis of their shared commitment to Italy. And the reply these soldiers got to their petitions was much less amenable than the reaction they got when they stopped a civilian on the street. Their petitions for Fiume pertinency were usually ignored, sometimes denied point-blank. Love of all things Italian was professed ad nauseam in postwar Fiume: when it wasn't, locals ran the risk of being charged with "inciting hatred among the nationalities," as had happened to young Francesco Pospek. But pertinency to the city-state—the one road to the privileges and benefits of localdom—was not on offer.

Nationality, Pertinency, and Citizenship

In April 1922, 26-year-old Nicolina Valacchini received two upsetting pieces of news from the Fiume school board: First, she was not going to receive an expected promotion. Second, she was going to lose her job. Neither was caused by any failure on Valacchini's part. On the contrary, the school board registered satisfaction with her service and had hoped to promote her. The problem: she had just married "an Italian citizen and had lost Fiume pertinency."[115] Pertinency was pertinency and laws were laws. Women's pertinency was determined by their husbands', period. It did not matter that Valacchini had already proved her qualifications for pertinency in 1920, submitting an application so in line with what the Fiume government looked for that she was made a pertinent almost immediately.[116] Nor did it matter that she was such an Italian nationalist that, as soon as she could, she voluntarily Italianized her last name from the Slavic-sounding Vlacancic she was baptized with to the Valacchini she preferred.[117] It was 1922. The Kingdom of Italy had bombed Fiume to force it to concede that Fiume would not be annexed to Italy. D'Annunzio and many of his legionnaires had left. On the map of Europe, diplomats had marked Fiume as an independent city-state. And the process of applying to belong to the city followed the same requirements it had since December 1918: Fiume pertinency was for Fiume locals, and women's pertinency was determined by marriage.

In cases like these, where the letter of the law blocked the privileges that Italian-oriented Fiumians believed they deserved, local authorities tried to find a solution. In this case, the Minister of Education, Salvatore Bellasich—the same man who had sent the outlandishly long telegraph to the Paris Peace delegation—found a compromise by fast-tracking Valacchini's husband's application for Fiume pertinency and proposing "the nomination to full [teacher's] rank of [Signora Raimondi-]Cominesi as of April with the obligation of presenting the decree of pertinency within three months."[118] Valacchini-Raimondi-Cominesi was lucky: her professional and economic condition was derailed only temporarily by Fiume's pertinency regime. If she had married a man holding a passport from the Kingdom of Serbs, Croats, and Slovenes; the Republic of Austria; the revamped Kingdom of Hungary; the Republic of Czechoslovakia; or the Kingdom of Romania, she would likely have found herself with little recourse: once she was listed as non-pertinent, the Italian nationalist Bellasich would not have thought twice of relieving her of her duties. For a local to remain local, love could not be identity-card blind.

Valacchini's predicament, its resolution, and the more negative outcome that would have befallen her if she had wed a man with a different passport point to the tensions of belonging in postwar Fiume. Nationalist politics held sway, but were still subsidiary to the rights of localdom. Fiumians stuck together, and if they looked to incorporate anyone from outside, Italy was the only acceptable option. As we have seen, any other arrangement was suspect: the offended police officer Castellicchio could not have been blunter when questioning the anti-Italian Fiumian clerk Francesco Pospek: "How [is this], you live here, you are pertinent here, you work here, and [yet] you speak against

Italy?"[119] Pospek belonged because he lived, worked, and was registered as Fiumian; within that framework, however, everyone knew that the Kingdom of Italy should be given a special standing.

Fiumians lived in a world of solidified local affiliations, intersecting with and sometimes challenging broader claims about nationality. To obtain rights, you had to have ties to the city. Leanings toward anything other than Italian national aims could land you in jail, though not get you banished. Overall, it was best to show Italian partisanship. But at the same time, nationality did not guarantee anything. The fact that in this setup locals didn't have citizenship is the key to unlocking the paradoxes of belonging in post-1918 Fiume. Starting in December 1918, belonging to Fiume was consistently described in terms of pertinency rather than with the seemingly more apropos word *citizenship*. In many ways, *citizenship* would have been the easiest word to use to describe what gave someone the right to partake in the city's body politic: since ancient Greece, ancient Rome, and then again in the medieval era, the body politic to which an individual belonged and through which he or she could claim rights was usually the metropole or city-state. Would not *citizenship* be the perfect word to define the new privileges and rights that only long-standing city residence granted after December 1918?

To answer yes to this question would be to ignore what leaving the category of citizenship empty provided. Without it, Fiume could transform the pertinency category—always employed and conceived as part of a triangular relationship with imperial citizenship and municipal residency—into something new. Before 1918, the power triangle left pertinency as a rights initiative of interest only to the vulnerable in need of poor relief and the wealthy eager to control city administration; after 1918 it became a means of consolidating the city against the wave of heavy immigration in a time of economic struggle. Certainly, Fiume's provisional government saw continuing the pertinency regime as helpful in ensuring that Italy would take over the citizenship slot. But it also speaks to how its leaders imagined that incorporation would run, with the city as a separate unit within a royal citizenship superstructure, not one that had been fully absorbed into a broader national belonging.[120]

What this meant in real terms was felt by all who lived or arrived in Fiume. Locals were pertinents, and their rights had to be protected and expanded. The newly arrived, no matter what their nationality, deserved no such provisions. Our next piece of the puzzle is to understand how the city promoted a strident Italian annexation mission while simultaneously strengthening a consolidated sense of localness among Fiume's heterogeneous body politic.

5

A Sense of Self

Propaganda and Nationalism

On January 20, 1920, when the accountant Béla Szécsey processed an eight-line supply order, he had no idea it would put his job at risk. It looked harmless enough: an authorization for "2 packages of lined paper, 2 packages of checkered paper, 1000 pieces of vignette-paper, [and] 10 balls of ribbons [in] national colors" to be delivered to the Fiume tobacco factory.[1] Szécsey did not explain the order; its purpose was clear. Ribbons in the national colors of Italy and a new batch of fancy paper shipments without sign or stamp from the prior Habsburg regime clearly adhered to the July 1919 government directives insisting that all "envelopes, office modules, etc. . . . be compiled only in the Italian language."[2] Use of the old Habsburg multilingual envelopes and eagle-engraved papers "eight months after the [Italian] National Council had taken up state powers" was, according to government officials, "a grave offense to the language of the country."[3] With the end of the Habsburg regime, the new Fiume government required all traces of non-Italianness to be erased so that citizens were "saved from the pain of running across the vestiges and emblems" of the Habsburg regime.[4] The Fiume tobacco factory had already warned the government that this initiative would take time, because of the costs involved and the enormous reserves of Habsburg-stamped paper on hand. Nonetheless, Szécsey's superiors had assured the government that as soon as possible, new supplies featuring "exclusively the Italian language" would be procured, "and only these will be used [in the future]."[5] Szécsey's order was just a step in the process of turning Habsburg Fiume into a postwar center of Italianness. Many such steps had been taken, and Szécsey was unconcerned about the day's events when he headed home after sending out the order.

His problems began the next day, when Fiume's education minister, the 30-year-old lawyer Salvatore Bellasich, somehow obtained a copy of the order. A furious Bellasich scribbled in the margin, "I'm stunned by this." Then he demanded that the tobacco factory initiate "an immediate disciplinary investigation against the employee" who had authored the order. The education minister was not irate because in a time of shortages the tobacco factory was using scant resources for propaganda paraphernalia like national ribbons and vignette paper. That was fine. Szécsey was in trouble because he had written the order "exclusively in the Hungarian language."[6]

Everything we've learned about postwar Fiume has prepared us to assume that Szécsey's Hungarian-language misstep was dangerous and rare. We know that Fiume reveled in performing Italian nationalist fervor. D'Annunzio's motto "Italy or death" was on the front pages of Fiume's newspapers; it was shouted by the mayor and municipal elites and sung by schoolchildren, housewives, workers, legionnaires, and everyone else. We also know that at least two waves of vandalism against Croatian signs and storefronts beset the town in 1919 and 1920, with locals shattering public emblems of the city's prior multilingualism. In such an environment, the education minister's outraged "I'm stunned by this" sounds about right, and one would guess Szécsey was fired posthaste. And if his pertinency papers were not in order, he might well have been expelled from the city for committing a "grave offense to the language of the country."[7] However, none of this occurred. Szécsey's boss, the 66-year-old Koloman Termatsits, assured the finance office and Bellasich that Szécsey "was a very calm and diligent employee, who fulfills his duties with the maximum zeal."[8] Termatsits wrote the director of the finance office to "propose an exception" for Szécsey, thereby excusing him from any disciplinary action.

In a world where "Italy or death" was the most chanted phrase, surely such indulgence was exceptional. But Szécsey's testimony during the

The Hungarian-Croatian bank after a July 1920 vandalism spree triggered by the news that two Italian soldiers had been killed by Croatians in Split (Dalmatia). Rioters specifically targeted businesses associated with Croatians and "foreign elements" in Fiume. Here D'Annunzio's forces clean up the shattered Hungarian-language bank sign.

investigation conducted four days later hints that leniency was more rule than anomaly. Szécsey explained that the problem had simply been that he ran short on time. In his own words, "Considering how late it already was getting, I prepared the order in the Hungarian language and gave it to my assistant . . . , forgetting without thinking about it to remind him to translate it into Italian." Szécsey ended his testimony by swearing that this error was a fluke, as all his other "notes concerning the delivery of various articles, deliveries effected by [him], bills, receipts, and in general all writings with interested parties were always conducted in the official language, that is in Italian."[9] Szécsey did not disavow writing the first drafts of his memos in Hungarian; that was normal operating procedure.

It's likely that much of Education Minister Bellasich's frustration with Szécsey's supply order stemmed from the fact that implementing Italian monolingualism in Fiume was proving difficult. When the first language law was issued, the tobacco factory wasn't alone in saying that enforcement would take time. In August 1919, the postal and telegraph services indicated that "they have been working for a while on substituting all the stamps, emblems . . . etc. etc. that until now were produced in two languages or exclusively in Hungarian," but that unfortunately full substitution will still take a long time.[10] The good news, according to the post office, was that "all printed materials destined to the public were already almost completely substituted"; only internal communications were still multilingual.[11] Around the same time, the railway office admitted the same thing: external communications utilized Italian only, but materials for internal office communications "were still in the process of being translated . . . and [non-Italian-language materials] were still being used."[12] Even the finance office, the office responsible for calling Szécsey to task, admitted in August 1919 to encountering the same problem: while external communications were almost completely in Italian, internal office communications still used the old Habsburg multilingual forms.[13] The Italian National Council, seeing how slowly the Italianization campaign was moving, suggested to the railway office a solution that mirrored precisely the defense Szécsey had made to exonerate himself; the government recognized that "the difficulties in substituting Hungarian with the language of the land for internal office communications are not slight. It is necessary however . . . to utilize every means—resorting perhaps to the work of translators—so that at least in direct communications with Fiume citizens" only Italian was used.[14]

Szécsey's avoidance of disciplinary action stemmed from the fact that many people used languages other than Italian. It was not a secret: government officials knew, and historians can see it in the hundreds of boxes of paperwork held in the Fiume archives. Wherever you look, the lived experience of the city's postwar multilingualism pops up: the doctor's note verifying a teacher's sick leave because of a nasty case of influenza, written in Hungarian (with no translation).[15] An anguished note from a mother explaining why she had abandoned her 5-month-old baby, conveyed in Croatian (with no translation attached).[16] Testimony of tram workers' office disputes, reportedly barked in Italian and Croatian.[17] Hotel employees' gossip about stolen cash, reportedly whispered in Slovenian, Croatian, Italian, Hungarian, and German.[18] Testimony in a child abuse case telling of the congenial environment in a local butcher shop, in which customers jested in Italian, Croatian, Hungarian, and Romanian.[19] Even legal professionals were no better: the justice department had to inform one of the city's most esteemed notaries of "the illegality of using the Hungarian language exclusively when authenticating public documents."[20] Apparently the notary in question, Fiume-born Federico Gelletich, had not considered authorizing documents in Hungarian a "grave offense to the language of the country."[21]

The archival sources revealing the city's everyday multilingualism are a direct result of the fact that Fiume's bureaucratic corps was multilingual. Why translate everything into one language (Italian), if pretty much everyone understood all the languages in play, both before and after the fall of the Habsburg regime? Applicants for jobs in the Fiume courts, police force, hospital, port, railways, fire department, and post office, as well as for any and all office clerk positions, displayed knowledge of at least two (preferably more) languages in their cover letters. As 28-year-old Fiume-born Ferlan Ruggero put it in his July 1920 application for a position in the police department's registry office, "I know all the languages spoken in this city."[22] Szécsey's aptitude with languages was part of the reason he had been hired in the first place. Even Minister Bellasich, so outraged about the Hungarian-language supply order, built his career (both before and after 1920) on his fluency in Italian and Hungarian, a fact noted by the 1970s Italian encyclopedia entry emphasizing that "during World War Two he held positions of trust for the Italian government in relation to Hungary, thanks to his economic and linguistic background."[23] Multilingualism helped push through paperwork, negotiate trade contracts, and neutralize disputes among a diverse body politic. The head of the tobacco factory refused to punish Szécsey for one of the skills most valued in the Fiume business climate, and leniency again proved the rule of the Fiume language politics game, even when Italian nationalist fervor was official policy.

On the most basic level, Szécsey's relatively tolerated language misstep reminds us once more that even as Gabriele D'Annunzio was insisting that Fiume was "the most Italian of cities," there was a much wider assortment of Fiumians than the Italian nationalist fanfare admitted. The Croatian, Hungarian, Slovene, German, Romanian, Czech, Slovak, and Yiddish speakers of the city still made their home there, and the dissolution of the Habsburg Empire did not suddenly silence their mother tongues or confine them to hearth and home. Instead, the lilt of non-Italian tongues was heard in Fiume's offices and workplaces, as well as in the cafés, bars, promenades, and marketplaces. Italian was now the lingua franca, but non-Italian language practices persisted throughout, as Szécsey's case showed. It was an open secret, if not state policy.

Unraveling this tension between open secret and state policy shows something fundamental in understanding how Fiume could remain as relatively stable as it was in the immediate postwar period. The reality is that in many ways the Italian nationalist Fiume government hid its city-state's non-Italianness rather than eradicating it. The details of this cover-up (and its limits) reveal the particularly layered and flexible initiatives that Fiume's propaganda machine (and the city dwellers who came into contact with it) utilized. On the surface, everything was to look and sound Italian. Below it, non-national, non-nationalist, and non-nationalizing elements persisted, if not flourished. Clerks whose mother tongue was Hungarian, like Szécsey, kept their jobs and compiled their data on multilingual Habsburg forms, while the government paid for translators to hide the fact that many of them did not think or draft in the language of Dante. How could this work? Why should it? And what were the limits of what could and couldn't be changed? By looking at some of the most conspicuous nationalizing propaganda campaigns between 1918 and 1921, including rules about flags, name-change laws, and school curriculum, we see how in even the most prominent arenas of propaganda and "nation building," Fiume Italianized its imperial structures rather than nationalizing its community, which is how Szécsey could coexist with Education Minister Bellasich and his "Italy or death" comrades-in-arms.

Flagging Fiume: The Visual Plebiscite of Fiume's "Italy or Death" Campaign

When contemplating nationalizing propaganda campaigns in postwar Fiume, the first image that probably comes to mind is the flags. Throughout contemporary newspaper reports, newsreels, contemporary photographs, and witness accounts, the vertical green, white, and red tricolor Italian flag dominates the imaginary of postwar Fiume. Internet searches reveal a similar preponderance of flags, as the waving and unfurling of Italian banners was a centerpiece activity in Fiume between 1918 and 1921. But these flags are not alone. They are shown amid crowds of mostly faceless people (men and women, old and young, seemingly rich and poor) who raised, cheered, and apparently adored said flags. These images give the impression that the Italian flag was a powerful indicator of the city's general will to join Italy. Propagandists like Fiume-born schoolteacher and amateur historian Edoardo Susmel emphasized that these images were especially impressive because Italian flags were hard to get, given that Fiume had been part of a kingdom at war with Italy for nearly four years. Susmel's descriptions of how "Fiume dressed its heartache in [Italian] tricolors, suffocated its indignation by unfurling [Italian] tricolors, [and] pacified its rage [by] covering itself in [Italian] tricolors" underscores what some of the most famous photographs of postwar Fiume suggest: the flags' omnipresence embodied postwar Fiumians' commitment to being Italian.[24]

Scholars of nationalism have considered the acts of displaying and routinizing the presence of flags a fundamental process in defining and solidifying "we-hood."[25] Most of these studies focus on how state bodies (governments) and popular movements (nations) intersect around the flag, noting that in the modern world, flags are to states what heraldic devices were to families: just as no family could be important without a heraldic device, no state could be recognized (by other states or its own population) without a flag. Flags mark where states begin and end, who belongs to the state by how they identify with it, and what values a state upholds (the green of Islam, the red of socialism, the stars of federalism). Flags are usually meant to characterize not just the iden-

Road connecting Fiume's main thoroughfare to the Governor's Palace, where D'Annunzio's Command had its headquarters. Note the Italian flags flying from almost every window.

tity of the government but that of the people attached to said government; they materialize the overlapping ideas of the state and the nation. The power of flags is not event driven, as Michael Billig has brilliantly made clear. Though waving or burning a flag can be a potent political act, the sheer banal, everydayness of flags hanging everywhere unquestioned, requiring mindless, unconscious ritual care, gives them the deepest of political meanings.

The preponderance of Italian flags (whether as events or as banal everydayness) throughout the Fiume cityscape from 1918 to 1921 attests to activists' belief that flags combined the production of a national sense of "we-dom" with the political push to annex themselves to the state whose flag they waved. Fiume's Italian National Council made displaying Italy's tricolor a priority. Schools were chided by the city's propaganda committee if the "Italian flag waving [outside their buildings] was too small."[26] If bigger ones were required, it was often the committee that supplied them. The loyalty oaths required of all city notaries asked them not only to swear to abide by "the laws and ordinances in force" but also to promise, "I will make sure that within a week's time from today, and constantly from then on, I will fly an Italian national flag in front of one of my office windows."[27] In a March 1919 letter to the Trieste branch of the Italian Kingdom's information office for operating troops, the Italian National Council made its reason for insisting that flags fly outside schools, centrally located offices, and houses explicit: "We need flags, many flags," the Council said, "to make of the roads and squares of Fiume a vast flowering of national colors, so as to give in these anxious days a visible sign of our intimate and great excitement—especially to foreign visitors."[28] The government's flag displays did impress visitors, like Riccardo Dina, the Italian colonel of the First Sardinian Grenade Regiment, who said that it was hard to forget Fiume's "innumerable flags that said so much in their expressive silence."[29]

What foreign onlookers were meant to understand from the "expressive silence" of the "innumerable flags" was precisely what we are led to believe today by the flag-filled photographs: Fiume was part of Italy, and the flags were a visual plebiscite, so to speak. But the meaning of the flags' presence or absence on the ground was much less clear. To some, the flag indicated Italian nationalist feeling or a commitment to have Fiume join Italy. For others, proudly displaying the Italian tricolor could mean something as simple as wanting to go to a party. This was the case for the August 15, 1920, celebration of Ferragosto, the annual Catholic observance of the Virgin Mary's assumption into heaven: attendees needed to show "the [Italian] tricolor ribbons" to gain entrance to the festivities in centrally located Piazza Dante.[30] No tricolor ribbons, no party. For schoolchildren, producing the Italian tricolor could mean the difference between bread and hunger: schools were told to limit free bread allocation to those children "wearing cockades in the Italian colors."[31] No colors, no food. "For those who come with cockades that are not the Italian colors," the school council elaborated, "they will not be permitted to enter the communal schools" at all.[32] As we saw earlier, flags waving proudly outside city notary offices did not show anything more than that the notaries were obeying their oath of office. We know nothing about what the August 15 partygoers, the schoolchildren and their families, or the notaries felt about those Italian colors. What we do know is that it was important for the Italian tricolor to be blazoned over as many buildings and people as possible. Fiumians might have appreciated the symbol, or they might have wanted to make their life easier. As long as you went along with promoting a vision of Fiume as Italian, the local government supported you. Questions about the sincerity of these efforts went unasked.

In such a climate, one could assume that the determinedly public act of taking a flag down would be costly. But even that varied in meaning and effect. For example, the Italian National Council denied a passport to the sea captain Marco Crentini because "he refused to navigate under the Italian flag," a clear sign (according to the government) that he was a "fanatical Yugoslav agitator."[33] On the other hand, the 32-year-old Fiume-born artisan Pietro Diracca suffered no repercussions for lowering the Italian flag outside his family's home. In fact, in testimony given to support his brother-in-law in a slander suit, Diracca explained he had taken down the flag "so as to avoid conflict, [Diracca] being an artisan, and therefore having to be in contact with people of different political sentiment."[34] In response to this statement, one of the lawyers added that "in the period of time after the fall of the Austro-Hungarian monarchy . . . many citizens did the same to avoid insult or persecution."[35] Diracca might have been an Italian nationalist afraid of publicizing his convictions. Or he could have been a disinterested onlooker to the nationalist fever taking over his neighbors (and potential clients). Or he could have been convinced that Fiume's interests would be best served by its being an independent state than by its being annexed to Italy. Two of his sisters were active Italian nationalist propagandists, while Diracca's brother-in-law expressed reluctance about an all-or-nothing campaign to annex Fiume to Italy. Which side did Diracca take? We can't say, just as we can't know what the "expressive silence" of the "innumerable flags" actually signified.

If looking at how flags were employed tells more about the impression they were meant to have on spectators than about the convictions of Fiumians, perhaps a better method of assessing how much flags reveal about local values is to look at where the flags came from and how people obtained them. As noted, propagandists at the time had made much of the omnipresence of the flags precisely because Fiume had been part of a Habsburg and Hungarian flag culture before and during the war, making Italian flags a rarity in the town. The idea here is that Fiume's flag waving was not passive: locals had to work to get those flags. Fiume Italian nationalists in the 1920s and 1930s even promoted a Betsy Ross, American-style myth that local flag production showed a spontaneous and particularly female annexation fervor. A case in point, again, is Edoardo Susmel's popular history of the Fiume Crisis published in the 1920s and republished in the 1940s. According to Susmel, the flags found at every window and outstretched arm were the work of Fiume women whose "hundreds of hands, thousands of hands singingly sewed the blessed tricolor."[36] Happy, melodic ladies doing their domestic duty to honor the nation is a common trope in most nationalist narratives, and it is as misleading here as it is elsewhere. Undoubtedly, more than one Fiume girl took needle to fabric to stitch together an Italian flag. Perhaps they enjoyed their work enough to sing a little ditty. But most of the materials were not produced by Fiume girls, and local women were not the sole or even the primary producers of Fiume's tricolored extravaganzas.

Before even tracing where the flags came from, one point must be made clear: the stuff of flag making was a precious commodity throughout the period from 1918 to 1921. Shipments into Fiume's port were rare, industrial production was geared to military needs instead of consumer products, and every day more shops and businesses closed. Fiume's families were anxious about survival in a time of rising unemployment and spiraling inflation. While before the war, petty thefts focused on luxury goods (watches, jewelry), by the end of the war, police reports abounded with thefts of depressingly mundane objects: food, cigarettes, coal, wood, pants, dresses, coats, sheets, shoes, shoe laces, socks, underwear, gloves—anything and everything was fair game when food and fabric were scarce. In the first years after the war, school authorities regularly reported either that children didn't come to school "because they didn't have any clothes to wear" or that they could not concentrate on their lessons because they were "barefooted, badly dressed and probably badly fed."[37] In light of this, school authorities indicated that feeding students "certainly served in increasing attendance."[38] Distributing clothing was harder, however, with one school admitting that it could not use the money the state provided to buy clothing "because of the lacking merchandise to buy shoes or other apparel clothing for poor students."[39] Pitiful letters like that from 44-year-old Fiume-born veteran Rodolfo Latcovich Fiumani fill the city archives. In his successful appeal for a stipend to purchase work clothing, Latcovich Fiumani described returning after four years at the eastern front to find his wife and seven children "barefoot and in rags . . . having sold almost all of [his] clothes to the point that only with difficulty could [he] remove the hated [Austro-Hungarian] uniform."[40] The government acquiesced to his request because he was an ardent Italian nationalist, but also because what he described was believable. Clothing was short because fabric was scarce. And if there wasn't enough fabric to clothe Fiume's children or reclothe its veterans, where did the fabric to produce all those flags come from?

Susmel's descriptions of the spontaneous efforts of "hundreds of hands" sewing does apply to the period immediately after the dissolution of the Austro-Hungarian Monarchy in late October 1918. As the principal of the leading Hungarian state school, Francesco Schneider, reported in his synthesis of the 1918–1919 school year, "In those days the homes of the city were flagged according to the sentiments and nationality of their inhabitants. Since the Hungarian flag can be easily transformed into an Italian flag or a Croatian flag, many times people tried to appropriate the school flag."[41] Schneider was adamant that the flagging of the city from the vestiges of his long-honored Hungarian flag did not happen under his watch ("I didn't give it [the school flag] to anyone"), but many Hungarian flags found new lives honoring other lands. In the few pictures we have of those first days, we can see the crazed outcropping of flags.[42] But if these pictures were in color, we

Postcard of the Fiume city center in November 1918. Note the mixture of flags, some with vertical stripes (Italian) and others with horizontal ones (Serb-Croat-Slovene).

would notice that the flags were more varied than later on: alongside the vertical-striped green, white, and red tricolor Italian flag, we would also see the horizontal-striped blue, white, and red tricolors of the Kingdom of Serbs, Croats, and Slovenes. Homespun, perhaps re-dyed, and patched together from the vestiges of their former Hungarian colors, the initial flags of Fiume were as far from a visual expression of a common national will as one could imagine. They were motley; they were makeshift; they openly desecrated the prior emblems Fiumians had grown up with and under whose banner they had fought a losing war. They also asserted divergent "sentiments and nationality," not just one.

After the Hungarian flags were used up, the flag onslaught did not end, even though fabric was still scarce. The transformation of the city from one dappled with Italian and Serb-Croat-Slovene national colors into one where only Italy's green, white, and red reigned occurred when the Italian troops arrived. Within days, the National Council of Serbs,

Croats, and Slovenes was ousted, and slowly but surely the blue, white, and red tricolors of the Kingdom of Serbs, Croats, and Slovenes disappeared from apartment windows and city offices. With the Italian National Council entrenched as the acting government, an avalanche of green, white, and red Italian flags enveloped the city. The local government, which directed the flagging, looked to the Italian military in mainland Italy for flags. In response to the Italian National Council's requests, the Italian military governor in Trieste sent four thousand Italian flags to the Fiume government in December 1918, with specific instructions to "distribute them among the primary schools of the city and surroundings."[43]

When the Italian military could not satisfy the local government's requests for fabric and flags, the Italian National Council looked to nationalist activist circles in Italy. A case in point is an October 1919 letter from the Fiume education minister Salvatore Bellasich to one of the most vociferous nationalist organizers in Milan, Benito Mussolini. Three years before taking over the Italian government, Mussolini was spending much of his time writing about Italy's rights to annex Fiume, characterizing the Fiume Crisis as a micro-case of how the Great Powers were denying Italy its rightful place on the world stage. Bellasich wrote Mussolini, hoping Mussolini would publish his letter in the many news outlets increasingly under his influence, saying, "Fiume wants to cover its indomitable Italic ardor in an immense flag. Fiume wants to be all [Italian] tricolor. Tell the Italian people that Fiume asks for nothing else but flags, flags, flags."[44] Such entreaties worked, because the "Italian people" (those who read Mussolini's paper and other nationalist publications) seemed willing to keep sending flags to Fiume government offices from places like Verona, Florence, Naples, Milan, and Rome.[45]

The flagging of Fiume was a government project, heavily bankrolled by Italian and military sources. Fiume's Italian National Council also augmented the flags from the mainland by paying local professionals to make flags. Monies were earmarked monthly for fabric needed in flag production and to pay local tailors and their workshops to sew the fabrics into flags.[46] Some happy, singing female volunteers may have helped, but they were not the primary architects of Fiume's Italian-flag

mania. So, while locals did wave those flags, the flags' appearance was
nurtured by government initiative and outsiders. The official nature of
Fiume's flagging was no secret; it was a lived experience. When buildings suffered damages because of all the flags attached to walls and
roofs, local businesses sent invoices for repair and reimbursement to
government offices, emphasizing, for example, that it was government
"employees who caused heavy damages to the roof of the Hotel Europa by displaying flags on more than one occasion."[47] The clear equation of the Italian flag with outside and top-down initiatives led some
Fiumians resentful of government policies to "attack" or "disrespect"
the Italian flag. Just months after the Italian National Council took over,
police files describing complicated "flag destruction" plots began to
grow.[48] To prevent these gestures of dissent, the police conducted several investigations and posted guards in front of important government buildings to protect the flag.[49] In March 1920, the issue came to
blows, with some of D'Annunzio's legionnaires beating up Fiume civilians for not displaying appropriate deference to the Italian flag.[50]

These examples of the drive to get "flags, flags, flags" and the coun-
teractions of resentment to their omnipresence lead to another question: Was the vision of Italian tricolor Fiume purely a performance from
above, one in which only the state-anointed participated? Or did even
those not favored by the local government have a genuine interest in
decking Fiume with Italian tricolors? Police records provide some answers. Apparently throughout 1919–1920 local interest in obtaining
Italian flags was high enough to warrant people breaking the law to
obtain them, often through good old-fashioned black-market capitalism. An examination of the testimony associated with the bust of a
black-market flag ring of three 20-something locals—the 22-year-old
unmarried Fiume-born domestic servant Lina Dolezal and two young
men, the 23-year-old Fiume-born veteran and bookbinder Pietro Gennari and the 24-year-old Fiume-born unemployed mechanic Casimiro
Derado—demonstrates that some Fiumians' interest in obtaining flags
extended to buying them illegally.[51] The Fiume government prosecuted
these youths because they committed theft, not because of what they
stole. We, instead, will consider what they stole and why.

Why would Fiumians steal and sell flags if the government was already distributing them? The testimony suggests that it was mostly about saving money. Government flag-distribution drives focused on schools, courts, and sectors linked to government services. For non-official Fiume, hoisting a flag outside your window or in front of your shop cost money. A lot of money. Private purchase of medium-size to large flags from the government cost around three hundred crowns or 190 lire, the equivalent of forty-eight days of unemployment payments for a male head of family in 1919.[52] Commissioning flags to be produced by local tailors (or producing them oneself) was difficult, as one witness reported, because "they had to await the necessary fabric from the [Italian] Kingdom."[53] The female member of the black-market flag-selling ring, Dolezal, admitted they sold the flags for one-third the government price, between eighty and one hundred crowns each. This was still quite a hefty sum, the equivalent of what it would cost to legally purchase three pairs of "luxury leather shoes" or two "luxury silk shirts for women."[54] Dolezal, Gennari, and Derado's price was not based on the cost of obtaining the flags, as the flags they sold were stolen from military bases, schools, and other official quarters. They set prices according to how much they thought they could get for them—a good bit of money, even if significantly less than the government price.

The three were aware that they were taking a risk. First, how do you explain how such young, impoverished, and unaffiliated youths had access to so many flags? Gennari's job in the ring was to find the flags; he worked in the city's propaganda office and knew where flags were stored, how to get them, and which guards could be tricked into handing them over. Dolezal testified that Gennari advised her that if she was caught with the flags to claim she had "received the flags from an Ardito [D'Annunzio] soldier."[55] Both the flags' actual provenance and the excuse for having them confirmed what everyone knew: flags were available through the city government and the military. Dolezal's and Derado's success in selling them also reveals something else: possessing and displaying the flags was not a sign of government sanction, as their provenance was not as simple as it seemed. The government might have been the primary distributor of the flags, but displaying flags did not indicate government affiliation.

Dolezal, Gennari, and Derado's customers were local businesspeople whom they approached from the street. Four customers testified, explaining why they had trusted the youths enough to hand over cash for the flags. Enrico Jugo, a 41-year-old Fiume-born clothing-store owner, explained that he had purchased a flag from Derado because he had been looking for one and because he "knew a family Derado," so he thought he "was having to do with a respectable person."[56] Olindo Padoani, a 48-year-old Fiume-born businessman, explained his purchase by saying he "knew the youth by sight as he had been in [Padoani's] office for social occasions related to [his] children."[57] Padoani also added that Derado had used as references "other distinguished citizens and so therefore [he] purchased without suspicion 2 flags for 200 crowns."[58] Witnesses in the trial against Dolezal were all women who ran their own businesses. Giovanna Cappa, a 41-year-old Fiume-born widowed shopkeeper, testified that Dolezal came to her store "offering to sell [her] a national flag made by her [own hand] and that the profits earned would be given to a family in need."[59] The 30-year-old Dubrovnik-born Enrichetta Domich claimed that Dolezal entered her musical instrument store and succeeded in selling her one even though she "had no need to purchase the flag."[60] Dolezal apparently convinced Domich that the provenance of the flag was respectable by saying that the aforementioned Cappa, a friend of Domich, "had purchased two flags for propaganda reasons."[61] No one testified that the youths had misrepresented themselves as somehow linked to a government or state initiative; it was simply that they had flags to sell and people wanted to buy them. The testimonies corroborate that outside government-engineered spectacle, people were interested in obtaining flags "for propaganda reasons." Private citizens spent hard-earned cash on flags—so much so as to give crafty youths the idea of making a profit from it. The redressing of Fiume with the Italian tricolor was not just engineered from above or without; it reverberated throughout.

Naming and Nationalism: Fiume's Peculiarly "Italian" Families

Clearly there were locals (including those outside government circles and even outside the law) who could and did aid in presenting a mono-lithic vision of Fiume as Italian. But what about more personal aspects of redressing the city as nationally Italian? Were locals willing to re-make their multilingual, multiethnic, and multicultural personal lives to promote the idea of Fiume as Italian only? If so, what were their priorities? If not, what does that say about commitment to Italianizing the city from below?

A good way to answer these questions is to analyze the name-change legislation introduced in Fiume in March 1919, when the city govern-ment allowed pertinents to change their family names as they saw fit. In the Hungarian Kingdom before World War I, the ability to change family names was essentially limited to women who took their hus-bands' names, people who changed their religion, or those taking on feudal titles. Changing one's family name to indicate a different ethnic affiliation was a privilege accorded only with the consent of the Hun-garian government, and this consent was typically only granted to those wishing to make their names sound more Hungarian. Essentially, family names were not tools for creating local cohesion. If someone immi-grated to the Habsburg Empire or moved from one part of the Austro-Hungarian lands to another, his or her surname was not altered for purposes of linguistic homogeneity or community building. While im-migrants to the Americas regularly had their last names "simplified" to more easily integrate into an English-speaking, Spanish-speaking, or Portuguese-speaking local context, when immigrating within the Habsburg Empire, individuals kept the family names with which they arrived, unless they wanted to do the extra paperwork to Hungarianize their surnames to match the national identity with which their kingdom hoped they would increasingly identify.[62]

Even when local usage meant that the spellings of names changed, official records did not follow suit, as the goldsmith Edoardo Csabrian knew all too well. Born in Fiume in 1848, Csabrian was the son of immigrants whose official state paperwork retained the Hungarian spelling of the family name. Nonetheless, throughout Csabrian's lifetime, in local school rolls, guild associations, and the odd newspaper mention, his name was spelled Italian-style as "Zabrian." Even the name on his storefront went by the Italian-friendly "Zabrian."[63] Eduardo Csabrian petitioned all the way through his 70s to have the official spelling changed in the population registers, arguing he had never used "Csabrian" in his daily life and was known by all as "Zabrian." But his protests fell on deaf ears. As long as there was an Austria-Hungary, his name remained Csabrian.[64]

Not everyone resented this Habsburg policy. Well into her late 40s the Fiume-born schoolteacher Emma Zbožensky continued spelling her last name as her identity papers indicated, the way her Czech-speaking ancestors preferred. Zbožensky carefully wrote the diacritic ž in all her correspondence, even though the post office, school meeting minutes, and local office announcements regularly wrote it in letters that an Italian-language typewriter could handle, the semi-Italianized "Zbozensky."[65] But in the official registrars of the Austro-Hungarian state itself, except in very special circumstances, names did not change, regardless of locality, typewriter capacity, or personal desire.

The Habsburg state's resistance to permitting surname changes came from the importance family names had in classifying individuals. In the first paragraph of every cover letter, job applicants provided their first name, their last name, their maiden name (if applicable), the first name of their father, their place of birth, their year of birth, and sometimes, depending on the job, their civil and pertinency status. When registering a marriage, the birth of a child, or a divorce, heads of family provided baptismal or birth records of all the parties concerned, which included all the first names, family names, and birthdates of forefathers, foremothers, and offspring. When questioned by the police or giving testimony in court, individuals identified themselves with their first name, their last name, the first name of their father, their age, and sometimes their place of birth. Without this linkage between name, family lineage, and year and place of birth, identifying or finding people within the Habsburg lands was impossible. The difficulty of tracking people without such information can be seen in correspondence between Trieste and Fiume municipal offices, when Trieste employees told Fiume officials that they could not deliver official decrees to Fiume pertinents living in Trieste using only the first and last names provided by the Fiume office. As they said, with so many "other people carrying the same first and last name currently living in this city . . . more personal data was necessary."[66] In 1906, residents of the Hungarian Kingdom (including Fiume) read that the Hungarian interior minister József Kristóffy was under investigation for having altered his family name in church records (from Kristo to Kristóffy) without state approval.[67] The resulting scandal hurt Kristóffy's career, as changing one's surname held sinister implications: family names anchored individuals into a stable social and economic context, and changing them suggested a desire to mislead or hide from these systems. In essence, surnames, combined with family lineage and age, functioned much as social security numbers or identity card numbers do today; they were the means by which a person's creditability and potential for criminality were determined. Changing last names implied a desire to hoodwink these webs of creditability.

For a booming port city like Fiume, its population growing by 30 percent every ten years through immigration from all across and outside the Habsburg lands, the enforced stability of family names created a civic culture filled with a rainbow of ethnic surnames, many of which were a mismatch with the way their holders thought of themselves. Within Fiume and much of the Adriatic, as Maura Hametz reminds us, a surname did not signify national belonging, in part because, within the Habsburg realms, family names were almost immutable, while hearts and minds were not.[68] In Fiume, schooling, intermarriages, broader family and business connections, and other relationship networks were more important than the paternal lineages demonstrated by a surname. For example, in applying for Fiume pertinency in 1919, Giovanni Lukinčić declared he had been living in Fiume since 1886 and nursed "pure" Italian nationalist sentiments; his pertinency application passed without a hitch because, though his last name—with its diacritic-filled spelling—pointed clearly to a Croatian heritage, police

confirmed he had always exhibited the Italian nationalist sentiment he
proclaimed.[69]

Italians arriving in Fiume after 1918, whether soldiers from the
Kingdom of Italy or D'Annunzio's legionnaires, were apparently confused by (if not cynical about) Fiume's culture of surnames. Passport
controls going in and out of Fiume were a never-ending site for the
acting out of this incomprehension. In 1920, for example, during a rou-
tine check of identity papers of the passengers on a train arriving from
Trieste to Fiume, the Italian lieutenant colonel Vittorio Margonari refused to cooperate with local police, calling the Fiume police agent Alberto Novach "nothing but a nasty little Croat."[70] When inspecting
documents of travelers moving from Fiume out toward the Italian-
occupied lands, Italian soldiers checking papers at the borders had to
regularly accept Fiume government-issued decrees attesting, for example, that 24-year-old Fiume-born university student Bruno Fuerst,
33-year-old Fiume-born mechanic Giovanni Blasich, and 25-year-old
Fiume-born student Letizia Ramous were all of Italian nationality, even
though they did not have Italian citizenship and their surnames seemed
to bespeak other ethnic ties.[71] These police authentications were required because otherwise Italian military personnel were quick to assume that a surname's ethnic lineage indicated a traveler's national
identification. Thus, Michele Polonio-Balbi passed through military
borders without questioning, even though in Fiume circles the Polonio-
Balbi family was rumored to be of "strong Croatian sentiment." It was
"thanks to the Italian last name" that he "succeeded in passing without
difficulty the border, evading the necessary inspections."[72] If Fiume officials had manned the borders, Polonio-Balbi would have found permission to travel difficult.

No Fiumian would assume a surname's ethnic markers predicted an
individual's national sentiment. Just reading the last names of Fiume's
Directive Committee of the Italian National Council, the group most
publicly committed to an Italian nationalist-annexationist agenda for
the city, makes that clear. Alongside the Italian-origin last names of Ga-
rofolo, Gigante, Mini, Nascimbeni, Venutti, and Vio were many more
names with Croatian, Slovene, Hungarian, and German origins, in-

cluding Baccich, Bellasich, Blau, Burich, Codrich, Corossacz, Gotthardi, Grossich, Host, Lenaz, Meichsner, Nicolich, Ossoinack, Prodam, Rubinich, Rudan, Schittar, Springhet, and Stiglich. In January 1919, when Fiume notables Mario Blasich, Antonio Grossich, and Andrea Ossoinack presented a memorandum to Woodrow Wilson in Rome demanding Fiume be annexed to Italy because they, like all Fiumians, were "brothers of blood, language, and culture" to Italy, no Fiumian doubted their conviction, even though their last names suggested that their ancestors might have disagreed.[73]

The March 1919 name-change law provided the Fiume body politic a tool to render national affiliation more intelligible. It was not an attempt to change the prior Habsburg state's policies regarding family names; family names continued to be one of the primary means for administrative tracking.[74] The March 1919 name-change law, instead, "provided authorization to reintegrate or rectify family names of Italian origin as well as to change or modify foreign family names."[75] Just as the Fiume government Italianized the names of boulevards, quays, streets, schools, parks, institutes, and even mountain retreats, so the government encouraged private citizens to do the same with their family markers. Avenue Deák—honoring one of Hungary's most important politicians—became Avenue Vittorio Emanuele III—Italy's king at the time.[76] Why should Fiumians not do the same with the names plastered on their identity papers and storefronts? In essence, the law hoped to help Fiumians clear away traces of former non-Italian connections and flag their families as Italian.

Campaigns to nationalize family names were common among modernizing, expanding, and centralizing states before and after World War I.[77] In the 1840s, for example, the Spanish colonial government forced Spanish-language surnames on the Filipino communities living under its rule; in the 1880s French colonial offices forced local Algerians to take surnames completely alien to their own naming systems. In the 1890s the Hungarian Kingdom sent out pamphlets to civil servants throughout the realm telling them how they could Magyarize their surnames to demonstrate their state pride; simultaneously the United States forced Anglo-friendly family names on Native Americans living on its reservations. In the 1920s Mussolini's Fascist state forced those with foreign family names to replace them with Italian surnames, and in the 1930s Mustafa Kemal Atatürk's Republican government required all its citizens—regardless of ethnicity—to register with Turkish-language surnames.[78] To an extent, Fiume's name-change law shared the goals of these initiatives: it hoped to make a common national culture more legible and use it as a building block of its political, social, and economic community. The difference was that Fiume's 1919 law allowed Fiumians to *voluntarily* Italianize their family names, without any standards, guidelines, or requirements except that new surnames had to be "strictly Italian" and could not replicate those of patrician or famous families.[79] Everyone who wanted could change their name; no one had to. There was no commission created to enforce or encourage locals to do it; no system to ensure that only the worthy or suitably nationalist could Italianize. And almost no attention was paid to what a "strictly Italian" surname really entailed.

The majority of those who took advantage of the name-change law were exactly those one would expect: Fiume pertinents wanting to re-baptize themselves as the "proper Italians" they felt themselves to be. A prime example is 41-year-old Fiume-born sculptor Giovanni Marussich. Marussich saw naming as a way to express Italian national sentiment, as his five children's names show. The name of Marussich's first son, Garibaldi, born in 1909, celebrated the most charismatic of Italy's founding fathers. Marussich's first and only daughter, Anita, born in 1911, was named in honor of Garibaldi's wife, who had died campaigning with her husband in his 1849 battle against the Habsburgs. The name of Marussich's second son, Dante, born in 1912, paid tribute to the greatest Italian poet. The third son, Giovanni, born in 1916, was named for his father. Finally, the name of his youngest son, Redento Fiumano Libero, born in 1918, reflected his father's joy that the Habsburg Monarchy had dissolved and now his hometown could be joined to Italy. Redento Fiumano Libero translates to "redeemed free Fiumian," quite a name for an infant to pull off.

With the fall of the Austro-Hungarian Monarchy, Marussich saw his chance to couple his children's patriotic Italian first names with a de-

Croatianized surname. He was so excited by the prospect that he submitted a petition before the name-change law was written, asking the government to "remove from [his] surname the 'ch' ending, evidently applied by someone who once controlled the birth registries."[80] Marussich knew that he was as Italian as they come, so the *-ch* ending of his family's name could only have been the work of some Slavophile priest centuries earlier (Marussich was not just a proud Italian nationalist, he was also a proud atheist and Slavophobe).[81] One can only imagine the emotions this struggling sculptor must have felt seeing his name written in official documents after 1919 as Giovanni Marussi, father of Garibaldi, Anita, Dante, Giovanni Jr., and Redento Fiumano Libero.[82] Few other Fiumians dedicated their naming practices to Italy's cause as completely as Marussich did, but between 1919 and 1921 other Fiumians used his shortcut to remove their Slavic heritage from their surnames.[83] Cutting out the *-ch* turned Codrich into Codri, Lazzarich into Lazzari, Millich into Milli, Sarinich into Sarini, and Tominich into Tomini. Just like that, these families' names matched the Italian identities so important to the heads of households who filled out the name-change applications, with just enough of the original family names left to keep ancestral continuity and the sounds of home alive.[84]

Not everyone who wanted to Italianize their last names could or wanted to apply the easy fix that the Marussichs and Lazzarichs did. Some went further. Brosich became Ambrosi, Dorcich became Dorini, Milec became Miletti, and Virtich became Vitti. Another popular option was to emphasize a similarity in sound while getting rid of the obvious *-ch* marker. In this way, Barbich became Barbis; Martich, Martis; and Petrich, Petris. For those families, protecting the aural integrity of their names trumped their desire to adopt "strictly Italian" last names, as the *-is* suffix, though present in some parts of Italy, usually denoted an Iberian heritage. But as there were no rules telling Fiumians what was and what wasn't Italian, the changes went through.

It was harder for applicants who had ethnic Hungarian and German names to retain the sonic integrity of their surnames. Those with short surnames had it easier; they just changed the spelling and added an Italian suffix, changing Kobl to Cobelli, Bruss to Brussati, Festö to Festa,

Frankl to Franchi, Stebel to Stebellini, and Vidmar to Vidali. However, those with longer names usually had to choose between integrity of sound and meaning. The Apfelthaller, Katz, and Mayer families chose to preserve some sound continuity with their new Italian surnames, opting for Alberti, Conti, and Marini, respectively. The Schneeberger and Kuschlig families prioritized the meaning of their names, anointing themselves Monteneve and Baciotti, respectively.

Most name changes tried to retain as many links to an ancestral heritage as possible, but nonetheless some families' choices would likely have shocked their grandfathers and all the other fathers before them. Many heads of households decided that the best way to Italianize was to feminize by using maiden names or those from the female line. Perhaps 38-year-old Antonio Crast was worried about his choice, for when he decided his mother's maiden name of Demori was his best option, he noted in his application that Demori was also his father's grandfather's last name, implying he was not disavowing his father's line. Maria de Huszár, a 21-year-old Fiume schoolteacher, gave no explanation when she decided her mother's maiden name was the way to go, re-creating herself in 1919 as Maria Cicuta, though the new name did not keep her from visiting her father's family in Budapest throughout her lifetime. With the recent death of her husband, Mariano Besjak, 28-year-old Feliciana Besjak decided to return to her Italian-sounding maiden name, Tremari. One might expect the Besjak family to disapprove, as Feliciana's decision meant that her three underage children no longer bore their father's name. Apparently, it was not a problem, and just a year later Feliciana's sister-in-law, Giuseppina Besjak, changed her name to Tremari, thus taking the maiden name of her dead brother's widow.

The acceptability of substituting Italian-sounding maiden names in place of fathers' or husbands' surnames was not omnipresent, however, as can be seen by the only case of the Catholic Church refusing to accept a name change the government had approved. When the two Fiume-born Kotschken brothers—45-year-old bureaucrat Alberto and 42-year-old priest Adolfo—applied to change their names to Rossini, their mother's maiden name, the Fiume state immediately granted their request. But in November 1921, when church registry offices caught up with all of the paperwork from the Fiume Crisis, Fiume's central parish office wrote the city magistrate to say that it "approves all the changes and corrections to surnames [submitted], except for the correction of the surname Kotschken to 'Rossini' in that it involves a grave injustice to filial piety on the part of the applicants."[85] What set the Kotschken case apart from the Crast-Demori, de Huszár-Cicuta, Besjak-Tremari, and similar name changes was that the applicants' father was still alive (and had chosen to keep his German-sounding surname), while the mother whose maiden name they were adopting was long dead. For the church officials, this lacked the necessary patriarchal respect. And though the Fiume state ignored the church's refusal, the issue of moving to the female line was a tense one for all concerned, even though the reason was to go Italian while still keeping it in the family.

The most intriguing name changes are those that signaled a complete reinvention or rupture with prior family naming patterns. How can you not want to know more about 47-year-old mechanic Francesco Ursić, who changed his surname to Dal Fiume, literally meaning "from the river," though he probably meant it to mean "from Fiume"? Mistakes in Italian grammar aside, this choice is surprising because Ursić was neither from Fiume nor a river. He was from Trieste, and his wife, 44-year-old Martina Krulčić, was from a little village in Istria.[86] Did 30-year-old Fiume-born construction worker Ettore Lust change his surname to Politei because of a long-standing love of all things ancient Greek, or was he a committed republican, hoping that the dissolution of the Habsburg Monarchy meant that his family would no longer be ruled by a king (the approximate translation of *politei* being "republic"), a radical idea in a political climate where the government was working so hard to join the monarchical Kingdom of Italy?[87]

These questions emphasize the qualitative difference between the redressing of communities via the hoisting of flags and the intimate implications of national name-change policies within a heterogeneous ethnic population. These rebrandings lasted beyond the shelf life of a political moment or a flag fluttering in the wind and rain. In most name-change regimes, as discussed earlier, individuals had little to no choice. In the 1920s, Italian Fascist procedures were automated, with handbooks produced indicating how foreign surnames should be Italianized and some families with foreign surnames even receiving news in the mail that their names had been changed.[88] In Fiume, on the other hand, whether and how to change surnames was left to individuals. Some families named Dorcich changed their names to Dorini; others chose Dori. Some families named Mayer chose to change their names to Marini, probably to keep some sound continuity. But families named Iskra also chose Marini, probably to honor the pseudonym a son used while fighting in the Italian military (more on this later). The Fiume state did not intercede, seemingly unworried that new family associations came into being between the different Marini clans, that new names with decidedly non-Italian endings entered the rosters, and that potentially politically resistant surnames like Politei would show up forever on Fiume's electorate list.[89]

That a name-change regime would be so laissez-faire is surprising, but even more surprising, especially considering the endless Italian nationalist fanfare flooding Fiume's streets, houses, bulletins, and newspapers, is how few people changed their names at all. Between the issuing of the name-change law in April 1919 and the end of the Fiume Crisis in January 1921, only 161 head-of-household pertinents registered to Italianize their names, in a city of over 50,000 inhabitants made up mostly of families with non-Italian surnames. Only four members of Fiume's Directive Committee of the Italian National Council chose to Italianize their surnames (Springhet became Springhetti, Gotthardi became Gottardi, Prodam became Proda, and Codrich became Codri). Fiume's Italian nationalist president, Antonio Grossich, displayed no interest whatsoever in making his surname more Italian by changing it to the similar-sounding Grossi, even though it would have taken little effort and would have given him a name that could be quite appealing for a head of state (Grossi means "big" or "great"). Even the Education Minister Salvatore Bellasich, who had fought to have the unfortunate accountant Béla Szécsey punished for writing a supply order in Hungarian, made no move to transform his Slavic-sounding surname into something like Bellasis, Bellasini, Bella, or even Bellis. It appears that while Italian nationalists in Fiume thought writing in a language other than Italian was "a grave offense to the language of the country," signing one's name with a non-Italian surname posed no such offense.[90]

The best way to understand this conundrum is to look at the Italian nationalists in Fiume who were even more celebrated as the spearheads of Fiume's annexation to Italy than Grossich or Bellasich. Who were these overwhelming figures? They were not politicians. The most admired nationalist figures in postwar Fiume were the young men who had fled Fiume during World War I to fight with Italy against the Habsburg Monarchy. In many ways, their incomparable nationalist credentials make sense, for these men fought for Italy against their own state, meaning that on a battlefield they could easily be shooting at neighbors or classmates, all in the name of love for Italy. In the press and in political circles, the feats of this small group proved that Fiume had a vibrant Italian national culture even before the Habsburg state had dissolved. Though few in number, those who survived became the most celebrated symbols of Fiume's willingness to risk all to become one with Italy. Often emphasized when discussing their feats was the fact that their decision to fight for Italy had put their own families at risk, with some of their family members called to police headquarters or even accused of treason and sent to internment camps. Because of these risks, Fiume soldiers who fled Austria-Hungary to enlist in the Italian army shed not only their Habsburg military uniforms but their surnames as well, hoping to protect family members from Habsburg state retribution. The 24-year-old Giovanni Host arrived at the rank of captain in the Italian Arditi shock troops division as Giovanni Venturi; 29-year-old Fiume-born Enrico Horitzky served as a lieutenant in the Italian artillery division as Enrico Orsini; 21-year-old Luigi Hlaich received his Italian army pay as Luigi Lacini; and two Fiumians who were awarded Military Crosses also fought and survived with Italian pseudonyms: 21-year-old Rodolfo Fabjan received his as Rodolfo Negrelli, and 25-year-old Leone Spez as Leone Quarnari.

When armistice was declared, these soldiers returned to Fiume as quickly as possible, intent on organizing Fiume's immediate incorporation into Italy. They were pivotal in orchestrating D'Annunzio's September 1919 arrival. And when the name-change law was proclaimed, all of them took pen to paper to request Italianization of their surnames. But what they asked for was not a substitution; it was an addition. Giovanni Host became Giovanni Host-Venturi; Enrico Hortizky proudly signed his name Enrico Horitzky-Orsini. Leone Spez did not rise in the Fiume ranks as Leone Quarnari, but instead as Leone Spez-Quarnari. Even Luigi Hlaich chose to keep his original last name, though it was undoubtedly almost impossible for most Italian speakers to pronounce (in Italian, the letter *h* goes unpronounced; the Slavi *hl* sound is beyond comprehension to most Romance-language speakers). It would always be Hlaich-Lacini, pronunciation problems be damned. These Fiume veterans of Italy's WWI military proudly kept their original Slavic-, Hungarian-, and German-origin surnames, never worrying that they diminished their claims to Italianness. If anything, the addition of their Italian noms de guerre reminded everyone that they were not just Italians in heart and mind; they had also voluntarily risked their lives and their families' lives for Italy.

The Fiume state's concerted efforts to paper over its multiethnic character with language laws and flagging initiatives (supported from both the top down and the bottom up), combined with the state's and the populace's disinterest in promoting or controlling a name-change Italianization campaign, might seem to indicate that nationalist propaganda initiatives only went skin deep, perhaps to avoid inciting dissent by forcing the issue of how Italian Fiume and its locals really were or wanted to be. But examples like state leaders who avoided name-change initiatives and the WWI veterans who Italianized their names while keeping their non-Italian ones point to another explanation: in Fiume most Italian nationalists did not see a multiethnic (non-Italian) heritage as disqualifying to true Italianness. If anything, a name like Host-Venturi, Horitzky-Orsini, or even Hlaich-Lacini was as Italian as one could be. And this peculiar form of Fiume-Italian nationalism that focused more on how one asserted Italianness (through chosen language use, flags, and political activity) than on lineage was not new or the result of the chaos of 1919. It was part of a Fiume-specific, multiethnic-heritage Italian nationalism that had started before the war but came to full fruition in the immediate postwar period.[91] And perhaps the best way to understand how someone like Minister of Education Bellasich could demonize a clerk for writing in a language other than Italian and beg Mussolini to tell "the Italian people that Fiume asks for nothing else but flags, flags, flags," while declining to Italianize his own last name, is to look at how the Fiume school system went about creating a nationalist Italian mindset in a particularly Fiume-centric way.

Schooling Fiume: Stability and Discipline in an Italianizing World

When the Habsburg Empire dissolved in October 1918, school officials did not immediately begin Italianizing Fiume's curriculum. In part, this was because bigger problems loomed. Like the rest of Europe (and the world), Fiume was beset by the Spanish Flu. For everyone, the first priority was to control the epidemic and lower the death count. In September 1918, just three weeks into the academic year, city officials closed the schools, as over 60 percent of the student body and many teachers had shown evidence of Spanish Flu contagion.[92] When Hungarian forces deserted the city in late October 1918, there was no effect on classrooms because they were empty. The arrival of Italian, British, American, and French forces in November 1918 brought no change because schools remained closed. Only in mid-December 1918, just weeks before the Christmas and New Year's festivities, did the municipal government decide it was safe to let Fiume's children begin to return to the classroom.[93]

It was only a beginning, because it proved difficult to reopen the schools. Many students were still sick. With no money or materials arriving from an imperial metropole, heating and lighting supplies were low. Fiumian winters are cold; like many towns of the upper and eastern Adriatic, the city gets hit hard by the winter Bura winds (Bora in

Italian), and the cold, moist, dark winter months quickly rendered the stone school buildings frigid. Without proper heating and lighting supplies, Fiume's schoolrooms felt like crypts, especially to under-nourished children and teachers wearing whatever scraps of clothing had survived four previous tough winters. As late as March 1919, one school principal decided to ignore the new daylight saving ordinances decreed by the city government because "with the little light, insuf-ficient heating and the lacking clothing and shoes from which stu-dents suffer," school needed to be held during the warmest, lightest times of the day.[94]

Containing the effects of the Spanish Flu and managing buildings with few resources would have been enough to preoccupy staff, but Fi-ume's political situation compounded these problems. When the for-eign troops arrived in November 1918, the Inter-Allied military leaders repurposed the empty school buildings as barracks. When school was to be reopened in December 1918, the city government wanted the sol-diers moved out immediately, but the Inter-Allied command ignored the government's decree.[95] In January 1919, most school buildings had still not been evacuated. Powerless against Inter-Allied commanders, the city government decided to try to make room for as many students as possible by creating reduced-hour teaching shifts in the few avail-able buildings, with most of the older students cycled through and the younger ones left out.[96] That was one approach. Another school prin-cipal decided to prioritize boys' access to schooling over girls', arguing that "even if they [the girls] lost an entire year of education, this would not be as detrimental to them as it would be if the boys continue with the limited hours they have now."[97] Such priorities resulted in many girls receiving no instruction whatsoever, as one principal noted that with the American troops' occupation of her building, "school must be closed, to the great detriment to those [female] students forced to lose the scholastic year."[98] A year after the war ended, one school council meeting reported, "Only four schools in the territory are open (in one building there are two schools and weekly lessons of 3 and 3 on alter-nate days) and only one boys' school in the city is functioning, with limited hours because of the overwhelming number of students. All because the school buildings are occupied by the military."[99]

Things did not improve significantly when the Inter-Allied troops left, mostly because they were quickly replaced by D'Annunzio's followers. The Italian National Council decided that the legionnaires and the children would share school buildings. Unsurprisingly, this, too, proved less than ideal. Teaching staff went into great detail in their discussions at school council meetings about how intolerable the setup was: "The toilets, constructed for children, are badly adapted for adult use causing daily floodings," with the resulting smell proving "more than monstrous."[100] School corridors were a madhouse of foot traffic with the "continual shouting of people with no regular [military] service."[101] Outside was little better. Playgrounds and victory gardens were overrun with bored soldiers "shooting their guns, even during hours of instruction."[102] The noise was not rifle practice. Hungry legionnaires were hunting whatever birds they could.[103]

No one was surprised at the end of the 1918–1919 school year when student outcomes proved beyond unsatisfactory. As explained at one school council meeting in January 1920, "Having reviewed the didactic programs [of the previous year] the teaching faculty revealed that current school conditions had paralyzed all the initiatives of the teaching faculty, whether concerning instruction or discipline."[104] Many were concerned about what it would mean for the prospects of Fiume's youth if they failed to learn how to read, write, and calculate adequately to survive in the increasingly bureaucratized world of the twentieth century. Equally worrisome was the issue of inculcating discipline in students.

These worries were both literal and metaphorical. In day-to-day terms, teachers immediately noticed a changing ethos within the student body. There were some quite extreme cases, such as that of the 18-year-old Arturo Colacevich, who yelled out to his teacher in the middle of class, "We're sick of you!"[105] After several warnings and many failing report cards, Colacevich and his ilk were expelled to protect "the discipline and prestige of the school and its teachers."[106] The most common example of the discipline problem, however, was a general lack of interest in education and disregard for state ordinances. Teachers admitted in their school council meetings that the majority of cases

> of indiscipline most probably must be attributed to both the nomadic life to which children have grown accustomed during the too-long inauspicious years of war and armistice and to the little effort parents have demonstrated in supervising and educating their children, let alone instilling upon them the importance they should give to schooling.[107]

Blaming parents for children's lack of dedication is a time-honored practice, but as another school council report clarified, the times really had trained children (and their parents) to disregard education and civic order. Students avoided school because of the "indulgence of the troops" stationed in the city: soldiers played with children, gave them treats, paid them for menial tasks, and generally enjoyed occupying their time. Children were "distracted by the street which offered continuous entertainments," and parents seemed uninterested in offsetting the trend, or powerless to do so.[108] Because of "the large number of children under the age of 12 who had never even been registered in a school" and because "many parents preferred for their children to beg or even steal [instead of going to school]," teachers felt school was no longer a priority for many Fiume families.[109] Some teachers suggested increasing fines to families (and even their landlords) for allowing children to run wild.[110] Others thought it was a question of time spent in school, and pushed for Christmas holidays to be annulled so children could catch up.[111] But the most common option was to approach this as a question of civic culture that could be solved by re-creating the "solemnity experienced within the schools in the 'ante bellum' years."[112]

There is something peculiar about school officials and members of Fiume's Italian National Council calling for a return to an antebellum educational culture—that is, the Habsburg system. Just as they were pulling down Habsburg banners and hoisting up Italian flags and enforcing Italian-only language laws, they were publicly hailing the fact that their school system could end the Habsburg model of multilingual national "hypocrisy" and become "a temple to Italianness."[113] The nationalist strain in reworking the school system was put most bluntly by the Italian National Council's propaganda office in January 1919, which stated,

> For us it's not enough that teaching abstains from putting forward conflicting political views: from today on we want every teacher to inculcate the most pure national sentiment within our children. It is not enough for us to instill in our children a simple admiration for Italy. No! We want their hearts to feel how great, magnanimous, and civil our Italy is, and how only Italy, and no other, is our Patria.[114]

For decades, nationalists across Europe and beyond had identified the schoolroom as a key location for nationalizing heterogeneous, cross-class, ethnic, and linguistic populations. Italian nationalists in postwar Fiume repeated many of these ideas: the school had "as its holy function to educate Italianly [*italianamente*] the minds and hearts of the growing generation"; once it reached the children, Italian national pride could "penetrate into the family of every single student."[115] Considering these goals, we would expect the government, the school council, and the teachers to begin to completely transform education from its antebellum approach. But that is not what happened.

On closer examination, it is apparent that what the government and teaching staff actually did in the schools was much more multivalent. Without a doubt, from the first moments of the 1919 school year there was a changed curriculum. Before 1918, Fiume had two school tracks: the Hungarian-language imperial schools (higher-ranked schools attended by those hoping for government jobs and white-collar futures, with language instruction in Hungarian and Italian) and the Fiume city schools, which were Italian-language based but included mandatory Hungarian courses. By January 1919, Hungarian-language courses at the city schools had been canceled, and families of children at the imperial schools were informed that "only students whose mother tongue was Hungarian, meaning that at home Hungarian is commonly spoken," could continue taking their courses in Hungarian.[116] "All

A Fiume teacher leading students waving Italian flags and cheering on a parade.

others [students whose mother tongue was not Hungarian—the majority of students enrolled] must attend courses given in Italian."[117] At the end of the 1918–1919 school year, the city government announced that all the imperial schools in the city would be closed, as they believed the German-language imperial schools in the former Habsburg regions currently occupied by the Italian military had been.[118] Classrooms were still filled with the same combination of "children hailing from Italy, Germany, Austria, and students from the Hungarian schools," not to mention the overwhelming majority in many of Fiume's schools of mother-tongue Croatian and Slovene speakers.[119] What was different was that schools now offered only one language for upward mobility: Italian.[120]

Transitioning education to Italian-language-only certainly fulfilled the expectations of Fiume's most virulent Italian nationalists. But the management of this transition was more about reinstituting a Fiume-specific civic culture and dealing with the discipline problem than about Italianizing the youth. In short, emphasis was not placed where nationalists in the Kingdom of Italy would have expected. The postwar curriculum focused on infusing a sense of political order in which all locals, regardless of ethnicity or language, followed city rules (which might or might not conform to the norms of the Kingdom of Italy).

For example, in the switchover to the Italian-language-based system, Hungarian-trained teachers were not fired en masse and replaced by teachers shipped in from Italy. Instead, Fiume teachers were re-educated to teach in Italian. In the summers of 1919 and 1920, the Fiume government sent a handful of local teachers to Florence to attend a summer school in Italian language, literature, and culture.[121] Supplementary courses were also held in and around Fiume "for those teachers who are not in complete possession of the language in which they need to teach."[122] In the summer of 1919, eighty-five Fiume teachers voluntarily signed up to participate in an intensive Italian course sponsored by the Italian occupying forces in Opatija (just a thirty-minute train ride southwest from the Fiume city center).[123] During the 1919–1920 school year, Fiume teachers who had been trained in Hungary were required to take after-school Italian courses. These courses were not to be taught by teachers from mainland Italy. Instead the government specifically detailed how all instruction had to be provided by "(male and female) Fiumian teachers."[124] Fiume's educational initiatives focused on retooling for a new era of *italianità* (Italianness), but not to the extent of changing the ethnic or cultural makeup of its students or teachers.

The formula of keeping local teachers for local students was not just a pragmatic way of coping with the fact that the majority of the population of Fiume did not speak Italian as their mother tongue. It was also a curricular decision intended to resolve the discipline problem. As the Italian National Council explained in 1920 to missionaries who applied to open a medical dispensary, kindergarten, and women's school in Fiume, the plan would not get local government approval unless it proved "completely Fiumian."[125] "Completely Fiumian" meant, first, that any staff hired by the humanitarian organization would need to be made up of locals, to protect "Fiumian interests."[126] But it also meant that the schools had to share the city's priorities—that is, they had to instill a "Fiumian" worldview, something the city government admitted that it "rightly guarded jealously."[127]

This emphasis on protecting a sense of being Fiumian even amid the push for Italian-language training was not a postwar development: it had been the modus operandi of city educators for decades. Fiume's teachers wrote their own textbooks for courses in Italian, Hungarian, and geography (and got them approved by the Budapest-based Education Ministries). Teachers did all this extra work in part to make money, but also out of a firm commitment to ensure that lesson plans were connected to issues that "concern us directly," and to avoid materials produced outside Fiume "that do not correspond at all to our needs."[128] Fiume educators and local elites were so jealous of their right to determine what they would teach and how they would teach it that before the war, the entire corps of Fiume teachers voted against overseeing textbooks for Italian-language learning for Hungarian schools. Their reasoning is clear, if surprising: they did not want to oversee how Hungarians learned Italian because they wanted "no inconsistencies in their deliberations"—that is, their intention not to use Budapest-produced scholastic materials.[129] If they were involved in determining what imperial schools would teach, what would stop Budapest officials from pushing imperial textbooks on their city classrooms? In essence, even before the war, Fiume teachers (and the many city administrative units above them) preferred to give up a say in kingdom-wide curricular decisions to protect local curricular independence.

After the war, the insistence on protecting and promoting a specifically Fiumian worldview continued—indeed, it increased. To understand what this worldview amounted to, we can look at how principals, the school council, and individual teachers approached the teaching of geography. As reported in the minutes of the December 1918 school council meeting, "The geography curriculum will remain unchanged[;] . . . geography will be taught on the basis of the old curriculum with due reservations and modifications rendered necessary following the new conditions of the city."[130] Keeping the curriculum the same while modifying content according to the changed postwar, post-Habsburg, Italian nationalist Fiume political climate might seem contradictory, but Fiume educators had worked out how everything could change while still staying the same, even in their (seemingly imminent) Italian nation-state future.

In the decades before the war, Fiume teachers had developed a detailed step-by-step geography program to respond to the processes of expanding imperial states and newly forming national ones (especially in the Balkans). In fact, two different Fiume schoolteachers produced new geography textbooks that reflected both city initiatives to foreground Fiume's special status and the changes caused by the political reorganization of the lands of Austria-Hungary with *Ausgleich* (dualism), the dismemberment of Ottoman holdings in the wake of the many Balkan Wars, and the voracious expansion of European imperial states in the eastern and southern Mediterranean.[131]

The Fiume geography curriculum worked on the principle of big to small. Before even looking at cities, regions, or states, for three hours a week 7- and 8-year-olds learned the concepts of "Horizon. Form of the Earth. Means of orientation on a globe and a map. The Earth's movements. Astronomical zones and seasons. Earth's constituent parts. Horizontal and vertical morphology. Rivers and lakes. Man."[132] From earth forms, focus shifted to "The geographic division of Hungary—Rivers of Hungary. The Great [Hungarian] Plain. The Little [Hungarian] Plain. Simple cartographic sketches."[133] In the next lessons, students were pushed to imagine their own maritime and Balkan regional world: "The plateau southeast of the Drava and Sava [Rivers]; the [Adriatic] littoral."[134] From the region, lessons then widened again to consider Europe and beyond, emphasizing "The physical geography of Europe. Austria, the Balkan peninsula, the Italian peninsula, the Iberian peninsula, France, Switzerland, Germany, Belgium, Holland, the British archipelago, Scandinavia, Russia. The physical and political geography of Asia."[135]

The tone of these lessons was not universalist. As one Budapest-based geography professor explained in his 1913 evaluation of Fiume-produced geography textbooks, the emphasis was on providing "the Italian[-speaking] student with a clear vision of those lands, to which his own autonomous city [that is, Fiume] plays an integral part in public law."[136] In essence, geography classes before World War I gave a telescopic vision of Earth, humankind, the Hungarian Kingdom, the Balkans, the Adriatic, Europe, and beyond from the starting point of how the Fiume city-state fit into these bigger pictures. And up until war was declared, every school put in regular requests for new "topographic maps in large format of Fiume," "pictures representing the city of Budapest," "geographic maps representing Europe, the Austro-Hungarian Monarchy, and Hungary," and that is about it.[137] Lists of school holdings after the war made no mention of maps of the southern hemisphere, the Americas, or Asia. Students only saw maps of Fiume, the Hungarian Kingdom, the Austro-Hungarian Monarchy, and Europe (in that order of frequency). To supplement class work, teachers organized field trips, taking students on a mountain trip every year to the source of the Fiumara River, which emptied into the Adriatic on the eastern border of the city center.[138] Older students took class trips to the centers of power and culture most intertwined with Fiume's political economy; girls' high schools received city subsidies to take students to Venice; boys' high schools received funds to visit Budapest.[139] Geography lessons in prewar Fiume were Fiume centered, reverberating out to the regions, metropoles, and states that the corpus separatum was linked to politically, economically, and culturally.

Teachers could fulfill the December 1918 school council's directives to keep "the geography curriculum . . . unchanged . . . with due reservations and modifications rendered necessary following the new conditions of the city" because geography lessons had always been centered on Fiume itself.[140] The core of this curriculum could be kept, even increased, while making substitutions here and there to deal with the dissolution of Austria-Hungary. How did this work? The "Didactic Curriculum" reversed the order of the lessons. Instead of starting with space, Earth, Earth's component parts, or Earth's horizon, students would learn geographic fundamentals by starting from the most local of local spaces. As one teacher outlined, the first geography lessons would now start from the home, with children schooled to think geographically according to these categories:

Geography
The child within the family. Love and responsibility towards particular members of the family. The family as a small society. The school society considered as a bigger society. Responsibilities towards the teacher and fellow students. Many families together form a bigger society called a *comune* [municipality]. Idea of a village, town, and city. Civic representatives and the mayor. Place of residency and place of birth. Patria = responsibilities to it.[141]

Instead of learning how to read a map by finding an earthly orientation as they had before the war, students were now invited to walk their neighborhoods, read a map of the city, and give directions. Students would also be taught the names "of the city's most important buildings and squares" and would be taught the basic physical geographic concepts of terms such as "hills, mountains, plains, woods, fields, meadows, vineyards," and so on.[142] After the first year, geography was what you could learn about Fiume and through Fiume. Beyond that? The school council was very clear: "Instead of the geography of Hungary, the geography of the Adriatic Lands should be introduced."[143]

In essence, students were still being taught to think outward from Fiume, but with the Fiume core taking center stage and the rest of the world approached ever more gradually. After students learned about Fiume, the next level in the geography curriculum (replacing the Hungarian Kingdom) focused on the "Adriatic Lands" like this:

The Istrian peninsula. Orography and Hydrography. The major cities and towns. Population; agriculture, industry and commerce.
The Croatian Littoral.
Dalmatia. Fishery, cities, islands. Agriculture, industry, commerce.
Italy. Natural and political borders. Seas, gulfs, straits, principal canals. Lakes and major rivers of Italy. The Alpine and Apennine

mountain ranges with their highest points. Plains. Regions and principal cities. Agriculture, industry, commerce, communications. Government and administrative divisions.[144]

Gone were the lessons on the Great Hungarian Plain and the Little Hungarian Plain and those on the southeast Balkan regions of the Drava and Sava River basins. Instead Fiume was described as the center of an Adriatic regional world (including Istria, coastal Croatia, Dalmatia) linked naturally to the Kingdom of Italy's mountains, rivers, plains, and cities. Only after absorbing that information would students tackle Earth's movements, space, and Europe.[145] In a geographic sense, as another school council meeting emphasized, the initial geography classes could remain "on the whole unaltered because they treat the *luogo natio* [birth place]," but with the recommendation that "when discussing the city constitution of Fiume, the teacher should mention the new state of things and the functions of the Italian National Council."[146] After students learned about the geological formations, economies, and populations of the region, it was "opportune to teach the geography of Italy and its new borders in place of that of the ex-Monarchy."[147] Local knowledge outweighed all; the city government trumped the Kingdom of Italy. Far from teaching children "to feel how great, magnanimous, and civil our Italy is, and how only Italy, and no other, is our Patria," as the propaganda office had proclaimed, schools taught Fiumians that, though circumstances had changed, Fiume remained the real "Patria," one that could be incorporated into the Italian Kingdom much as it had been into the Hungarian Kingdom.[148]

Imperial Fiumian Italianization

On April 3, 1919, cars transported a host of Fiume politicians, a military escort, and Lady Anna Maria Grazioli—the wife of the Italian general then overseeing the Inter-Allied command in Fiume—to Plasse, a village on the northern outskirts of the city-state. Though just a thirty-minute walk up the steep, winding road northwest from the city center, Plasse was to Fiume what any low-income agricultural village would

The Plasse girls' school event was much larger than this nuns' school's festivities given to honor D'Annunzio. The trappings, however, were the same: flowers, gifts, and children displaying gratitude and enthusiasm for Italy.

be to the big, industrializing metropole it fed with manpower and foodstuffs: rustic, dotted with factories, with residents who lived both parallel to city life and connected to it. Lady Grazioli and company made the trip in order to be thanked by Plasse's girls' elementary school for the supplies of food, shoes, books, and clothes donated by the Italian city Genoa.[149] Having participated in many such celebrations at Fiume's other schools and hospitals over the previous weeks, Lady Grazioli knew the drill. The celebration played out like the rest, with the school bedecked with flowers, Italian flags, pictures of the king of Italy, and tricolor ribbons. Children presented bouquets to Lady Grazioli as if she were the Italian queen Elena herself.

After mementos had been given to Lady Grazioli, children from the school recited Italian nationalist poems and sang Italian soldiers' songs about risking their lives for their beloved Italian flag. The school's principal, 53-year-old Fiume native Maria Voncina, gave a formal speech hailing everything Italian and emphasizing how much they appreciated (and still needed) help from the Italian motherland. There were more songs, some emotionally manipulative speeches from the school's oldest and youngest prized pupils, more flowers, and after two hours or so Lady Grazioli's motorcade drove back down to the city center. To Lady Grazioli these ceremonies must have meshed perfectly with what Fiume's fervent Italian nationalist enterprise intended, demonstrating that every Fiumian, young and old, wanted nothing else but to profess their Italianness. And, of course, the school celebration unfolded precisely as our histories of postwar Fiume have led us to imagine. Postwar Fiume was a center for nationalist activism, predictable in its methods and its message. It was textbook: when the empires of Europe fell away at the end of the war, communities rich and poor, central and peripheral, pushed away their imperial pasts and celebrated nationalism as the vital organizing principle for constructing and surviving the future. The Plasse girls' school celebration was just one of hundreds of thousands of similar events happening throughout Europe toward that effect.

As she told colleagues at the next school council meeting four days later, Principal Voncina took pride in the event she had orchestrated, especially because she had pulled it off in a very poor district, where the majority of the student body spoke Croatian or Slovene as their mother tongue, still learning the Italian they recited in the celebration. The Fiume notables present praised Voncina, and in her report to the school council she agreed with principals from the other Fiume schools that Lady Grazioli "appeared deeply moved with demonstrations of affection for our Patria and flattered by the welcome shown to her."[150] Eleven days after the event, however, Voncina had to report something very different. Apparently two city government representatives, who were extreme Italian nationalists, had questioned Voncina's teachers individually, trying "to extort a written document declaring that [Voncina] prohibited students from singing patriotic songs" and weakened the patriotism of the event.[151] Some teachers eagerly provided these documents, while others refused. Amid the tension, parents of two students decided it was best to take their children out of the school altogether.

Voncina contextualized this surprising turn of events by admitting she had "strongly recommended teachers avoid those songs that sow hatred in the hearts of those who should only be open to kind feelings."[152] Though it is unclear which songs Voncina meant, there were many Italian nationalist tunes that could have upset the students and their families. The canon of Italian nationalist songs at the time included quite a few choruses like, "All of us, all of us will die before we become Slav!" or "Our civilization has never been Croat. No! No! It's true."[153] Perhaps Voncina also decided Italian war songs rallying soldiers to kill every last Habsburg soldier were inappropriate, as most of the pupils' fathers had been drafted to fight (and perhaps die) in service to the Habsburg armies. Whichever songs were censored, Voncina explained that it was not through a lack of patriotism or an effort to thwart Fiume's annexation bid. She insisted that throughout her twenty years of teaching she had worked to "diffuse [her] maternal language [Italian] in this zone."[154] Her words were not empty rhetoric, for even before the war, under the Hungarian administration, she had coupled her supply orders for "maps of Europe, the Austro-Hungarian Monarchy, and Hungary" with book requests for the Italian nationalist texts penned by authors including Giovanni Pascoli and Giosuè Carducci.[155] Voncina was a long-standing Italian nationalist, but for her, patriotism and Italian nationalism did not mean provoking hatred.

This was not the first time Voncina had had to defend herself and her methods. Months before, in January 1919, Fiume's propaganda office had demanded she be fired, though it admitted that she had not performed any political actions or expressed any opinions against government dictates and that she instilled "admiration for Italy" in her school.[156] Nonetheless, the propaganda office wanted a teacher with a "more pure national sentiment."[157] The propaganda office's demands were pushed aside, however, and Voncina retained her position. After the Lady Grazioli celebration, the propaganda office's urgings were

again ignored; the nationalist press in Fiume described Voncina's celebration as a success, and she kept her job well beyond D'Annunzio's
time in Fiume.

   This chapter began and ends with stories of near firings because of
nationalist politics, just two of hundreds such files that exist in the archives of the 1918–1921 Fiume Crisis. Together they help show the
complexities of postwar Italian nationalism in a city where over half
the population did not speak Italian as its mother tongue. The reason
this period did not explode into continuous moments of internal strife
and communal violence was not that Fiume was immune to or unin-
volved in campaigns for Italianization. As we have seen, in the immediate postwar period a large proportion of the local populace actively
worked to remake the multilingual, multiethnic port city into an Italian
urban community. Multilingual signs, the Habsburg emblems, Hungarian flags, the maps of central Europe, and Hungarian-language
spelling drills were all gone, replaced by an Italian-only official linguistic culture, with Italian flags, Italian maps, Italian monuments,
Italian street names, and Italian commemorations. Fiume underwent a
self-propelled Italianization campaign that was supported by military
and civilian efforts in the Kingdom of Italy, but was not forced on the
city by outsiders.

   Italianization was definitely the postwar Fiume project. However, nationalization, as the term is commonly understood, was not. Unlike in
the territories newly occupied by the Italian armed forces to the west
and north of Fiume (Tyrol, Trieste, and Istria, among others), in Fiume,
pertinents not of Italian heritage or not native Italian speakers were
not pushed out of the civic order, unless they obstinately refused to play
along with the Italianization project. They kept their jobs: some received
translators to bridge the language gap; others, including schoolteachers,
received the necessary training to function in an Italianized civic culture, to be "in complete possession of the language in which they need
to teach."[158] The student body remained diverse, a mix of Italian, Croatian, Hungarian, Slovene, German, Romanian, and Czech speakers;
the difference was that while before the war they had to excel in both
their Italian and Hungarian classes, now only Italian mattered. Some

families shed markers of a non-Italian ethnic heritage through name changes, but the absolute majority kept their family names regardless (or because) of the national cultures with which they were associated.[159] It was a political era of Italianization, and those who resisted these initiatives suffered the consequences, including fines, firings, and, in extreme cases, expulsion from the city-state. This pressure was undoubtedly felt and resented. A new wave of insecurity touched the lives of all, since jobs could be lost because of Italianization missteps. Students might be subjected to some pretty odious teachings that could lead their parents to take them out of school. None of this was ideal, and many probably yearned for prewar times or hoped for the day when Italianization was replaced with Yugoslavization. But Italianization stopped short of what it later became: one was at risk if one was not amendable to making Fiume look and feel Italian, but no one was required to actually be Italian.

So what is the difference between this Fiumian Italianization and what we call nationalization? In the Voncina case, it was the difference between how the Plasse school celebration performed nation under her direction and the way the propaganda office wanted the ceremony to go. Put simply, Fiumians did not opt to transform their laws, lives, lessons, or selves into what was expected or required of a citizen of the Kingdom of Italy. They willingly (sometimes illegally) decorated their landscapes with Italian "flags, flags, flags," but most showed no inclination to reject their multiethnic backgrounds.[160] Language laws, flag initiatives, name-change laws, and lesson plans all pushed for the same thing: Fiume should look and feel Italian, but Fiume and Fiumians could and did choose what was and was not Italian. Future generations were not schooled to think of the world Italo-centrically. Italy was put into Fiume's curriculum by keeping Fiume central and changing what surrounded it, replacing the Habsburg Empire with Italy. And people who tried to push for a complete recasting of Fiume as Italian-only were on the whole ignored. This was both state policy and an open secret.

The difference here goes to the heart of the question of how non-Italian Fiume could coexist with the nationalist agendas of the more extreme elements of the Italian National Council and D'Annunzio's regime. The provisional government Italianized the Fiume-centric imperial structures they already had, rather than extending them into new nation-state policies of national integration. Maria Voncina closed her letter defending her methods of diffusing an Italian patriotism by saying that she needed "calm and serenity to continue the complicated work" of leading her peripheral, ethnically mixed, low-income girls' school as she had done for the last fourteen years. On the whole, it appears most Fiumians (though not all) shared Voncina's goals and priorities: to continue what they had been doing, but this time "Italianly" instead of "Habsburgly." Rather than a story of leaving imperialism through nationalization, their history was one of transitioning to a new form of locally centered imperialism, with Italy standing in for the Habsburgs.

Conclusion

When Empire Disappears

When Gabriele D'Annunzio's Christmas of Blood petered out on New Year's Eve 1920, it seemed like Maria Voncina's lesson plans infusing Italian nationalism with mutual respect and ethnic sensitivity were just what Fiumians needed for the future that awaited them. In January 1921, D'Annunzio and most of his legionnaires left Fiume; the city was declared a Free State under League of Nations and Italian protection; Fiume's border with the Kingdom of Serbs, Croats, and Slovenes was set at the Fiumara River, dividing Fiume from Sušak; and elections to transform the city's provisional government into its permanent one were scheduled. Political parties vied for power, working hard (and often illicitly) to round up votes. In April 1921, Fiume's first president was the man who had been elected Fiume's mayor in 1914—Riccardo Zanella.[1] As he had in 1914, Zanella ran on a platform of Italian nationalism, Fiume exceptionalism, and locals above all else, just the kind of thing Voncina and other Fiume educators had been teaching their students all along. But without the broad infrastructures and investments of a metropole to back the city's trade, Fiume's economic woes continued, currency remained unstable, and unemployment grew, along with worry and dissatisfaction.[2] The former boom town continued to struggle, while across its western border Benito Mussolini "marched" on Rome and the Kingdom of Italy became increasingly fascinated with the promises of authoritarianism. A year and a half after D'Annunzio left Fiume, a Fascist putsch (engineered by a coalition of ex-legionnaires and Fiume locals) ousted Zanella and declared the city's virtual annexation to Italy

People cross a temporary bridge connecting Fiume to Sušak, installed immediately after the Christmas of Blood. Life went on after January 1921, but unfortunately for most, it kept getting harder every year.

along very different lines from those of 1918–1921. Now the Italian mad-*repatria* that Fiumians joined was Fascist, and the teachings of someone like Voncina lost out to the stances of people like the propaganda office employees who had tried to have her fired just a few years earlier.

Mussolini's official annexation of the city to Italy in 1924 instigated a remaking of Fiume along textbook nationalist, Italian centralist lines. Gone were programs aimed at making Fiume look and feel Italian while keeping it functioning much as it had before the war. The pragmatic exceptionalisms Fiumians had hoped would give them a leg up once they were reabsorbed into a big state never came to pass. Crown-lire exchange rates never arrived at the 1 to 1 everyone had hoped for; by 1924 the now meek and exhausted Fiumians gratefully accepted the 2.5-to-1 rate Italy offered. Laws were no longer a mash-up of Hungarian priors, Italian additions, and Fiume-only innovations: now the laws enforced from Palermo to Venice were instated en masse in Fiume, regardless of community wishes. Women lost the vote, divorce became illegal, and tax codes benefited Rome, not Fiume's regional trade. Pertinency disappeared from the citizenship rolls: with the 1924 annexation, Fiume pertinents had to opt for Italian, Serb-Croat-Slovene, or some other citizenship, with nothing in between except statelessness. Fiume pertinents who chose not to become Italian lost the right to state employment. Under these conditions, many Croatian- and Slovene-speaking Fiumians moved across the river to Sušak, where their ethnic identification bolstered their rights instead of impeding them. Name changes were no longer voluntary—there were specific Fascist protocols about how they were enacted. Fiume's textbooks and geography lessons were replaced by the national curriculum. Under Mussolini, Habsburg Fiume was decisively annulled in a way it had not been at any of its earlier crisis points—not the dissolution of Austria-Hungary, the arrival of Inter-Allied troops, Woodrow Wilson's diplomatic pronouncements, the takeover of the Italian National Council, the arrival of D'Annunzio and his followers, the Christmas of Blood, or the international recognition of the Free State of Fiume. Though the majority of locals remained, the contours of their world now reflected the desires of their new empire in formation, the Fascist one, and not the old one, the Habsburg one, whose legacy had lived on for so long.

Does it matter that this transformation came about six years after the date our history books have taught us to expect? Does it matter that extreme nationalism and Fascism did not overwhelm Fiume when armistices were signed or when D'Annunzio came driving in? I spent most of the last decade in the researching and writing of this book because I believe the answer is yes. It matters both for a better understanding of why things happened the way they did and because it can keep us from making easy assumptions that can lead to some pretty terrifying conclusions.

First, learning how Fiumians navigated currency conversions, maneuvered through hodge-podge legal systems, and manipulated citizenship regimes while orienting their children to see the world as a Fiume-centric enterprise with Italy filling the role once inhabited by the

Habsburgs lets us see the incredible activism—both inside and outside state bureaucracies—of locals working to remake their worlds after their empire disappeared. The histories of post-imperial successor states were different from those of the victor states. In Italy, France, and Great Britain, officials hoping for order in the face of strikes and workers' movements tinkered with existing systems to provide new welfare initiatives, suffrage, and pay increases to satiate veterans and an exhausted home front. But the defeated living amid the "embers of empire" had the same problems as victor states, just with less money, fewer resources, and no government in place.[3] The practicalities of surviving the chaos of dissolution induced many to retain imperial practices as best they could in order to chart the twentieth-century unknown that awaited them. *Nation* might have been on everyone's lips in 1918, but in how their worlds were remade, locals living in the defeated states allowed (or chose, or preferred) for empire's structures to live on.

Second, turning a blind eye to these stories gives the impression that the relative ease with which D'Annunzio and his legionnaires came to Fiume was a testament either to the universality of Italian nationalist commitment or to a charisma so powerful that it let D'Annunzio brainwash a whole town into serving his will. Neither is true. When we understand the initiatives Fiumians took to survive dissolution, we can see how a city so ethnically and linguistically varied managed to weather the D'Annunzian fanfare without too much violence. The methods employed by Fiumians to instill order and continuity allowed D'Annunzio to make his nest in the town without the bloodshed, burnings, or mass rapes perpetrated by the paramilitary groups that occupied civilian communities in Poland, Estonia, Ukraine, and elsewhere. In essence, Fiume's methods to survive its empire's demise created the space for the stories that have papered over those struggles. Reexamining the former lets the how and why of the latter be seen in the world in which they played out, no longer obscured by the fantastical aura they have enjoyed thus far or the teleology of what came later. It lets us see that nationalism was a powerful political ideology in post-WWI Europe, but that there were other things going on that directly subverted nationalist teachings and blossomed under cover of its emblems. When we study the power of charisma, populism, postwar para-militarism, and proto-fascism by looking at the Fiume case, we must be very careful not to forget the older structures that Fiumians—officials and non-officials alike—used to contain violence and recapture prewar prosperity.

This scramble to create a state out of the structures of empire did not just shape Europe's smallest successor state, Fiume—it characterized all the postwar successor states. If little Fiume had problems stabilizing, nationalizing, and controlling its currency, imagine what befell the populations living in newly forming Poland, which had its three prewar currencies (German, Russian, and Habsburg) still circulating along with the newly stamped currencies and forgeries that came after 1919. If Fiumians took advantage of the opportunity to pick and choose which laws to follow, which to dump, and which to add between the prewar Hungarian order and the new Italian one they assumed would be theirs, imagine the opportunities and risks in newly forming Czechoslovakia, which had two different prewar legal systems (the Austrian and the Hungarian) to choose between, plus all the enticements of starting from scratch. If in Fiume the city was inhabited mostly by people who did not have pertinency, what must have befallen the population of postwar Vienna—the capital of the empire—where immigrants had poured in for decades looking for work? In fact, pertinency was ripe for manipulation across post-Habsburg Europe, where those seen as undesirable were denied employment, welfare, or the right to remain if they could not provide appropriate documentation of their prior imperial status. Jews in Poland, Germans in Czechoslovakia, Slovenes in Italy, Romanians in Austria, Serbs in Hungary, and the poor, unemployed, or newly arrived everywhere found themselves in danger of being cast out of their homes and denied state services because of the reinterpretation of imperial norms. And finally, if the Fiume school council felt it had to recast lesson plans to bridge the old world with what the world could or should be, imagine how much more deeply entrenched and contradictory the legacies of empire must have been in the lesson plans of the Kingdom of Serbs, Croats, and Slovenes, where curriculum needed to be created for lands as diverse as post-Ottoman

Skopje, post-Hungarian Novi Sad, post-Serbian Belgrade, post-Bosnian/Habsburg Sarajevo, post-Austrian Dubrovnik, and post-Croatian/Hungarian Zagreb. What Fiumians did to cobble together the old and the new was echoed throughout post-imperial Europe, with greater or lesser success. These processes are important because they structured how life would be led, the expectations locals had, and how violently the aftereffects of the "national question" would play out. And not only are they important, they must be reintegrated into the interwar histories in a way that, on the whole, they have not yet been.[4]

Reanchoring history in this transition period from empire is important not just because it lets us understand better what was going on in the immediate aftermath of World War I. It is vital because the consequences of this transition period did not end in in the mid-1920s when most of Europe's successor states solidified their nation-state structures. The legacies of empire did not end with the formation of the nation-states, they just disappeared from the story, subsumed within the broader narrative progression from World War I to extreme nationalism to fascism to World War II to the Holocaust.

One way to see the costs of overlooking this history is through the lens of the scandal surrounding Giovanni Palatucci, the so-called Italian Schindler. Almost immediately after World War II, Palatucci was hailed a hero of the Holocaust by the Israeli state and later honored as a "Righteous among Nations." He was commemorated for using his position as a Fiume police officer to shield Jews from a racialist, bureaucratized anti-Semitic world. He was celebrated for falsifying documents and organizing private ships to help Jews fleeing eastern Europe to enter Italy or Palestine, for destroying police files identifying Jews living in Fiume, and for arranging safe havens in Switzerland or Italian detention centers far from the concentration camps where Fiume Jews would have met their deaths. Slowly but surely throughout the 1960s, 1970s, 1980s, 1990s, and 2000s, the entire world jumped on the honoring-Palatucci bandwagon: Pope John Paul II named him a twentieth-century martyr; the Italian government awarded him a posthumous Gold Medal for Civic Merit; and even New York City's Mayor Michael Bloomberg designated May 18 as Giovanni Palatucci Courage to Care

Day. All of this global attention was mostly fed by reports that he had died in 1945 in the Dachau concentration camp because he had used his position in Fiume's police commissariat to save over five thousand Jews. The idea that a policeman and devout Catholic would risk everything to save Jews in a time of almost universal anti-Semitism was something many wished not only to honor but also to use as a lesson. The Washington, DC, Holocaust Museum created a special exhibit showcasing Palatucci. The New Jersey public school system approved a state curriculum that focused almost entirely on him, emphasizing that he embodied Italians' unwillingness to execute Adolf Hitler's demands to eradicate the Jews of Europe. In classrooms across the United States' eastern seaboard, schoolchildren were taught to think of Palatucci's role in the Holocaust as a "little recognized but remarkable aspect of this history that actually leaves the researcher with some sense of cautious optimism."[5]

In 2013, cautious optimism turned into shame when first Italy's *Corriere della sera* and then the *New York Times* published front-page articles recharacterizing Palatucci, the Italian Schindler, as a Nazi collaborator.[6] These articles—and others worldwide—reported that historians from Italy and the United States had been investigating allegations that Palatucci's acts of bravery were a fraud perpetrated by family members in the immediate post-WWII period in order to receive a subsidy from the Italian government.[7] Local historians pointed out that there was no way five thousand Jews could have been rescued in Fiume because in the 1940s only circa five hundred were still housed there, and of those a higher percentage were sent to die in Auschwitz than anywhere else in Mussolini's Italy.[8] Reports that Palatucci had destroyed documents to protect Jews from Nazi roundups were similarly debunked, as the documentation designed to monitor and eventually round up those Jews were still in the local archives, along with notes showing that Palatucci himself had helped produce them. Perhaps the most distressing part was the paper trail showing that it was Palatucci's Fascist superiors (and not him) who organized ships to transport fleeing eastern European Jews to Palestine—not to save them, but to limit the number arriving in Italy while also creating moneymaking opportunities for Fiume's shipping agents. The head of New York University's Primo Levi Center summarized the utter wrongness of celebrating Palatucci as a "Righteous among Nations," asserting that research produced by a dozen scholars reviewing nearly seven hundred documents made it clear that Palatucci was "a willing executor of the racial legislation and—after taking the oath to Mussolini's Social Republic, collaborated with the Nazis."[9]

In light of these revelations, agencies in the United States quickly and quietly wiped Palatucci off their list of Holocaust heroes (though in Israel and Italy many still claim his righteousness): the Holocaust Museum in Washington, DC, removed him from its galleries; the Anti-Defamation League rechristened the award given out in his name; New York City canceled Giovanni Palatucci Courage to Care Day; and New Jersey schools stopped having their students hold mock trials based on Palatucci's unjust murder for his heroic acts.

How could such a colossal mix-up have happened? How could a Fascist police officer and collaborator whose work was essential for the killing of Fiume's Jews have been transformed into a Holocaust hero? In part, the answer lies with those who desperately wanted to believe in the kind of hero Palatucci represented: Catholics, Italians, Italian-Americans, law-and-order representatives, and the fledgling state of Israel (which was eager for European Union allies) pushed the Palatucci narrative, unaware that it was untrue, but uninterested in confirming its veracity because of the needs it fulfilled. But the other reason the story went unquestioned was that Palatucci died in Dachau. Why would a Fascist Italian functionary wear the striped uniform of the despised if he had not tried to save Jews? The well-documented police orders and court rulings damning Palatucci to death were not consulted, because a concentration camp death could only equal Holocaust tragedy, or, when a gentile was involved, Holocaust heroism.

Here is where we see how cutting out the transition period of Europe's post-WWI experiences proves dangerous, for Palatucci was not sent to Dachau because of the histories we know, the ones that torment our consciences. Instead, his arrest, torture, and deportation to Germany are tied to the long shadows cast by Fiume's post-imperial past:

he died in Dachau for offering information to enemy British agents in exchange for promises that Fiume would be made independent once more. Born in a small southern Italian town over five hundred miles from Fiume and only 10 years old when D'Annunzio made his triumphant entry, Palatucci seems an unlikely martyr for a sovereign Fiume. But he lived in Fiume for seven years, formed friendships with former members of Fiume's Italian National Council, and spent his time— drinking coffee, playing billiards, swimming in the Adriatic, walking the city's promenade—with people who had lived Fiume's prosperous Habsburg past and its strapped post-Habsburg future. He occupied a world in which the legend of the city's corpus separatum status and its resultant wealth held sway. He also lived in its present, where without its autonomy, without a metropole promoting its infrastructures and pumping it with capital, and in the throes of Mussolini's failed war, Fiume wilted into provincial impoverishment. It is unlikely that any of these influences pushed Palatucci to risk his life, but living there, he knew of "the other path" its locals had trodden before and after 1918 and had not forgotten. Historians agree it was Palatucci's Italian nationalism, combined with a fear of Josip Broz Tito's Yugoslav partisans, that led him to collude with the British against Fiume's Nazi occupiers. His time in Fiume had convinced him that Fiume's Italianness could only be saved from German undoing or Yugoslav absorption by reanimating the immediate postwar world.

The commemoration of a Fascist functionary as a Holocaust hero is not just sickening; it is a cautionary tale reminding us not to look at the interwar period as a seamless march from World War I to nationalism to fascism to World War II to genocide. Other factors, seemingly anachronistic, also held sway. D'Annunzio's Fiume adventure was as much the result of charismatic nationalism as it was the by-product of the enduring structures of Habsburg imperialism. Palatucci's death in Dachau was prompted by firm beliefs in the importance of Italian nationalism, but also by an older, peculiarly Fiumian, Habsburg Italian nationalist version of it. Emphasizing the importance of the chaos that dominated the economic, legal, social, political, and cultural experience of successor-state Europeans after World War I will help us rebel against the easy, linear narratives that have led to the flawed histories we have trusted too long, the histories that have made fascism and its violence seem the inevitable consequences of the energies set loose in 1918. Nothing was inevitable; everything was the construct of time, place, and choices. Understanding that an era did not end in 1914, 1918, or even 1938 broadens our understanding of why so many Europeans participated the way they did in the tense decades of the 1920s, 1930s, and 1940s. Untangling past imperial norms shows us how and why an imperialist nationalist like D'Annunzio could take the spotlight in multiethnic Fiume. But in a broader sense, foregrounding the post-imperial reminds us why nation-states in the mid-twentieth century were fraught enterprises whose inherent contradictions (not just in ideals but also in lived experiences) triggered so many of the frustrations that led to much of the world we know.

NOTES

ACKNOWLEDGMENTS

ILLUSTRATION CREDITS

INDEX

Notes

Abbreviations

HR-DARI: Hrvatski Državni Arhiv u Rijeci (Croatian National Archives in Rijeka)

AFV: Vittoriale degli italiani—Archivio fiumano (Vittoriale of the Italians Fiume Archive)

JHSC: Johns Hopkins Special Collections

All documents from the Vittoriale and Rijeka archives were written in Italian in their originals, unless otherwise noted. All translations were made by the author, also unless otherwise noted. Personal names are spelled as they were in the documents consulted.

Introduction

1. Gino Berri, "Le giornate di Fiume: L'aspetto e la passione della citta'," *Corriere della sera*, January 4, 1921. All translations throughout this book were made by the author unless otherwise cited.

2. "Dopo due giorni di tregua," *La vedetta d'Italia*, December 31, 1920.

3. For a thought-provoking new book reconstructing how Italy's racial laws and the onslaught of the Holocaust decimated Fiume's Jewish population, see Sanja Simper, *Židovi u Rijeci i liburnijskoj Istri u svjetlu fašističkog antisemitizma (1938.–1943.)* (Zagreb: Židovska vjerska zajednica Bet Israel u Hrvatskoj, 2018). According to her work, in 1910 Jews made up circa 3 percent of Fiume's population, in 1938 circa 2 percent. Ibid., 99.

4. For a new analysis of what happened to people who fled what would become Yugoslavia for post-WWII Italy, see Pamela Ballinger, *The World Refugees Made: Decolonization and the Foundation of Postwar Italy* (Ithaca, NY: Cornell University Press, 2020).

5. Ljubinka Toševa-Karpowicz, William Klinger, and Giuseppe Parlato are the three historians of early twentieth-century Fiume / Rijeka who have formulated much of what we know about the political, economic, and social mechanisms that shaped the city from 1867 until 1924. Unfortunately, most of their work is found in articles, hard-to-access monographs, and unpublished dissertations, primarily in Croatian and Italian. Nonetheless, they have filled

in the most blanks about how the city formed, functioned, and unraveled. For a well-written narrative history of nineteenth- and twentieth-century Fiume, based on a synthesis of the Italian-language historiography and including an extensive discussion of the Italian domestic, foreign policy, and military influences on Fiume, see Raoul Pupo, *Fiume città di passione* (Rome: Laterza, 2018). For the best English-language accounts of what happened in Fiume after World War I, see Michael Arthur Ledeen, *The First Duce: D'Annunzio at Fiume* (Baltimore: Johns Hopkins University Press, 1977); J. N. Macdonald, *A Political Escapade: The Story of Fiume and D'Annunzio* (London: J. Murray, 1921). For a new bilingual Croatian-English book recently published that summarizes much of the current narrative of the Fiume Crisis and includes fascinating images and archival details, see Tea Perinčić, *Rijeka ili smrt! (D'Annunzijeva okupacija Rijeke 1919–1921). Rijeka or death! (D'Annunzio's occupation of Rijeka, 1919–1921)* (Rijeka: Naklada Val, 2020). There is an almost gargantuan historiography of pre- and post-WWI Fiume (the city, not D'Annunzio's regime) that was written mostly for specialist audiences speaking to those camps interested in showcasing the city's rightful Croatian, Italian, Hungarian, or Communist revolutionary heritage. These works of scholarly commitment have kept a history of the city outside the narrative of the D'Annunzio occupation alive and have painstakingly unearthed much useful information about what its inhabitants experienced. Worth special mention are the many volumes and articles published by Silverio Annibale, Amleto Ballarini, Ferdo Čulinović, Ervin Dubrović, Antonella Ercolani, Ilona Fried, Danilo Klen, Antonio Luksich-Jamini, Daniel Patafta, Luigi Peteani, Mihael Sobolevski, Giovanni Stelli, and Igor Žic, among still others. Over the past few years, a new wave of Rijeka historians has begun to publish, overturning prior politically oriented fascinations of Fiume's pre-WWII history and already leading to rich results that reposition Fiume/Rijeka's history within the broader historical landscape of nineteenth- and twentieth-century Europe. Of special note are the recent articles and forthcoming volumes by Marco Abram, Vanni D'Alessio, Ivan Jeličić, Ágnes Ordasi, Francesca Rolandi, Sanja Simper, Péter Techet, and Gianluca Volpi. Reading works by all the authors listed has given me key insights into the workings of Fiume before and after World War I. However, unless explicitly cited, the materials and arguments of this book are based on what I found in the archives.

6. For an interesting article discussing the particular variant of Habsburg nostalgia lived politically and culturally in today's Rijeka, see Péter Techet, "Post-habsburgische Erinnerungspolitik als unreflektierte Nostalgie oder als antinationalistisches Gegennarrativ im heutigen Rijeka?," *Zibaldone* 68, no. 2 (2019): 119–131.

7. George Mosse, *Masses and Man: Nationalist and Fascist Perceptions of Reality* (New York: Howard Fertig, 1980); Emilio Gentile, *The Sacralization of Politics in Fascist Italy* (Cambridge, MA: Harvard University Press, 1996).

8. "Eia! Eia! Eia! Alalà!" is based on the ancient Greek war cry "Ἀλαλά." D'Annunzio introduced it among aviators during World War I and instilled it as the official war cry of his legionnaires in Fiume. For the twenty years of Mussolini's control of Italy, it was used as an official Fascist military war cry.

9. Emphasis on the non-Fascist elements of D'Annunzio's time in Fiume has taken center stage in Italian historiography of late, with particular emphasis on D'Annunzio and his followers' focus on libertarian, corporatist, and anti-traditional politics. For a brilliant discussion of how the histories of D'Annunzio in Fiume have developed, see the forthcoming article by Natka Badurina, "D'Annunzio a Fiume: La violenza politica, l'etica e la storia," in *Atti del Convegno Fiume 1919–2019: Un centenario europeo tra identità, memorie e prospettive di ricerca, Vittoriale degli Italiani* (Milan: Silvana Editoriale, 2020).

10. Claudia Salaris, *Alla festa della rivoluzione: Artisti e libertari con D'Annunzio a Fiume* (Bologna: Il Mulino, 2002). The analogy of D'Annunzio's Fiume to 1960s counterculture movements began in the historiography of Fascism produced in the 1970s, most famously in the works of Renzo De Felice. It is now a common trope, most notably by Gabriele Marconi, *Le stelle danzanti: Il romanzo dell'impresa fiumana* (Florence: Vallecchi, 2009).

11. Mark Mazower, *The Dark Continent: Europe's Twentieth Century* (New York: Knopf, 1999). For the most explicit mirroring of Mazower's larger argument for Europe focusing on the Fiume-D'Annunzio story, see Raoul Pupo and Fabio Todero, *Fiume, D'Annunzio e la crisi dello stato liberale in Italia* (Trieste: Irsml Friuli Venezia Giulia, 2010).

12. Robert Gerwarth, *The Vanquished: Why the First World War Failed to End* (New York: Farrar, Straus and Giroux, 2016); George L. Mosse, *Fallen Soldiers: Reshaping the Memory of the World Wars* (New York: Oxford University Press, 1990). Gerwarth's work is the most synthetic and widely read on this topic, but there have been a host of other fascinating studies showing how the "war did not end," especially in east central Europe, with special attention paid to veterans and paramilitary groups. For a representative sample of this florid field, see Robert Gerwarth, ed., *War in Peace: Paramilitary Violence in Europe after the Great War* (Oxford: Oxford University Press, 2013); and Julia Eichenberg and John Paul Newman, eds., "Aftershocks: Violence in Dissolving Empires after the First World War," special issue, *Contemporary European History* 19, no. 3 (2010). For a fascinating extension of this thesis to the region of the northern Adriatic, see Borut Klabjan, "Borders in Arms: Political Violence in the North-Eastern Adriatic after the Great War," *Acta Histriae* 26, no. 4 (2018): 985–1002.

13. J. Adam Tooze, *The Deluge: The Great War, America and the Remaking of the Global Order, 1916–1931* (New York: Viking Adult, 2014).

14. Pankaj Mishra, *Age of Anger: A History of the Present* (New York: Farrar, Straus and Giroux, 2017), 4.

15. For an excellent new study on how the D'Annunzio media cult infected large swathes of young Italian men and women in the immediate postwar period, see Marco Mondini, *Fiume 1919: Una guerra civile italiana* (Rome: Salerno Editrice, 2019).

16. Timothy Snyder, *Bloodlands: Europe between Hitler and Stalin* (New York: Basic Books, 2010); Omer Bartov and Eric D. Weitz, *Shatterzone of Empires: Coexistence and Violence in the German, Habsburg, Russian, and Ottoman Borderlands* (Bloomington: Indiana University Press, 2013).

17. Emily Greble has made a similar point in a recent forum on post-WWI Europe looking at Muslims' experiences in the post-imperial Balkans. Emily Greble, "The Uncertain 'Wilsonian Moment' for Muslims in Yugoslavia: Reframing Historiographical Conversations through Minority Experiences," within the forum "Trasformazioni e transizioni imperiali sulla scia della Grande guerra (1917–1923)," *Passato e presente* 2019, n. 106, 36.

18. Hannah Arendt, *The Origins of Totalitarianism* (New York: Harcourt, 1951), 261.

19. Pieter M. Judson, *The Habsburg Empire: A New History* (Cambridge, MA: Belknap Press of Harvard University Press, 2016), 448.

20. Ibid., 449.

21. Erez Manela, *The Wilsonian Moment: Self-Determination and the International Origins of Anticolonial Nationalism* (New York: Oxford University Press, 2007).

22. Petition to Italian National Council and Mayor by city administrative employees against decision to close job openings, May 30, 1919, 541 Općina Rijeka 1918–1945, Prezidijalni Spisi: 95/1919, HR-DARI.

23. Capitaneria del porto, Minutes of meeting to reorganize Fiume's maritime administration, January 26, 1920, prot. 466, cass. 46, AFV.

1. Concealing Histories

1. "To Carry Petroleum in a Steam-Ship," *New York Times*, December 27, 1883.

2. "Brings a Cargo of Beet Sugar," *New York Times*, March 12, 1896.

3. "Japan Orders Torpedoes in Italy," *New York Times*, October 13, 1904.

4. "From Readers: Restriction of Immigration in Various Countries and Mr. Whelpley's Book," *New York Times*, July 22, 1905.

5. "Steamship Pool to Be Sued as Trust," *New York Times*, March 31, 1910.

6. Woodrow Wilson, "Fourteen Points," in *Joint Session of the United States Congress* (January 8, 1918).

7. In the personal archive of the geographer Isaiah Bowman, Fiume was among a list of fourteen cities of Austria-Hungary for which a map was commissioned in 1918 by the American Geographic Society, which he ran, so as to be prepared for peace negotiations in Paris 1919. See "List of Maps commissioned by the Inquiry in preparation for the Paris Peace Conference," January 31, 1925, Isaiah Bowman Papers, MS 58, Series 13, Box 3, Folder 22, JHSC.

8. Lawrence E. Gelfand, *The Inquiry: American Preparations for Peace, 1917–1919* (Westport, CT: Greenwood, 1976), 327.

9. The history of how Fiume's corpus separatum got reinstated is a fascinating and still deeply divided one. For more information, see Ljubinka Karpowicz, "Riječki corpus separatum 1868–1924" (PhD diss., Univerza Edvarda Kardelja v Ljubljani, 1986). Giovanni Stelli, *Storia di Fiume: Dalle origini ai giorni nostri* (Pordenone, Italy: Edizioni bibliotcca dell'immagine, 2017). "Semi-independent" here refers to how Fiume's municipal government issued its own regulations and ran its own city government with the oversight of a Hungarian-appointed governor, who was responsible to Hungary's prime minister and commercial minister. As Hungary's government pushed for greater and greater centralization around the turn of the century, tension around how independent Fiume was or could be of Hungarian administrative practices was a point of much political contention, leading to increasing commitment among many Fiumians for an "autonomism" (aka continued semi-independence) platform.

10. Ivan Jeličić, "Nell'ombra dell'autonomismo: Il movimento socialista a Fiume, 1901–1921" (PhD diss., Universita' degli Studi di Trieste, 2016), 47.

11. For a wonderful discussion of language and dialect diversity in Fiume/Rijeka, see Vanni D'Alessio, "Divided Legacies, Iconoclasm and Shared Cultures in Contested Rijeka/Fiume," in *Borderlands of Memory: Adriatic and Central European Perspectives*, ed. Borut Klabjan (Oxford: Peter Lang, 2018).

12. Throughout the book I refer to the Hungarian Kingdom and Habsburg Hungary. The more precise terminology (though less regularly used) would be the Lands of the Crown of Saint Stephen (*A Szent Korona Országai*), also known as Transleithania, which comprised all the non-Austrian-held territories of Habsburg Europe (except Bosnia-Herzegovina), and included the Kingdom of Hungary, the Kingdom of Croatia-Slavonia, and corpus separatum Fiume. As the Lands of St. Stephen were directly controlled by Budapest, I have chosen to emphasize the semiautonomy of Croatia-Slavonia and Fiume under Hungarian rule instead of using the terminology of Crown of Saint Stephen. Bosnia-Herzegovina was jointly administered by Hungary and Austria.

13. Jeličić, "Nell'ombra dell'autonomismo," 89.

14. William Klinger, "Dall'autonomismo alla costituzione dello Stato—Fiume 1848–1918," in *Forme del politico: Studi di storia per Raffaele Romanelli*, ed. Emmanuel Betta, Daniela Luigia Caglioti, and Elena Papadia (Rome: Viella, 2012), 56.

15. From the list of works consulted, especially important were the human geography studies of the Balkans produced by the Serbian geographer Jovan Cvijić. See "List of reports and maps of Inquiry," July 13, 1918, Isaiah Bowman Papers, MS 58, Series 13, Box 3, Folder 14, JHSC. For analysis of Cvijić's take on human geography, see Jeremy W. Crampton, "The Cartographic Calculation of Space: Race Mapping and the Balkans at the Paris Peace Conference of 1919," *Social and Cultural Geography* 7, no. 5 (2006): 731–752.

16. Apparently, before the Paris peace talks both the progressive journalist Walter Weyl and the geographer Major Douglas Johnson reported to the Inquiry on the Fiume issue. During the Paris peace talks, the British *Times* editor Wickham Steed submitted reports on Fiume, and Lieutenant Colonel Sherman Miles traveled to Fiume to issue on-the-ground reports of the situation.

17. Sherman Miles, "A report on Fiume by Lt. Col. Sherman Miles," March 26, 1919, Isaiah Bowman Papers, MS 58, Series 13, Box 7, Folder 17, JHSC.

18. "Memorandum of Italian claims according to the Treaty of London line in Dalmatia, as presented to Commissioner Henry C. White," January 25, 1919, Isaiah Bowman Papers, MS 58, Series 13, Box 7, Folder 17, JHSC.

19. Isaiah Bowman, *The New World: Problems in Political Geography* (Yonkers-on-Hudson, NY: World Book, 1921), 265.

20. "Black Book," 41–42, Isaiah Bowman Papers, MS 58, Box 13.13, JHSC, quoted in Wesley J. Reisser, *The Black Book: Woodrow Wilson's Secret Plan for Peace* (Lanham, MD: Lexington Books 2012), 93–129.

21. Article 5: "A free, open-minded, and absolutely impartial adjustment of all colonial claims, based upon a strict observance of the principle that in determining all such questions of sovereignty the interests of the population concerned must have equal weight with the equitable claims of the government whose title is to be determined."

22. Article 10: "The peoples of Austria-Hungary, whose place among the nations we wish to see safeguarded and assured, should be accorded the freest opportunity of autonomous development"; Article 9: "A re-adjustment of the frontiers of Italy should be effected along clearly recognizable lines of nationality."

23. For a fascinating analysis of Wilson's stance regarding eastern European nation making, see Larry Wolff, *Woodrow Wilson and the Reimagining of Eastern Europe* (Stanford, CA: Stanford University Press, 2020).

24. Reisser, *Black Book*.

25. Wilson ordered the US delegation's steamship the *George Washington* to be ready to depart in mid-April 1919. John Maxwell Hamilton and Robert Mann, *A Journalist's Diplomatic Mission: Ray Stannard Baker's World War I Diary (from Our Own Correspondent)* (Baton Rouge: Louisiana State University Press, 2012), 327.

26. David Lloyd George, *Memoirs of the Peace Conference* (New Haven, CT: Yale University Press, 1939), 2:541.

27. Still the best work analyzing the Italian diplomatic and political intrigues surrounding the Paris Peace Conference and Italy's "Adriatic Question" remains Paolo Alatri, *Nitti, D'Annunzio e la questione adriatica*, SC/10 (Milan: Feltrinelli, 1976). For a good synthesis of the longer-term clashes around Italian diplomatic and political interests in the

Adriatic, see Marina Cattaruzza, *Italy and Its Eastern Border, 1866–2016* (New York: Routledge, 2017).

28. "Minutes of the Supreme Council: Italian Claims and Policy in Asia Minor," May 1919, Isaiah Bowman Papers, MS 58, Series 13, Box 4, Folder 9, JHSC.

29. "Discussion of the Adriatic Problem in the Supreme Council of the Peace Conference," 1919, Isaiah Bowman Papers, MS 58, Series 13, Box 1, Folder 3, JHSC.

30. Ibid.

31. The Italian delegates had successfully convinced all that "the question was not a boundary adjustment between two Allied nations, Italy and Serbia, but between Italy and territories formerly Austrian . . . [comprising] Croats and the Slovenes." According to the Italian delegation, the Serb-Croat-Slovene delegation was not an Entente power but instead represented those who for the most part fought *against* the Entente, and Italy's foreign minister "absolutely refuse[d] either to dismiss or to dispute with his enemies." Ibid.

32. "Statement of President Wilson Regarding the Disposition of Fiume," *Chicago Tribune*, April 24, 1919, Paris edition. As for the Treaty of London, Wilson reassured Italians that for Italy "on the north and northeast her natural frontiers are completely restored, along the whole sweep of the Alps . . . to the very end of the Istrian peninsula, including all the great watershed within which Trieste and Pola lie." To explain why he was blocking the rest of what Italy had been promised at the Treaty of London, Wilson pointed out that Dalmatia and many of its islands had undoubtedly been pledged because "here and there on that coast there are bodies of people of Italian blood and connection, but also, and no doubt, chiefly, because it was felt that it was necessary for Italy to have a foothold amidst the channels of the eastern Adriatic in order that she might make her own coasts safe against the naval aggression of Austria-Hungary." To this, Wilson again had an answer he was sure would convince: there was nothing to worry about because "Austria-Hungary no longer exists" and there would be a League of Nations–enforced "limitation of armaments and . . . adequate guarantees . . . of equal and equitable treatment of all racial or national minorities." Italy would thus be protected from naval attack. And thanks to the League of Nations' supervision, Italian speakers living within the Kingdom of Serbs, Croats, and Slovenes could live freely, without mistreatment. Wilson ended his appeal to the Italians by reminding them that "interest is not now in question, but the rights of peoples, of states new and old, of liberated peoples and peoples whose rulers have never accounted them worthy of right. . . . These, and these only, are the principles upon which she [America] can consent to make peace. Only upon these principles, she [America] hopes and believes, will the people of Italy ask her to make peace." Ibid.

33. Hamilton and Mann, *Journalist's Diplomatic Mission*, 341.

34. Ibid., 326.

35. Noriko Kawamura, "Wilsonian Idealism and Japanese Claims at the Paris Peace Conference," *Pacific Historical Review* 66, no. 4 (1997): 503–526.

36. Isaiah Bowman, Manuscript pages of "Disarmament and Security Tribute to G. L. Beer," Isaiah Bowman Papers, MS 58, Series 13, Box 2, Folder 15, JHSC.

37. This Wilsonian moment anti-imperialist nationalism argument in China is most famously made by Erez Manela, *The Wilsonian Moment: Self-Determination and the International Origins of Anticolonial Nationalism*, Oxford Studies in International History (New York: Oxford University Press, 2007). Also see Pankaj Mishra, *From the Ruins of Empire: The Intellectuals Who Remade Asia* (London: Picador, 2012).

38. "Lodge Favors Italy's Demand," *Spokane Chronicle*, April 30, 1919.

39. Quoted in Crampton, "Cartographic Calculation of Space," 747.

40. Daniela Rossini, *Woodrow Wilson and the American Myth in Italy: Culture, Diplomacy, and War Propaganda*, Harvard Historical Studies (Cambridge, MA: Harvard University Press, 2008).

41. Daniela Rossini, "Italy: An Object of Demonstration in Wilson's Foreign Policy. Retrospects of the Fiume Appeal of April 23, 1919," *Revue française d'études américaines* 61 (1994): 225–234.

42. Sherman Miles, "A report on Fiume by Lt. Col. Sherman Miles," March 26, 1919, Isaiah Bowman Papers, MS 58, Series 13, Box 7, Folder 17, JHSC; "Discussion of the Adriatic Problem in the Supreme Council of the Peace Conference," 1919, Isaiah Bowman Papers, MS 58, Series 13, Box 1, Folder 3, JHSC; National Council of Rijeka (Fiume)-Susak, *The Question of Fiume* (Paris: Lang, Blanchong and Cie, 1919), 7; Isaiah Bowman, Manuscript pages of "Disarmament and Security Tribute to G. L. Beer," Isaiah Bowman Papers, MS 58, Series 13, Box 2, Folder 15, JHSC; "Lodge Favors Italy's Demand"; Giordano Bruno Guerri, *D'Annunzio* (Milan: Mondadori, 2008), 229.

43. As Judson puts it so well, "The lack of a specific date on which the Habsburg Empire came to an end tells us something important about both the circumstances and the meanings of its fall." Pieter M. Judson, *The Habsburg Empire: A New History* (Cambridge, MA: Belknap Press of Harvard University Press, 2016), 441.

44. Quoted in William Klinger, "Le origini dei consigli nazionali: Una propsettiva euroasiastica," *Atti: Centro di Ricerche Storiche-Rovigno* 40 (2010): 466.

45. The initial national council founded in Zagreb was named the "Slovene, Croat, Serb" council. Only later, when the new kingdom was officially declared, did the order of this change to "Serb, Croat, Slovene." For more information on the original foundation of the Zagreb council, see Ivo Banac, *The National Question in Yugoslavia: Origins, History, Politics* (Ithaca, NY: Cornell University Press, 1988), 127–138.

46. Quoted in Daniel Patafta, "Privremene vlade u Rijeci (listopad 1918.—siječanj 1924.)," *Časopis za suvremenu povijest* 38, no. 1 (2006): 199. For more information on Lenac and his cultural ties to both Italian and Yugoslav-Croatian cultural worlds, see the article by Natka Badurina, "Kako pamtiti D'Annunzijev pohod na Rijeku," *Dometi* (forthcoming).

47. Quoted in Daniel Patafta, "Promjene u nacionalnoj strukturi stanovništva grada Rijeke od 1918. do 1924. godine," *Časopis za suvremenu povijest* 36, no. 2 (2004): 687.

48. Jeličić, "Nell'ombra dell'autonomismo," 282.

49. For a fascinating article investigating socialist and worker-party involvement in the immediate post-WWI Fiume situation, see Ivan Jeličić, "Uz stogodišnjicu rijeckog Radnickog vijeca: Klasna alternativa nacionalnim državama na sutonu Monarhije," *Časopis za povijest Zapadne Hrvatske* 12 (2017): 63–84.

50. The majority of the historiography on Fiume follows this Italian annexationist platform, as for most of 1918–1920 it predominated in city politics and controlled municipal government directives. For a quick summary of the cultural, political, and economic arguments made, see Andrea Ossoinack's memo to Italian foreign minister Tommaso Tittoni in Paris: Andrea Ossoinack, Petition to Foreign Minister Tittoni, July 31, 1919, cass. 247, Quest. Fiume 5, AFV. See also the Fiume delegation's speech to Woodrow Wilson in Rome: Deputazione fiumana, Fiume Delegation Speech to Woodrow Wilson, January 3, 1919, cass. 241-1919, prot. 415, AFV.

51. For a concise summary of these arguments, see the pamphlet prepared for the 1919 Paris delegation of the Kingdom of Serbs, Croats, and Slovenes, available in the *Agramer Tagesblatt*, March 15, 1919, as well as in "La questione di Fiume: Testo del memoriale

presentato dai delegati S.H.S. alla conferenza della pace e sua confutazione," April 5, 1919, cass. 241-1919, prot. 415, AFV.

52. For a concise summary of these arguments, see the many articles and volumes published by Giovanni Stelli, as well as Ljubinka Karpowicz, "Biografia politica di un autonomista: Ruggero Gottardi," *Quaderni: Centro di Ricerche storiche-Rovigno* (1983–1984), 39–64; and the forthcoming publication by Ivan Jeličić, "Redefining Fiumians and Italianity: The Ambiguities of the National Building Process in the Former Habsburg-Hungarian Corpus Separatum, 1914–1921" (unpublished manuscript, 2019).

53. Klinger, "Dall'autonomismo alla costituzione dello Stato."

54. Jeličić, "Nell'ombra dell'autonomismo," 282. For the best analysis of the relationship of prior political status with the formation of political power after World War I, see the forthcoming article "The Political Elites in Fiume and Its Challengers, 1918–1924" (unpublished manuscript, 2020). For greater detail on the involvement of socialist organizations in Fiume's administration, see Jeličić, "Uz stogodišnjicu riječkog Radnickog vijeca."

55. For an explanation of why Serb troops (which were stationed outside Fiume) were not included within the official Inter-Allied command stationed in Fiume, see Ferdo Čulinović, *Riječka država: Od Londonskog pakta i Danucijade do Rapalla i aneksije Italiji*, Mala historijska knjižnica, vol. 7 (Zagreb: Školska knjiga, 1953), 45–48.

56. The Fiume annexationist propagandist Edoardo Susmel explained the importance of choosing Grossich as president with these words: "The old liberal [Grossich] was not just autonomist; he was irredentist. It was not in vain that the young built all their trust in him: in him they found the point of connection of all the Italian tendencies in Fiume." Edoardo Susmel, *Antonio Grossich nella vita del suo tempo, 1849–1926* (Milan: Treves Treccani Tumminelli, 1933), 194.

57. Information on Antonio Vio Jr.'s background and prior service experience within Fiume politics from Jeličić, "Political Elites in Fiume." Special thanks to Jeličić for pointing out the importance of reconfirming Vio as mayor.

58. Antonio Grossich, Speech addressed to Francesco Grazioli, April 26, 1919, cass. 241-1919, prot. 2868, AFV. Consiglio nazionale italiano, Invites Grazioli to assume powers over Fiume on behalf of Kingdom of Italy, April 26, 1919, cass. 241-1919, prot. 2866, AFV.

59. Mario Jechel, Description of Fiume's press office, May 5, 1919, cass. 241-1919, prot. 3143, AFV.

60. Consiglio nazionale italiano, Correspondence between Italian National Council and Milan postcard publishing house, March 12, 1919, cass. 30, prot. 1550, AFV.

61. "Vado a votar per Fiume italiana," *La vedetta d'Italia*, October 28, 1919.

62. Arturo Chiopris, List of women to be included in electoral list, September 19, 1919, 541 Općina Rijeka 1918–1945, Opći spisi L57/19, kut. II: Chiopris, Arturo, HR-DARI.

63. Alfredo Fletzer, Attempt to register 16 widows to vote, September 17, 1919, 541 Općina Rijeka 1918–1945, Opći spisi L57/19, kut. I: Fletzer, Alfredo, HR-DARI.

64. Lino Petrilla, Report of Anna Candelari's behavior, October 29, 1919, 541 Općina Rijeka 1918–1945, Opći spisi L59/19, HR-DARI.

65. Maria Sustovich, Voter registration request, October 20, 1919, 541 Općina Rijeka 1918–1945, Opći spisi L57/19, kut. III: Sustovich, Maria, HR-DARI.

66. Aurora Kolmann, Voter registration request, September 10, 1919, 541 Općina Rijeka 1918–1945, Opći spisi L57/19, kut. III: Kolmann, Aurora, HR-DARI.

67. One of my favorite examples is that of the housewife Elena Mihich, who used her voter registration form also as a means to correct the spelling of her maiden name, Pezelj,

from the incorrect Italianized version Peretti. Elena Mihich, Voter registration request, September 23, 1919, 541 Općina Rijeka 1918–1945, Opći spisi L57/19, kut. III: Mihich, Elena nata Pezelj, HR-DARI.

68. Edoardo Susmel, *La marcia di Ronchi: Centoquarantanove tavole fuori testo con numerosi documenti inediti* (Milan: U. Hoepli, 1941), 37. For a hilarious fictional account of the Fiume ladies celebrating the arrival of the Italian sailors, see the novel by Viktor Car Emin, still not translated from the original Croatian, but definitely deserving translation. Viktor Car Emin, *Danuncijada: Romansirana kronisterija riječke tragikomedije 1919–1921* (Zagreb: Zora Matica Hrvatska, 1977).

69. For a fascinating example of a contemporary American news article emphasizing that "Italian Fiume" was an invention of the provisional government, see Elbert Francis Baldwin, "The Question of Fiume," *Outlook*, June 11, 1919.

70. For a vivid account of how the media fed this vision of Fiume as a national issue demanding and deserving Italians' attention, see Marco Mondini, *Fiume 1919: Una guerra civile italiana* (Rome: Salerno Editrice, 2019).

71. Ledeen, *First Duce*, 67.

72. The exact numbers of how many followed D'Annunzio that first day are hard to determine. The original forces to begin D'Annunzio's march to Fiume (from Ronchi) were about 200. Estimates of how many entered Fiume alongside D'Annunzio range around 1,000–1,500 (many deserters from Pittaluga's own forces just as D'Annunzio entered Fiume).

73. Gabriele D'Annunzio, "Lettera ai Dalmati," *Il popolo d'Italia*, January 15, 1919.

74. Guerri, *D'Annunzio*, 223.

75. The term *fiumanesimo* actually existed before D'Annunzio's arrival in Fiume (and the historical studies thereof), to denote an "intrinsically Fiume way of life and thinking," deeply connected to the city's prewar Autonomy movement. For more information on autonomism and fiumanesimo, see the many works of Giovanni Stelli, including his recent master narrative of Fiume history Giovanni Stelli, *Storia di Fiume: Dalle origini ai giorni nostri* (Edizioni biblioteca dell'immagine, 2017).

76. Renzo De Felice, *D'Annunzio politico: 1918–1938* (Rome; Bari: Laterza, 1978), 28.

77. Emilio Gentile, *The Origins of Fascist Ideology, 1918–1925* (New York: Enigma Books, 2005), 151. This synthesis of his definition is from pages 134–154.

78. Guerri, *D'Annunzio*, 199.

79. For an English-language description of D'Annunzio's flight over Vienna, see Lucy Hughes-Hallett's biography, where she gives the following apropos description: "'The Sky over Vienna,' d'Annunzio announced: 'On the wind of victory arising from the rivers of liberty, we have come only for the joy of the daring deed . . . Viennese! We could now be dropping bombs on you! Instead we drop only a salute.' The people of Vienna were urged to reject their own government, and to plead for peace. 'If you wish to continue the War—continue it! You will thereby commit suicide.' A further 100,000 copies were dropped of a rather blunter and more explicit message, composed by Ugo Ojetti, written in German and urging the citizens of Vienna to save themselves and their city by surrendering." Lucy Hughes-Hallett, *Gabriele D'Annunzio, Poet, Seducer and Preacher of War* (New York: Knopf, 2013), 442–443.

80. For an excellent English-language narrative history of Italians' experience during World War I, see Mark Thompson, *The White War: Life and Death on the Italian Front, 1915–1919* (New York: Basic Books, 2009).

81. For the best English-language narrative explaining how D'Annunzio occupied Fiume, see Ledeen, *First Duce*.

82. For an excellent analysis of why and how Italian men decided to join D'Annunzio in Fiume, see Mondini, *Fiume 1919*.

83. For the full text of the modus vivendi presented to Fiume's Italian National Council (and the greater populace of the city), see "Il 'modus vivendi' proposto a Gabriele d'Annunzio dal Governo italiano," *La vedetta d'Italia*, December 2, 1919. For an English-language description of the politics surrounding the modus vivendi moment, see Ledeen, *First Duce*, 131–135.

84. Gabriele D'Annunzio, "*L'urna inesausta*," December 19, 1919, Special Collections and University Archives, Gabriele D'Annunzio Collection (MS 763), University of Massachusetts Amherst Libraries; Raoul Pupo, *Fiume città di passione* (Rome: Laterza, 2018), 116.

85. The clearest analysis of the modus vivendi moment can be found in Alatri, *Nitti, D'Annunzio*, 323–328. Also see Giuseppe Parlato, *Mezzo secolo di Fiume: Economia e società a Fiume nella prima metà del Novecento* (Siena: Cantagalli, 2009).

86. For a discussion of the links between D'Annunzio's Fiume experience and Mussolini's "March on Rome," see Giulia Albanese, *La marcia su Roma* (Bari: Laterza, 2008).

87. Just one of many such examples is this 1919 confirmation of city residency: Magistrato civico, Confirmation of Maria Bertinazzo's residency, February 6, 1919, 541 Općina Rijeka spis, Opći spisi LI/1919, Bertinazzo, Maria, HR-DARI.

88. Not much work has been done on Fiume's World War I experience and, as per Ivan Jeličić's suggestion, it would be interesting to know whether D'Annunzio's continued emphasis on "Austrian" instead of "Hungarian" perfidy helped mend some political fences between Fiumians and D'Annunzio's command. This is a topic that should be further explored. A first step in this can be found in Jeličić, "Redefining Fiumians and Italianity."

89. Consiglio nazionale italiano, Letter informing Hungarian Republic of Fiume's independence, December 12, 1918, cass. 28, prot. 250, AFV.

90. Comitato direttivo, Letter informing banks that Italian National Council taking over all powers of Hungarian State, November 28, 1918, cass. 28, prot. 58, AFV.

91. Consiglio nazionale italiano, Letter to Italian Navy informing about different state responsibilities in Fiume under D'Annunzio, September 16, 1919, prot. 5960 + allegato, cass. 242-1919, AFV.

92. Reggenza italiana del Carnaro, Confirmation of all state employees until otherwise notified, September 23, 1920, 3, predmet 2, str. 5 (2. niz), HR-DARI.

93. For an excellent new study of the Green Cadres, see the work of Jakub Beneš, especially Jakub Beneš, "The Green Cadres and the Collapse of Austria-Hungary in 1918," *Past and Present* 236, no. 1 (2017): 207–241.

94. Timothy Snyder, *Bloodlands: Europe between Hitler and Stalin* (New York: Basic Books, 2010); Robert Gerwarth, *The Vanquished: Why the First World War Failed to End* (New York: Farrar, Straus and Giroux, 2016).

95. Servizi pubblici della città di Fiume, Refusal to provide nationality information of Fiume police force, October 25, 1920, cass. 49, prot. 637, AFV.

96. For the running column on non-Italian "Italian nationalists," see the articles in *Primorske novine* beginning on February 3, 1919. For an explanation of the column's title, see "I nuovi Italianissimi," *Primorske novine*, February 3, 1919.

97. Letter denouncing corruption of officials within the Italian National Council, January 26, 1919, prot. 613, cass. 29, AFV.

98. Parlato, *Mezzo secolo di Fiume*, 14.

2. Follow the Money

1. Giuseppe Maranini, *Lettere da Fiume alla fidanzata* (Milan: Pan, 1973), 111–113.

2. Ibid., 60–61.

3. Ibid., 81–84.

4. Ibid., 42–43.

5. Ibid., 67–69.

6. Census figures will be discussed at greater length in Chapter 4. Suffice it to say that in the 1910 census, 49 percent of city-dwellers declared their mother tongue Italian, 26 percent Croatian, 13 percent Hungarian, 5 percent Slovene, 5 percent German, and 2 percent an amalgamation of other tongues.

7. Maureen Healy, *Vienna and the Fall of the Habsburg Empire: Total War and Everyday Life in World War I* (Cambridge: Cambridge University Press, 2004).

8. Maria née Serdoz Diracca, Pre-trial testimony—Bydeskúty character defamation trial, August 11, 1920, 761 Krivični predmeti 1920, 208, HR-DARI, 7.

9. Maranini, *Lettere da Fiume alla fidanzata*, 60–61.

10. Borislavo Gjurić, Police statement, April 17, 1919, 1108 Opći spis 1919, 813 spis 3, HR-DARI.

11. Nicolò Kuprešanin, Police statement, April 17, 1919, 1108 Opći spis 1919, 813 spis 2, HR-DARI.

12. Giorgio Roosz, Police statement, May 25, 1919, 1108 Opći spis 1919, 868, HR-DARI.

13. Gabriele Stejćić, Police statement, April 28, 1919, 1108 Opći spis 1919, 721 spis 1, HR-DARI.

14. Paolo Neumann, Police statement, February 19, 1920, 761 Krivični predmeti 1920, 98 spis 1, HR-DARI.

15. Danilo L. Massagrande, ed., *I verbali del Consiglio Nazionale Italiano di Fiume e del Comitato Direttivo 1918–1920* (Rome: Società di studi fiumani, Archivio Museo storico di Fiume, 2014), 137. In the article, the move to stamp crowns in the Kingdom of Serbs, Croats, and Slovenes was explained as a necessary initiative to help control currency flows and stabilize a fixed exchange rate between the Serbian areas that used the dinar currency and the ex-Habsburg lands (made up mostly of Bosnia and Herzegovina, Croatia-Slavonia, Dalmatia, and Carniola) that used the crown. Just as Fiume elites were reluctant to brand their money and border up their cash inflows and outflows, Natasha Wheatley and Quinn Slobodian have also noted how Austrian financial elites saw the breakup of the Habsburg Empire and the formation of smaller national states as a worrisome challenge to free-market global trade, one that needed to be resolved with extra-governmental systems. Natasha Wheatley, "Central Europe as Ground Zero of the New International Order," *Slavic Review* 78, no. 4 (Winter 2019), 904. Quinn Slobodian, *Globalists: The End of Empire and the Birth of Neoliberalism* (Cambridge, MA: Harvard University Press, 2018), 43.

16. Danilo L. Massagrande, ed., *I verbali del Consiglio Nazionale Italiano di Fiume e del Comitato Direttivo 1918–1920* (Rome: Società di studi fiumani, Archivio Museo storico di Fiume, 2014), 142.

17. Ibid., 27. The one arena where the members of the Italian National Council trusted their own expertise over that of Italy was maritime trade: here they determined with little fuss that Fiume needed to become a customs-free port and actually decided to do it without waiting for Italy, saying that Italy's bureaucracy was too slow to resolve this in time. Ibid., 152.

18. For a discussion of Fiume's economic potential before and immediately after the war, see Stefano Petrungaro, "Una cruciale periferia: Fiume," in *Porti di frontiera: Industria e commercio a Trieste, Fiume e Pola tra le guerre mondiali*, ed. Laura Cerasi, Rolf Petri, and Stefano Petrungaro (Rome: Viella, 2008). Also see Giuseppe Parlato, *Mezzo secolo di Fiume: Economia e società a Fiume nella prima metà del Novecento* (Siena: Cantagalli, 2009), 46–56.

19. For a succinct discussion of how and why Hungary invested so heavily in the development of Fiume, see chapter 1 of the forthcoming volume based on the dissertation by Tyler James Callaway, "Hungary at the Helm: Austria-Hungary's Global Integration during the Age of Empire" (PhD diss., New York University, 2019). In 1908, the total value of state investment in the city and port was valued at 60,000,000 crowns, not including 2,800,000 crowns in equipment, 8,200,000 crowns in warehouse construction, and 10,000,000 crowns for the railway plant. The Hungarian Ministry of Commerce and Royal Hungarian State Railways funded most of Fiume's development. The Ministry of Commerce spent approximately 50,650,000 crowns on construction and 1,860,000 crowns on labor.

20. Callaway, "Hungary at the Helm." See especially chap. 4.

21. Massagrande, *I verbali del Consiglio Nazionale Italiano*, 125.

22. For an excellent discussion of the Italian state's shifting policies regarding economic aid to Fiume, see Paolo Alatri, *Nitti, D'Annunzio e la questione adriatica*, SC/10 (Milan: Feltrinelli, 1976). Also see Parlato, *Mezzo secolo di Fiume*. In December 1919, the Italian National Council was told point blank that Italy's prime minister, Francesco Saverio Nitti, "did not intend to resolve the economic question before the political question." Massagrande, *I verbali del Consiglio Nazionale Italiano*, 402.

23. Massagrande, *I verbali del Consiglio Nazionale Italiano*, 164.

24. Ibid., 174.

25. In July 1919 Fiume's mayor put these views most precisely when he announced in an Italian National Council meeting, "It is therefore the painful political situation of the city that has provoked the current absurd economic situation: the city has no way to change or radically correct this situation because this depends on events and circumstances beyond our power and our will." Ibid., 35.

26. Though both Italy and the Kingdom of Serbs, Croats, and Slovenes experienced extreme economic pressures after World War I, Italy's position was far stronger, as seen by the fact that within three years after the war (and before Mussolini took power) most of its economy had returned to prewar levels. The Kingdom of Serbs, Croats, and Slovenes, however, would not approach the economic wealth of Italy until World War II, if then. Often mentioned in Italian National Council meetings and in diplomatic pamphlets was the argument against the city's incorporation into the Kingdom of Serbs, Croats, and Slovenes because Fiume required attachment to an industrial, capital-investing state like Italy, not an unindustrialized, agriculturally oriented "poor state" like the Kingdom of Serbs, Croats, and Slovenes. For excellent synthetic articles presenting the very different postwar economic situations of both countries, see Fabio Degli Esposti, "Post-war Economies (Italy)," in *1914–1918-Online: International Encyclopedia of the First World War*, ed. Ute Daniel et al. (Berlin: Freie Universität Berlin, 2015), https://encyclopedia.1914-1918-online.net/article/post-war_economies_italy; and Ian Innerhofer, "Post-war Economies (South East Europe)," in Daniel et al., *1914–1918-Online* (2017), https://encyclopedia.1914-1918-online.net/article/post-war_economies_south_east_europe.

27. Massagrande, *I verbali del Consiglio Nazionale Italiano*, 402.

28. Already by December 1918 the Fiume state and the Hungarian state had negotiated that Hungary would continue to pay the salaries and pensions of all those who were not reconfirmed as employees or dependents of the Fiume state. Special initiatives were also taken to provide for Fiume's Hungarian schools in the first year of transition, as well as its railway workers.

29. Massagrande, *I verbali del Consiglio Nazionale Italiano*, 180.

30. For general discussions of the currency chaos and stamping procedures in the wake of the dissolution of the Habsburg Empire, see Elmus Wicker, "Terminating Hyperinflation in the Dismembered Habsburg Monarchy," *American Economic Review* 76, no. 3 (1986): 350–364; Karl Schlesinger, "The Disintegration of the Austro-Hungarian Currency," *Economic Journal* 30, no. 117 (1920): 26–38; Rudiger Dornbusch, "Monetary Problems of Post-communism: Lessons from the End of the Austro-Hungarian Empire," *Weltwirtschaftliches Archiv* 128, no. 3 (1992): 391–424; Ivan Berend and Gyorgy Ranki, "Economic Problems of the Danube Region after the Break-Up of the Austro-Hungarian Monarchy," *Journal of Contemporary History* 4, no. 3 (1969): 169–185; Georges de Ménil and Mathilde, "Breaking Up a Customs Union: The Case of the Austro-Hungarian Empire in 1919," *Weltwirtschaftliches Archiv* 130, no. 3 (1994): 553–575; Rawi Abdelal, "Purpose and Privation: Nation and Economy in Post-Habsburg Eastern Europe and Post-Soviet Eurasia," *East European Politics and Societies* 16, no. 3 (2002): 898–933; Peter M. Garber and Michael G. Spencer, *The Dissolution of the Austro-Hungarian Empire: Lessons for Currency Reform* (Princeton, NJ: International Finance Section, Department of Economics, Princeton University, 1994); and Richard Roberts, "A Stable Currency in Search of a Stable Empire? The Austro-Hungarian Experience of Monetary Union," History and Policy, October 1, 2011, http://www.historyandpolicy .org/policy-papers/papers/a-stable-currency-in-search-of-a-stable-empire-the-austro -hungarian-experie.

31. Radmila Matejčić, "Krune Citta di Fiume i problemi valute u Rijeci od godine 1918–1924," *Numizmatičke vijesti* 20 (1963): 54–71. There has been some work on nonstate actors keeping cross-regional crown networks alive, including through "crown hoarding," in the different successor states. For example, see Mira Kolar-Dimitrijević, *The History of Money in Croatia, 1527–1941* (Zagreb: Croatian National Bank, 2018); J. van Walré de Bordes, *The Austrian Crown, Its Depreciation and Stabilization* (London: P. S. King and Son, 1924); and Stephen G. Gross and S. Chase Gummer, "Ghosts of the Habsburg Empire: Collapsing Currency Unions and Lessons for the Eurozone," *East European Politics and Societies and Cultures* 28, no. 1 (2014): 252–265.

32. Máté Rigó notes an "amateurism" in currency conversion procedures similar to that exhibited in Fiume throughout post-WWI Europe. For a fascinating analysis of how currency conversions fared in post-Habsburg Romania compared with post-German Alsace-Lorraine, see Máté Rigó, "Transcending the East-West Divide: Towards a European History of Post-1918 Transitions," within the forum "Trasformazioni e transizioni imperiali sulla scia della Grande guerra (1917–1923)," *Passato e presente* 2019, n. 106, 41.

33. Del Bello-Smoquina-Zustovich-Velcich-Fischbein counterfeiting trial, 1920, 761 Krivični predmeti 1920, 10 spis 86, HR-DARI, 35.

34. Ibid., 23–25.

35. Maria née Butković Tisma, Statement for appeal—Giorgio-Darinka Tisma rape trial, July 14, 1920, 761 Krivični predmeti 1920, 190 spis 23, HR-DARI.

36. Comando dell'Esercito italiano in Fiume d'Italia, Ufficio Informazioni, Women interrogated for traveling to Bakar, June 26, 1920, cass. 249 Uff. info. Com. Esercito It., 27 giu. 1920, prot. 1802, AFV.

37. Stefania née Diracca Stefan, Appeal trial testimony, August 20, 1920, 761 Krivični predmeti 1920, 208 spis 24, HR-DARI.

38. Questore, Complaint of body searches performed on women, June 7, 1920, cass. 40, prot. 2797, AFV.

39. Paolo Rukavina, Complaint of 540 crowns sequestered, December 11, 1919, cass. 36, prot. 7467, AFV.

40. Consiglio nazionale italiano, Decree controlling speculation of Italian lire, April 3, 1919, 3, predmet 1, HR-DARI, 31. Consiglio nazionale italiano di Fiume, Decree on stamping Austro-Hungarian banknotes in Fiume Territory, April 9, 1919, 3, predmet 1, HR-DARI, 35–36.

41. Consiglio nazionale italiano, Decree setting fixed exchange rate of Fiume crown to Italian lira, April 9, 1919, 3, predmet 1, HR-DARI, 34.

42. Sezione d'approvvigionamento, Rations office warns of lacking Fiume crowns, July 31, 1919, cass. 34, prot. 5448, AFV.

43. Sezione d'approvvigionamento, Rations office warns of lacking Fiume crowns, August 10, 1919, cass. 34, prot. 5448, AFV.

44. Magistrato civico, Request on how to proceed with taxation without sufficient Fiume-crowns available, July 2, 1919, cass. 33, prot. 4818, AFV. Note on backside of business complaints indicates second round of stamping should resolve the problem (dated January 28, 1920).

45. Borsa Mercantile, Complaint about lacking small denomination bills, February 16, 1920, cass. 45, prot. 956, AFV.

46. Lazarus Fabbriche Cussar, Skull, Warning on need to fire employees unless receive small-denomination bills, February 24, 1920, cass. 45, prot. 1052, AFV.

47. Ufficio Informazioni, Intercepted messages from Danubius factory, November 20, 1919, cass. 249, prot. 288, Uff. info. Com. Esercito It., AFV.

48. Magistrato civico, Complaints of workers' representatives, February 3, 1920, cass. 38, prot. 874, AFV.

49. Vio Zoris, Letter to the economic finance office of the city military command, March 10, 1920, 761 Krivični predmeti 1920, 189, HR-DARI, 2.

50. Vio Zoris, Second letter to the economic finance office of the city military command, March 13, 1920, 761 Krivični predmeti 1920, 189, HR-DARI, 3.

51. Vio Zoris, Letter to the economic finance office of the city military command, March 10, 1920, 761 Krivični predmeti 1920, 189, HR-DARI, 2.

52. Clemente Marassich, Letter to Fiume city magistrate requesting to forestall employing him, October 3, 1919, 42 Školsko vijeće Rijeka 1919, Opći Spis 198, HR-DARI. Marassich was one of the most outspoken pro-Italian annexation journalists in Fiume. He changed his last name to Marassi in 1919 and later became D'Annunzio's rector of labor under his short-lived Carnaro Regency.

53. Giuseppe Stefan, Letter to Fiume school council asking for job reinstatement, April 9, 1920, 42 Školsko vijeće Rijeka Opći Spis 1920, 139, HR-DARI.

54. Enrico Bombig, Letter to Fiume city magistrate regarding problems receiving Fiume pension, February 12, 1919, 541 Općina Rijeka 1918–1945, D68/1901, Opći spisi 4204, HR-DARI.

55. Enrico Bombig, Letter to Fiume city magistrate rejecting payment of Fiume pension until annexation, May 20, 1919, 541 Općina Rijeka 1918–1945, D68/1901, Opći spisi 12445, HR-DARI.

56. Magistrato civico, Complaints of workers' representatives, February 3, 1920, cass. 38, prot. 874, AFV.

57. Magistrato civico, Request for Bombig family to be given government's official exchange rate, July 28, 1919, cass. 34, prot. 5238, AFV.

58. Massagrande, *I verbali del Consiglio Nazionale Italiano*, 103.

59. Ibid., 20.

60. Parlato, *Mezzo secolo di Fiume.*

61. Consiglio scolastico, Minutes, December 8, 1918, 42 Školsko vijeće Rijeka 1919, Opći Spis 19, HR-DARI.

62. Consiglio scolastico, Minutes, January 16, 1919, 42 Školsko vijeće Rijeka 1919, Opći Spis 22, HR-DARI.

63. Consiglio scolastico, Minutes, March 10, 1919, 42 Školsko vijeće Rijeka 1919, Opći Spis 22, HR-DARI.

64. Carlo Todiseo, Letter to Italian National Council explaining 300 lire gift, March 10, 1919, cass. 241-1919, prot. 1714, AFV. As a sidenote, the three hundred lire were promptly converted into crowns to purchase food and clothing.

65. Civica Scuola Elementare di San Giovanni (Pehlin), Letter to Fiume school council describing visit of Italian dignitaries, April 15, 1920, 42 Školsko vijeće Rijeka Opći Spis 1920, 147, HR-DARI.

66. Consiglio nazionale italiano, Letter to Comitato Centrale Pro Liberati e Liberatori-Padova, July 31, 1920, cass. 241-1919, prot. 1164, AFV.

67. Károly Fischbein, Police testimony, December 31, 1919, 761 Krivični predmeti 1920, 10 spis 42, HR-DARI.

68. Ibid.

69. Giovanni Bonmartini, Testimony against Eugenio Casagrande, March 31, 1920, cass. 250, Comm. inch. uff. All. 7, AFV.

70. Schlesinger, "Disintegration of the Austro-Hungarian Currency," 27–29.

71. Ibid., 30–31.

72. Walré de Bordes, *Austrian Crown*, 236, quoted in Dornbusch, "Monetary Problems of Post-communism," 416.

73. Dornbusch, "Monetary Problems of Post-Communism," 414–416. Czech crowns were the highest-valued stamped crown (thanks to the new provisional states' extreme deflationary measures), so though many tried to forge the Czech stamp, unstamped bills were worth much less in Czechoslovakia than in the other successor states.

74. David Petruccelli makes this point as well and provides a fascinating glimpse into how post-WWI counterfeiting exploded throughout east central Europe, but also how networks of counterfeiting strengthened preexisting Habsburg networks, while triggering the formation of international policing administrations throughout all of Europe. David Petruccelli, "Banknotes from the Underground: Counterfeiting and the International Order in Interwar Europe," *Journal of Contemporary History* 51, no. 3 (2016): 507–530.

75. Yugoslav crowns did not even have a single national stamp. Instead local banks, credit institutes, and administrative offices throughout the ex-Habsburg lands of the newly forming Kingdom of Serbs, Croats, and Slovenes each created their own stamps, leading to even more

chaos and even more ease in counterfeiting. See Matejčić, "Krune Citta di Fiume i problemi valute."

76. Stamping was limited to higher-denomination notes because of fear of the cost and confusion that would arise from instituting another recall. By December 1919 D'Annunzio's command had two representatives within the Italian National Council's Credit Institute, in the hope that more oversight could lead to less corruption and chaos. Unfortunately, however, it appears that many in D'Annunzio's command also looked at the stamping campaign as an opportunity for illicit moneymaking.

77. "Verso la regolazione della nostra valuta," *La vedetta d'Italia*, October 10, 1919.

78. Associated Press, "Fiume Blockade Ordered by Italy," *New York Times*, March 1, 1920, quoted in Tea Mayhew, *Krvavi Božić 1920: Riječka avantura Gabriela D'Annunzija* (Rijeka: Pomorski i povijesni muzej Hrvatskog Primorja Rijeka, 2010), 82.

79. Consiglio nazionale italiano, Decree declaring all monies must be transferred to city credit institute for currency control, October 6, 1919, 3, predmet 1, HR-DARI, 75–77.

80. Matejčić, "Krune Citta di Fiume i problemi valute." In April 1919, on the first round of stamping, the Fiume provisional government had stamped 47,743,190 Fiume crowns. In October 1919, 120,094,240 Fiume crowns were submitted for restamping. Forged stamps were accepted at face value by the government and individuals received newly stamped crowns to replace their forged crowns, at no loss. Upon the September 1921 recall, circa 124,500,000 Fiume crowns were submitted, though only 120,094,240 Fiume crowns had been stamped by the Fiume provisional government in October 1919.

81. Associated Press, "Fiume Blockade Ordered by Italy." As a sidenote, currently, an unstable money supply in G20 countries is determined by the number of forged bills per million, not per hundred. A stable supply is anything below fifty forged notes per million circulated. See Grant Robertson, "Funny Money: How Counterfeiting Led to a Major Overhaul of Canada's Money," *Globe and Mail*, December 3, 2011.

82. Questura, Discussion of police's success at stemming forgery crisis, January 15, 1920, cass. 38, prot. 321, AFV.

83. All of the police reports and trial records are held in "Del Bello-Smoquina-Zustovich-Velcich-Fischbein Counterfeiting Trial," 761 Krivični predmeti 1920, 10 spis 86, HR-DARI.

84. The other four defendants were the 23-year-old unemployed mechanic and veteran Umberto Smoquina, the 23-year-old unemployed mechanic Vilibaldo Zustovich, the 26-year-old veteran and clerk at the Fiume tax office Bruno Velcich, and the aforementioned 38-year-old Hungarian investor and businessman Károly Fischbein.

85. Just a few examples of xenophobic articles equating counterfeiting with "national enemies" include "I nuovi decreti per la valuta," *La vedetta d'Italia*, October 11, 1919; "Verso la regolazione della nostra valuta; Ingordi speculatori," *La vedetta d'Italia*, September 26, 1919; "Gli strozzini sono avvisati," *La vedetta d'Italia*, September 24, 1919; "Ospiti non desiderati," *La vedetta d'Italia*, September 19, 1919; "Ancora strozzini e speculatori," *La vedetta d'Italia*, September 6, 1919.

86. Bürger escaped trial because she fled the city for her hometown, Villach, before the police could apprehend her.

87. Elvira née Teck Gattinoni, Police statement, December 4, 1919, 761 Krivični predmeti 1919, 43 spis 3, HR-DARI.

88. Giorgio Rora, Police statement, December 29, 1919, 761 Krivični predmeti 1920, 10 spis 29, HR-DARI.

89. Simeone Radovich, Court testimony, January 26, 1920, 761 Krivični predmeti 1920, 10 spis 86, HR-DARI, 22–23.

90. Antonio Bauk, Court testimony, January 26, 1920, 761 Krivični predmeti 1920, 10 spis 86, HR-DARI, 24.

91. Cosimo Domancich, Court testimony, January 26, 1920, 761 Krivični predmeti 1920, 10 spis 86, HR-DARI, 25–26.

92. Annone Erbisti, Police statement, December 27, 1919, 761 Krivični predmeti 1920, 10 spis 16, HR-DARI.

93. Renato Skarso, Police statement, December 27, 1919, 761 Krivični predmeti 1920, 10 spis 24, HR-DARI.

94. Elvira née Teck Gattinoni, Police statement, December 4, 1919, 761 Krivični predmeti 1919, 43 spis 3, HR-DARI.

95. Simeone Radovich, Court testimony, January 26, 1920, 761 Krivični predmeti 1920, 10 spis 86, HR-DARI, 22–23.

96. Ferdinando Cretich, Police statement, December 29, 1919, 761 Krivični predmeti 1920, 10 spis 27, HR-DARI.

97. Felice Derenzin, Court testimony, December 27, 1919, 761 Krivični predmeti 1920, 10 spis 86, HR-DARI, 28–30.

98. Ervino Fürst, Court testimony, December 27, 1919, 761 Krivični predmeti 1920, 10 spis 86, HR-DARI, 27. Military trials headed by D'Annunzio's command showcased how legionnaires, too, participated in these exchanges both to enrich themselves and to cover the debts incurred by D'Annunzio's command. For example, in March 1920 legionnaires Amedeo Freddi and Eligio Casini were apprehended in a car driving to Trieste with hundreds of thousands of forged crowns. The interpenetration of legionnaires' and Fiumians' counterfeiting and money exchange practices went all the way to the top of the pyramid: the Italian war hero and future Fascist organizer Ulisse Igliori blithely testified in March 1920 that he and the head organizer of D'Annunzio's command, Giovanni Giuriati, sold the Italian government seven million Fiume crowns at the rate of forty cents and then "went to the various banks looking for a rate of 23 or 24 cents." See Rettore per gl'Interni e per la Giustizia, Discussion of legal parameters surrounding imprisonment of Freddi and Casini for counterfeiting, October 6, 1920, cass. 50, prot. 230, AFV; and Ulisse Igliori, Testimony on money exchange ordered by D'Annunzio, March 26, 1920, cass. 250, Comm. inch. uff. All. 14, AFV.

99. Carlo Trevisani Scoppa, Letter titled Reserved-Personal, December 19, 1919, cass. 250, Comm. inch. uff. All. 38, AFV. The bank in question was the Banca Cooperativa di Fiume, and the operations were organized by Andrea Ossoinack, one of Fiume's most powerful businessmen and the city's representative at the Paris Peace Conference. According to Trevisani Scoppa, Ossoinack's negotiations with Igliori also supplied the bank with a profit of over two million Fiume crowns through these operations and perhaps even more if the one-to-one exchange rate was realized with annexation. Igliori, in fact, would rise very high politically. After the Christmas of Blood, he became a leading member of Mussolini's Fascist squads, helping organize the March on Rome, and rose to the level of head of Mussolini's militia, state deputy, and national consigliere. He also opened several construction firms that made a fortune building state-affiliated projects in Rome, Florence, and Trieste.

100. Ibid.

101. Giuseppe Maranini, *Lettere da Fiume alla fidanzata*, 60–61.

102. Ibid.

103. Zara Steiner, *The Lights That Failed: European International History, 1919–1933*, Oxford History of Modern Europe (Oxford: Oxford University Press, 2005).

104. For excellent synthetic essays, see Gross and Gummer, "Ghosts of the Habsburg Empire"; and Innerhofer, "Post-war Economies (South East Europe)." The case of Austria is the most well-known because of its hyperinflation, the League of Nations loan it triggered, and the arguments for Anschluss (unification of Germany and Austria) that the currency crisis helped inspire. For more information on the importance of economics in League of Nations initiatives in post-Habsburg Europe, especially Austria, see Patricia Clavin, *Securing the World Economy: The Reinvention of the League of Nations, 1920–1946* (Oxford: Oxford University Press, 2013).

105. L. B. Namier, "Currencies and Exchanges in an East Galician Village," in *Skyscrapers, and Other Essays* (London: Macmillan, 1931), 163–172.

106. Czechoslovakia is consistently cited as the most successful example of a successor state that fueled a rather harsh economic nationalist policy, resulting eventually in a relatively stable economic and political regime. For more on this, see Alice Teichova, *The Czechoslovak Economy 1918–1980* (London: Routledge, 2012). Fiume's neighbor is perhaps the most disastrous example of how crown conversion triggered more nationalist tensions between different communities within its lands, especially in Croatia. For more on this fascinating story, see the several publications by John Lampe on Balkan economic history, especially John R. Lampe, "Unifying the Yugoslav Economy, 1918–1921: Misery and Early Misunderstandings," in *The Creation of Yugoslavia, 1914–1918*, ed. Dimitrije Đorđević (Santa Barbara: Clio Books, 1980).

3. Legal Ins and Outs

1. Masovcević/Sluga trial records, 1920, 761 Krivični predmeti 1919, 40 spis 24, HR-DARI, 9.

2. Ibid., 10.

3. Ibid., 11.

4. Del Bello-Smoquina-Zustovich-Velcich-Fischbein Counterfeiting Trial, 1920, 761 Krivični predmeti 1920, 10 spis 86, HR-DARI, 14.

5. Giuseppe Maranini, *Lettere da Fiume alla fidanzata* (Milan: Pan, 1973), 60–61.

6. For discussions on the intrinsic "layered" nature of imperial sovereignty, see Jane Burbank and Frederick Cooper, *Empires in World History: Power and the Politics of Difference* (Princeton, NJ: Princeton University Press, 2010); and Lauren A. Benton, *A Search for Sovereignty: Law and Geography in European Empires, 1400–1900* (New York: Cambridge University Press, 2010).

7. Antonio Allazetta, Loyalty oath, June 12, 1915, 541 Općina Rijeka 1918–1945, Opći spisi 20059, B59/a/1925, HR-DARI.

8. Antonio Allazetta, Loyalty oath, April 22, 1917, 541 Općina Rijeka 1918–1945, Opći spisi 12821, B59/a/1925, HR-DARI.

9. Gemina Benussi, Loyalty oath, January 19, 1918, 541 Općina Rijeka 1918–1945, Opći spisi 2105, D17/1917, HR-DARI.

10. Francesco Gilberto Corossacz, Announcement of Fiume municipal elections, July 9, 1915, 22 Gradsko poglavarstvo Rijeka, L34/1915, HR-DARI.

11. Nicolò Gelletich, *Autonomia di Fiume—appunti storici e considerazioni—Studi di un vecchio fiumano* (Fiume: Mohovich, 1901), 5–6, 42–43. Another common metaphor used to

describe Hungary's relationship to Fiume was that of husband to wife, a point I am grateful Ágnes Ordasi clarified for me.

12. For a fascinating discussion of how this administrative structure within many parts of the Hungarian Kingdom reveals domestic Hungary's imperial setup, see Gábor Egry, "Regional Elites, Nationalist Politics, Local Accommodations: Center-Periphery Struggles in Late Dualist Hungary," in *Österreich-Ungarns imperiale Herausforderungen: Nationalismen und Rivalitäten im Habsburgerreich um 1900*, ed. Bernhard Bachinger, Wolfram Dornik, and Stephan Lehnstaedt (Göttingen: V&R Unipress, 2019).

13. Francesco Gilberto Corossacz, Announcement of Fiume municipal elections, July 9, 1915, 22 Gradsko poglavarstvo Rijeka, L34/1915, HR-DARI.

14. Autonomism—a movement of local patriotism that advocated continued self-government within Hungarian state initiatives, based on the particularities of the city's commercial trade and its Italianate-Hungarian-Croatian body politic—was such a widespread ideology that it won adherents from among all the economic-political ideologies gaining ground in the city landscape, from extreme free-capital liberals to radical socialists. There has been much work on the importance of Fiume autonomism in the early twentieth century. Of particular note are the many publications by Ljubinka Toševa-Karpowicz, William Klinger, Gianluca Volpi, and Giovanni Stelli. For a truly beautiful article showing how autonomist ideas, multicultural values, support for continued Italian cultural dominance, and socialist leanings played out together in Fiume, see Ivan Jeličić, "Sulle tracce di una biografia perduta: Samuele Mayländer," *Quaderni: Centro di Ricerche storiche-Rovigno* 26 (2015): 227–269.

15. For a discussion of Fiume's legal status and battles between the Free City and the Hungarian Kingdom between the 1870s and 1914, see Luigi Peteani, *La posizione internazionale di Fiume dall'armistizio all'annessione e il suo assetto costituzionale durante questo periodo* (Florence: C. Cya, 1940). Also see Amleto Ballarini, *L'antidannunzio a Fiume: Riccardo Zanella*, Città di vita (Trieste: Italo Svevo, 1995), chap. 1.

16. Request from Hungarian Royal Governor to Fiume Civic Magistrate for city's education statute, January 31, 1918, 541 Općina Rijeka 1918–1945, Opći spisi 3664, D22/1911, HR-DARI.

17. Fiume's chamber of commerce and industry budget report, March 31, 1919, 179 Trgovačko–Obrtnička Komora 1919, kut. 195, spis 2914, HR-DARI.

18. Camera di commercio e d'industria, Research into pension increase, September 18, 1918, 179 Trgovačko–Obrtnička Komora 1918, kut. 231, spis 2401, HR-DARI.

19. Magistrato civico, Fiume tax proposal on entertainments in aid of war widows and orphans, January 19, 1917, 541 Općina Rijeka 1918–1945, Opći spisi 29272, E145/1917, HR-DARI.

20. Camera di commercio e d'industria, Research into and petition for pension, September 18, 1918, 179 Trgovačko–Obrtnička Komora 1918, kut. 231, spis 2401, HR-DARI.

21. Lawsuit by Mario Rossi against Hartweg Dry Cleaners, May 31, 1918, 112 Gradjanski i Krivični predmeti 1918, 2257, spis 1, HR-DARI.

22. Antonio Grossich, Letter to the US Secretary of State [in English], December 21, 1918, cass. 241-1918, prot. s.n., AFV. Quarnero/Kvarner is the name of the gulf that opens up south of Fiume.

23. Gilbert Close, Letter to National Council of Fiume [in English], December 23, 1918, cass. 241-1919, prot. 44, AFV.

24. Press Illustrating Service, Letter to Antonio Vio, Mayor of Fiume [in English], March 3, 1919, cass. 241-1919, prot. 3039, AFV.

25. Federazione Società Irredentiste Italo-Americane, Letter to Antonio Vio, Mayor of Fiume [in English], May 15, 1919, cass. 241-1919, prot. 4680, AFV.

26. For a fascinatingly similar case about postal confusion regarding names and geopolitical shifts, see Peter Bugge, "The Making of a Slovak City: The Czechoslovak Renaming of Pressburg/Pozsony/Prešporok, 1918–19," *Austrian History Yearbook* 35, no. 1 (2004): 205–227.

27. Natasha Wheatley, "Central Europe as Ground Zero of the New International Order," *Slavic Review* 78, no. 4 (Winter 2019), 901.

28. Vladimir Lenin, "Decree on Peace, October 26, 1917," in *The Bolshevik Revolution, 1917–1918: Documents and Materials,* ed. James Bunyan and Harold Henry Fisher (Stanford, CA: Stanford University Press, 1961).

29. David Lloyd George, "British War Aims, January 5, 1918," in *English Historical Documents, 1906–1939,* ed. J. H. Bettey (London: Routledge and Kegan Paul, 1967).

30. Woodrow Wilson, "Fourteen Points, January 8, 1918," in *Our Documents: 100 Milestone Documents from the National Archives,* ed. Michael Beschloss (New York: Oxford University Press, 2006).

31. Addetti italiani al Tramvia elettrico, Appeal to Fiume Italian National Council to have Croatians fired, January 20, 1919, cass. 241-1919, prot. 604.a, AFV.

32. Antonio Vio, Speech to head of Inter-Allied Forces after clash with French troops, January 24, 1919, cass. 241-1919, prot. 414, AFV.

33. Ibid.

34. This is not to say that the general populace of Fiume supported the Italian National Council's right to act as the governing body. Throughout all the archives, memoirs, and contemporary newspaper accounts it is clear that many considered it filled with nepotistic, corrupt, and self-serving men. Many also did not agree with its general policy to push for annexation to Italy instead of accepting independence or pushing for annexation to the Kingdom of Serbs, Croats, and Slovenes. Nonetheless, the Italian National Council did act as the provisional government at the moment, and its "laws in force" were the laws of Fiume to which Fiumians were held accountable. For an example of a contemporary account that recognized how unpopularity and the power of legislation were seen as unwelcome yet undeniable bedfellows, see J. N. Macdonald, *A Political Escapade: The Story of Fiume and D'Annunzio* (London: J. Murray, 1921). Here the Jesuit priest went to great lengths in his scathing memoir of D'Annunzio's "escapade" to underscore the corrupt and bullying qualities of the Italian National Council; nonetheless, he summarized its new post-1918 power as such: "[The Italian National Council] gradually assumed more and more authority, until from a purely administrative, it became a legislative body." Ibid., 37. A similar, critical contemporary assessment of the Italian National Council's lacking rights to rule, yet recognition of its new legislative power, can be found in the edited memoir of Hungarian state bureaucrat Egan Lajos (which includes documents in Hungarian and Italian). Ágnes Ordasi, *Egan Lajos naplója— Impériumváltások Fiumében a kormányzóhelyettes szemével (1918–1920)* (Budapest: MTA Történettudományi Intézet, 2019).

35. Del Bello-Smoquina-Zustovich-Velcich-Fischbein Counterfeiting Trial, 1920, 761 Krivični predmeti 1920, 10 spis 86, HR-DARI, 14. Throughout her work, Ljubinka Toševa-Karpowicz has always maintained that the Italian National Council approached its modus operandi as lawyers would, in part thanks to the fact that many of them had studied law (mostly in Budapest and Vienna). For a work analyzing the generational aspect of this transition of Fiume elites from professionals solely dedicated to maritime trade to ones also in-

corporating law, see Ivan Jeličić, "Ekonomsko-socijalna struktura promicateljskog odbora riječkog Književnog kruga (Circolo letterario)," *Zbornik Kastavštine* 21 (2017): 323–341.

36. The Inter-Allied and D'Annunzio commands did try to influence or override local administrative authority (and often succeeded in doing so). This was especially true during the D'Annunzio period after March 1920, culminating in the September 1920 declaration of the Regency of Carnaro.

37. Antonio Allazetta, Loyalty oath, June 12, 1915, 541 Općina Rijeka 1918–1945, Opći spisi 20059, B59/a/1925, HR-DARI.

38. Antonio Allazetta, Loyalty oath, May 9, 1919, 541 Općina Rijeka 1918–1945, Opći spisi 10980, B21/1919, HR-DARI. In December 1918, many Hungarian state bureaucrats were also explicitly asked to recognize in writing the Italian National Council (and not the government in Budapest) as the rightful governing body of Fiume, or else face termination, though no loyalty oath was instated.

39. Elisabetta Sirola, Loyalty oath, June 28, 1920, 541 Općina Rijeka 1918–1945, Opći spisi 10980, Opći spisi 12840 D32/1920, HR-DARI. In her oath she used "Elisa" instead of her legal name, Elisabetta.

40. Consiglio nazionale italiano, Decree that all legal bulletins and official notices will be published in Fiume, January 22, 1919, 3, predmet 1, HR-DARI.

41. Consiglio nazionale italiano, Decree of new regulations for law exams and qualifications, January 25, 1919, 3, predmet 1, HR-DARI.

42. Ibid.; Elisabetta Sirola, Loyalty oath, June 28, 1920, 541 Općina Rijeka 1918–1945, Opći spisi 10980, Opći spisi 12840 D32/1920, HR-DARI.

43. Consiglio nazionale italiano, Decree of new regulations for property, loans, and rents in regards to Hungary, March 16, 1919, 3, predmet 1, HR-DARI.

44. Consiglio nazionale italiano, Decree replacing references to "Hungarian citizen" with "pertinent of Fiume" in law codes, April 2, 1919, 3, predmet 1, HR-DARI. Explanations on what "pertinent" meant are discussed in Chapter 4.

45. Ivančić vs. Rošić Fiume civil suit, November 9, 1918, 112 Gradjanski i Krivični predmeti 1918, 1157, HR-DARI.

46. Consiglio nazionale italiano, Decree that all legal bulletins and official notices will be published in Fiume, January 22, 1919, 3, predmet 1, HR-DARI.

47. Consiglio nazionale italiano, Response from the department of commerce, industry, and agriculture in regards to application for formation of hotel corporation, September 19, 1920, 541 Općina Rijeka 1918–1945, Opći spisi 11528, F3/1922, HR-DARI.

48. Antonio Vio, Speech to head of Inter-Allied Forces after clash with French troops, January 24, 1919, cass. 241-1919, prot. 414, AFV.

49. Throughout the minutes of the Italian National Council, fears about growing socialist and Bolshevik tendencies abound. Licenses and permission to remain in Fiume were also regularly denied to anyone suspected of working to promote Bolshevik ideas. Though these impediments were often put in place in conjunction with nationalist reasonings ("Croatian," "Slav," and "Yugoslav" were often used as synonyms for "Bolshevik" and vice versa), the fear of social revolution among Fiume's liberal conservative provisional government was real.

50. Stefano Szorger and Enrico Bérczi, Request for metal worker license, December 21, 1919, 541 Općina Rijeka 1918–1945, Opći spisi 31936, Q19/19, HR-DARI.

51. For the clearest and most well-researched analysis of the structural formation of Fiume's municipal and government structures, see Ljubinka Karpowicz, "Riječki corpus separatum 1868–1924" (PhD diss., Univerza Edvarda Kardelja v Ljubljani, 1986).

52. Consiglio nazionale italiano, Decree affirming Italian National Council government of Fiume, January 22, 1919, 3, predmet 1, HR-DARI, 6–12. Article 10 of this same document reiterates the Italian National Council's commitment to unifying Fiume with Italy: "Both the president and vice-president in a special meeting of the National Council have solemnly promised and will dedicate themselves with honor and all the powers they hold to achieve the unification of Fiume to Italy."

53. Ivančić vs. Rošić Fiume civil suit, November 9, 1918, 112 Gradjanski i Krivični predmeti 1918, 1157, HR-DARI.

54. Consiglio nazionale italiano, Decree affirming Italian National Council government of Fiume, January 22, 1919, 3, predmet 1, HR-DARI, 6–12.

55. Consiglio nazionale italiano, Decree substituting all Hungarian symbols of state with their Italian equivalent, March 27, 1919, 3, predmet 1, HR-DARI, 24–25.

56. Delegato all'amministrazione della Giustizia-Consiglio nazionale, Report on expected demonstration of "Croatian" lawyers who refused to take the required loyalty oath, June 21, 1919, cass. 241-1919, prot. 3970, AFV.

57. Woodrow Wilson, "Statement of President Wilson Regarding the Disposition of Fiume," *Chicago Tribune,* April 24, 1919.

58. Speeches by Antonio Grossich and General Grazioli regarding Fiume's proposed self-annexation to Italy, April 26, 1919, cass. 241-1919, prot. 2880, AFV.

59. Consiglio nazionale italiano, Decree giving state powers of Fiume to Italy, April 26, 1919, cass. 241-1919, prot. 2866, AFV.

60. Wilson, "Statement."

61. Consiglio nazionale italiano, Decree substituting the Hungarian penal code with the Italian penal code, March 27, 1919, cass. 241-1919, prot. 2164, AFV.

62. Wilson, "Statement"; Consiglio nazionale italiano, Decree that the Hungarian legal code will now be replaced with the Italian legal code, May 12, 1919, 3, predmet 1, HR-DARI, 51–52.

63. Consiglio nazionale italiano, Decree substituting the Hungarian penal code with the Italian penal code, March 27, 1919, cass. 241-1919, prot. 2164, AFV.

64. Ibid.

65. Camera di commercio e d'industria, Research into and petition for pension increase, September 18, 1918, 179 Trgovačko–Obrtnička Komora 1918, kut. 231, spis 2401, HR-DARI.

66. R. Esercito Italiano-Comando Supremo, Pamphlet outlining tax code for Venezia-Giulia, June 28, 1919, 541 Općina Rijeka 1918–1945, Opći spisi 22247, E145/1917, HR-DARI.

67. Eszter Cs. Herger, "The Introduction of Secular Divorce Law in Hungary, 1895–1918: Social and Legal Consequences for Women," *Journal on European History of Law* 3, no. 2 (2012): 138–148; Robert Nemes, "The Uncivil Origins of Civil Marriage: Hungary," in *Culture Wars: Secular-Catholic Conflict in Nineteenth-Century Europe,* ed. Christopher Clark and Wolfram Kaiser (Cambridge: Cambridge University Press, 2003).

68. Herger, "Introduction of Secular Divorce Law," 141.

69. Nenad Hlača, "Razvod braka u Rijeci početkom 20. stoljeća," *Zbornik Pravnog fakulteta u Rijeci* 8 (1987): 93–108.

70. Giuseppe Német, Testimony given to begin divorce proceedings, September 18, 1918, 112 Gradjanski i Krivični predmeti 1918, 1005, spis 1, HR-DARI.

71. Emerico Koós, Testimony given to begin divorce proceedings, October 3, 1918, 112 Gradjanski i Krivični predmeti 1918, 1065, spis 1, HR-DARI.

72. Giuseppina Sluga, Testimony given to begin divorce proceedings, March 12, 1920, 112 Gradjanski i Krivični predmeti 1918, kutija 719, 1006, HR-DARI.

73. Mark Seymour, *Debating Divorce in Italy: Marriage and the Making of Modern Italians, 1860–1974* (New York: Palgrave Macmillan, 2006).

74. Ibid., 74–78.

75. Consiglio nazionale italiano, Decree instituting universal suffrage, September 9, 1919, 3, predmet 1, HR-DARI, 68.

76. Edoardo Susmel, Letter to the Consiglio Nazionale Italiano di Fiume, June 13, 1919, cass. 241-1919, prot. 3859, AFV.

77. Corpo insegnante dell'Istituto Tecnico Leonardo da Vinci, Minutes, November 25, 1920, 42 Školsko vijeće Rijeka, Opći Spis 1920, Riječko Nacionalno vijeće 27, HR-DARI.

78. Ibid.

79. Hlača, "Razvod braka u Rijeci početkom 20. stoljeća."

80. For a fascinating case showing how Austrian subjects followed similar sneaky techniques to obtain a divorce in Hungary, see Ulrike Harmat, "Divorce and Remarriage in Austria-Hungary: The Second Marriage of Franz Conrad von Hötzendorf," *Austrian History Yearbook* 32 (2001): 69–102.

81. Serenissima Repubblica di San Marino, Telegraph, April 4, 1919, cass. 241-1919, prot. 2384, AFV. It would be fascinating to learn whether Fiumians knew anything about the high degree of autonomy awarded to Italy's North African colonies (in today's Libya) in the immediate postwar period. For more on this, see Roberta Pergher, "National Claims and the Rights of Others: Italy and Its Newly Found Territories after the First World War," in *Beyond Versailles: Sovereignty, Legitimacy, and the Formation of New Polities after the Great War*, ed. Marcus M. Payk and Roberta Pergher (Bloomington: Indiana University Press, 2019).

82. Serenissima Repubblica di San Marino, Telegraph, April 4, 1919, cass. 241-1919, prot. 2384, AFV.

83. Much has been written of late about the Carnaro constitution, especially because of its open challenges to the Italian state, its corporatist initiatives for the reorganization of labor, its supposedly non-chauvinist and egalitarian definitions of active citizenship, and its quirky emphasis that music should anchor social change. Though little of the document reflects Fiumian legal culture, two things within it do: universal suffrage and the right to divorce. For more on the Carnaro constitution, see Renzo De Felice, ed., *La Carta del Carnaro nei testi di Alceste De Ambris e di Gabriele D'Annunzio* (Bologna: il Mulino, 1973); Augusto Sinagra, ed., *Lo Statuto della Reggenza italiana del Carnaro. Tra storia, diritto internazionale e diritto costituzionale. Atti del convegno (Roma, 21 Ottobre 2008)* (Milan: Giuffrè, 2009); Enrico Serventi Longhi, *Alceste De Ambris. L'utopia concreta di un rivoluzionario sindacalista* (Milan: Angeli, 2011).

84. Leo Valiani, "Io ragazzo nella Fiume di D'Annunzio," *Nuova antologia*, no. 2185 (January–March 1993): 71–82. For two fascinating analyses of Valiani's family background and life in Fiume before leaving the town, see Ivan Jeličić, "The Waizen Family and Young Leo Valiani in Fiume," *Časopis za povijest Zapadne Hrvatske* 10 (2015): 25–42; and Vanni D'Alessio, "Leo Weiczen Valiani and His Multilayered Identities: An Introduction," *Časopis za povijest Zapadne Hrvatske* 10 (2015): 11–20.

4. Between City and State

1. Questura, Police report for arrest of Francesco Pospek, March 22, 1919, 1108 Opći spis 1919, 684, HR-DARI.

2. Ibid.

3. Ibid.

4. Ibid.

5. A fascinating detail about Castellicchio, who served in Fiume's police force well into Fascist Italy's absorption of the town, is that until 1929 he listed Croatian and German as languages he could speak. After 1929, he listed only German. Also, though born in Vodnjan (outside of Pula, Istria) and not Fiume, Castellicchio had lived in Fiume and worked as a member of Fiume's police force since 1910; he was well aware of how the city's pertinency regime worked, as well as the city's multiethnic makeup. He had also served in the Austro-Hungarian army, had been wounded on the eastern front, and had been treated in Galicia and Hungary before returning to Fiume to take up policeman duties for the new provisional government. Giovanni Castellicchio's personnel file, Osobni dosej Castellicchio Giuseppe, 53 Ured za povjedništva agenata javne sigurnosti osnaka P. I. A., HR-DARI.

6. Questura, Police report for arrest of Francesco Pospek, March 22, 1919, 1108 Opći spis 1919, 684, HR-DARI.

7. In fact, in the March 27, 1919, protocol generated to process Pospek's arrest, he is still listed as a pertinent of Celje (Cilli in the original) and not Fiume. It is possible that Castel-licchio recognized Pospek's new residency card as proof of pertinency or that Pospek pro-duced some other sort of documentation indicating he was a Fiume pertinent or that his per-tinency papers were in process. It is also possible that news of his new pertinency had not yet been made known to the police department that drafted the protocol. In the 1925 Fiume census (produced by the Italian Fascist regime), Pospek is still listed as living legally in Fiume, being unmarried, working as an "employee," and holding "Yugoslav citizenship," which if he was a pertinent he could have opted for. Census cards for individuals living in Fiume, January 1, 1925, Pospek, Francesco, 536 Anagrafska zbirka 1869-1958- Rijeka Osobni karton, HR-DARI.

8. A fascinating article that highlights the complicated relationship between nationality politics, citizenship rights, and localism in immediate postwar Greater Romania (though through very different means) can be found in Gábor Egry, "Navigating the Straits: Changing Borders, Changing Rules and Practices of Ethnicity and Loyalty in Romania after 1918," *Hungarian Historical Review* 2, no. 3 (2013): 449–476.

9. *Guida di Fiume* (Fiume: Minerva, 1915), 2.

10. Jeličić's data here is really quite extraordinary: Though German was not an official government language of Fiume, and only 5 percent listed it as their mother tongue, 24 percent of Fiume's population claimed to speak it. Of the 26 percent who declared Croatian as their mother tongue, only one-third asserted that they were monolingual, with the rest indicating that 54 percent of them knew Italian, 13.4 percent German, and 7.6 percent Hungarian. Less than one-quarter of those who identified German as their mother tongue claimed they were monolingual, with 48 percent saying they knew Italian, 32.8 percent Croatian, and 30.5 percent Hungarian. Among those who identified Hungarian as their mother tongue, 39 percent were monolingual, with 41.5 percent saying they knew German, 33 percent Italian, and 23 percent Serbian and Croatian. As neither those who claimed Italian nor those who claimed Slovene as their mother tongue represented a linguistic group omnipresent throughout the Hungarian Kingdom, the analysis of multilingualism put them in the composite group of "other." Within this Italian-Slovene other category, 45 percent asserted they were monolingual and 42.5 percent said they knew Croatian and Serbian, 17.7 percent German, and 6.2 percent Italian (meaning that of those who claimed Slovene as their mother tongue in this category, 54.7 percent knew Italian). Ivan Jeličić, "Nell'ombra dell'autonomismo: Il movimento socialista a Fiume, 1901–1921" (PhD diss., Universita' degli Studi di Trieste, 2016), 50.

11. The remaining Fiumians were either Muslim or followers of some version of "Eastern Catholicism," which was under the protection of Rome, but had rites resembling those of Orthodox Christianity.

12. For the difficulty of ascertaining exact figures on pertinency for 1900 and 1910, see Ivan Jeličić, "Nell'ombra dell'autonomismo: Il movimento socialista a Fiume, 1901–1921" (PhD diss., Universita' degli Studi di Trieste, 2016), 47.

13. There is a growing, fascinating field of study analyzing the transformations of pertinency within Austria-Hungary and what this category meant to people before and after the war, especially "unwanted" linguistic and religious groups after 1918. For an outstanding English-language synthesis of how this played out in the Austrian half, see Ulrike von Hirschhausen, "From Imperial Inclusion to National Exclusion: Citizenship in the Habsburg Monarchy and in Austria 1867–1923," *European Review of History—Revue européenne d'histoire* 16, no. 4 (2009): 551–573. An excellent resource for understanding all the influences on how this legal category was formed and then reformed in the nineteenth and early twentieth centuries, see Waltraut Heindl and Edith Sauer, *Grenze und Staat: Passwesen, Staatsbürgerschaft, Heimatrecht und Fremdengesetzgebung in der österreichischen Monarchie 1750–1867* (Vienna: Böhlau, 2000); and Helmut Rumpler, Peter Urbanitsch, and Ulrike Harmat, *Von der Stände- zur Klassengesellschaft*, vol. 9, pt. 1 of *Die Habsburgermonarchie 1848–1918: Soziale Strukturen* (Vienna: Austrian Academy of Sciences Press, 2010).

14. As Sylvia Hahn and others have shown, however, in hubs of employment most cities in the Habsburg Monarchy had similar rates of non-pertinents to pertinents in their citizenship rolls. See Sylvia Hahn, *Migration - arbeit - geschlecht: Arbeitsmigration in Mitteleuropa vom 17. bis zum beginn des 20. jahrhunderts* (Göttingen: V&R Unipress, 2008). Sylvia Hahn and Katharine Apostle, "Es gab noch nie so viel Migration wie heute (früher waren die meisten Menschen sesshaft)," in *Migration und integration. Fakten oder mythen?*, ed. Max Haller (Vienna: Austrian Academy of Sciences Press, 2019), 39–54.

15. For the complete list of rules on Fiume pertinency, see *Statuto della libera città di Fiume e del suo distretto* (Fiume: Stabilimento Tipo Litografico di E. Mohovich, 1872).

16. *Statuto della libera citta di Fiume e del suo distretto e regolamenti interni per la rappresentanza e delegazione municipali di Fiume* (Fiume: Battara, 1908), 5–9.

17. The Roma of Austria-Hungary appear not to have been included in this "universally assigned" pertinency regime, with heartbreaking consequences. For more on this, see Tara Zahra, "'Condemned to Rootlessness and Unable to Budge': Roma, Migration Panics, and Internment in the Habsburg Empire," *American Historical Review* 122, no. 3 (2017): 702–726. People living in newly annexed Bosnia and Herzegovina also did not participate in this Austro-Hungarian pertinency-citizenship culture, though Habsburg state officials and military personnel stationed in Bosnia-Herzegovina did. As a sidenote, the German lands and Switzerland also used a pertinency system to organize welfare, suffrage, and right to remain rights.

18. Giorgio Bayer, Application for pertinency, August 16, 1918, 22 Gradsko poglavarstvo Rijeka, Opći spisi L3/1918, 27412/18, HR-DARI. Bayer called the city of his pertinency Münsterberg (as was common at the time), not Ziębice.

19. Nemesia Haller Gambel, Application for pertinency, November 18, 1919, 541 Općina Rijeka spis, Opći spisi L95/1919, 29081/19, HR-DARI.

20. Giovanni Krmpotich, Application for pertinency, November 23, 1917, 22 Gradsko poglavarstvo Rijeka, Opći spisi L3/1918, 35149/17, HR-DARI. His name is variously spelled as Krmpotić, Krmpotic, and Krmpotich throughout his paperwork. Apparently he usually used the diacritic; the pertinency file is titled using the "ich" ending.

21. For an excellent example of this, see Ivan Jeličić, "Sulle tracce di una biografia perduta: Samuele Mayländer," *Quaderni: Centro di Ricerche storiche-Rovigno* 26 (2015): 227–269.

22. Sylvia Hahn, "Inclusion and Exclusion of Migrants in the Multicultural Realm of the Habsburg 'State of Many Peoples,'" *Histoire sociale/Social History* 33, no. 66 (2000): 307–324.

23. According to the 1910 census, 16,689 inhabitants of Fiume did not hold Hungarian citizenship.

24. For a very clear English-language analysis of Hungarian citizenship law, see Norbert Varga, "The Framing of the First Hungarian Citizenship Law (Act 50 of 1879) and the Acquisition of Citizenship," *Hungarian Studies* 18, no. 2 (2004): 127–151.

25. For fascinating work analyzing how Hungarian-Croatian citizenship, pertinency, and language requirements worked, see Ivan Kosnica, "Hrvatsko-slavonska pripadnost u Hrvatskoj i Slavoniji u nagodbenom razdoblju," *Hrvatska i komparativna javna uprava: Časopis za teoriju i praksu javne uprave* 14, no. 2 (2014): 465–492; and Ivan Kosnica, "Zapošljavanje u javnoj upravi u Hrvatskoj i Slavoniji (1868.–1918.) s obzirom na državljanstvo i hrvatsko—slavonsku pripadnost," *Hrvatska i komparativna javna uprava: Časopis za teoriju i praksu javne uprave* 18, no. 4 (2018): 617–641.

26. Francesco Bavec, Application for pertinency, September 16, 1916, 22 Gradsko Poglavarstvo Rijeka, Opći spisi L6/1916, HR-DARI.

27. Ibid.

28. Salvatore Bellasich, Telegram from Fiume relaying research into Italian language use amongst tombstones and ship names, March 15, 1919, cass. 241-1919, prot. 1834, AFV.

29. "La questione di Fiume: Testo del memoriale presentato dai delegati S.H.S. alla conferenza della pace e sua confutazione," April 5, 1919, cass. 241-1919, prot. 415, AFV. Their pamphlet also reinterpreted the Hungarian as such: "24,212 Italians, 6,493 Hungarians, 2,315 Germans, and 15,687 Yugoslavs," whereby they put figures of Croats and Slovenes into one "Yugoslav" category, something the Hungarian census did not do (and would never have done).

30. Ibid.

31. There is far too much literature on post-WWI census taking and nationalist-driven population calculations to mention here. For the case of Trieste, Maura Hametz and Ester Capuzzo have been publishing excellent work analyzing how censuses and pertinency rights were understood in the post-1918 period. A superb volume has recently come out that includes analyses of how plebiscites, censuses, and legal regimes were manipulated throughout the post-Habsburg, Egyptian, and Persian lands; see Roberta Pergher and Marcus M. Payk, eds., *Beyond Versailles: Sovereignty, Legitimacy, and the Formation of New Polities after the Great War* (Bloomington: Indiana University Press, 2019).

32. For wonderful work showing the heavy consequences that could ensue when forced to choose national affiliation, see Tara Zahra, "Imagined Noncommunities: National Indifference as a Category of Analysis," *Slavic Review* 69, no. 1 (2010): 93–119.

33. Emil Brix, *Die Umgangssprachen in Altösterreich zwischen Agitation und Assimilation* (Vienna: Böhlau, 1982).

34. Salvatore Bellasich, Telegram from Fiume relaying research into Italian language use amongst tombstones and ship names, March 15, 1919, cass. 241-1919, prot. 1834, AFV.

35. "Ordinance for Census of Fiume Inhabitants," *La bilancia*, December 11, 1918. The full ordinance read: "THE ITALIAN NATIONAL COUNCIL OF FIUME: believing it necessary in these

exceptional conditions to discipline in a rigorous and precise fashion the distribution and rationing of products of primary necessity; considering also the necessity of collecting all data to resolve the grave problem of unemployment; considering it opportune to release to every inhabitant an identification card in order to facilitate the enjoyment of food provisions that will be adopted by the authorities; believing that these elements cannot be enacted except through a census of all the inhabitants of Fiume. ORDERS! 1) all inhabitants of Fiume, excluding children under 15 years of age, to appear at the time and place indicated, to make a declaration of residency and receive an identity card; 2) transgressors will be punished with 15 days incarceration and if possible will be expelled from the city."

36. Comando del Corpo di Occupazione Interalleato (Ufficio Politico Militare), "Dati statistici sulla popolazione del territorio di Fiume risultati dal censimento fatto dal Consiglio Nazionale Italiano di Fiume nel dicembre 1918," 1919, Museo storico Fiume.

37. Questura, Police report for arrest of Francesco Pospek, March 22, 1919, 1108 Opći spis 1919, 684, HR-DARI.

38. Consiglio nazionale italiano, "Decree-Law: Substitution of Fiume Pertinency for Hungarian Citizenship," *La bilancia*, April 2, 1919.

39. Consiglio nazionale italiano, "Decree-Law: Abrogation of Hungarian Ministry of the Honvéd (Land Forces) Subsidy for Soldiers' Families," *La bilancia*, March 4, 1919.

40. Consiglio nazionale italiano, Request to Inter-Allied command that Danubius and Whitehead factories employ Fiume pertinent workers, May 31, 1919, cass. 241-1919, prot. 3582, AFV.

41. Consiglio nazionale italiano, "Decree-Law: On Pension Increases for Service Rendered to the State during the Last War," *La bilancia*, February 6, 1920.

42. Consiglio nazionale italiano, "Decree-Law: On Indemnity Payments for Fiume Railway Employees," *La bilancia*, March 16, 1920.

43. Consiglio nazionale italiano, "Decree-Law: On Provisional Subsidies for War Invalids and the Families of Fallen Soldiers," *La bilancia*, July 31, 1920.

44. Consiglio nazionale italiano, "Decree-Law: On Price Controls in Stores and Restaurants," *La bilancia*, July 15, 1919.

45. Consiglio nazionale italiano, "Decree-Law: Laws of Eviction," *La bilancia*, February 5, 1920.

46. Consiglio nazionale italiano, Report of Arturo Gerö's expulsion, January 8, 1919, cass. 241-1919, prot. 60, AFV. His place of pertinency was listed as "Nagymegyer."

47. Consiglio nazionale italiano, Report of different people expelled from city, September 21, 1920, cass. 243-1920, prot. 189, AFV.

48. Ibid.

49. Ibid.

50. Questura, Police report on Maria Svat's restitution of her employer's wallet and expulsion, February 26, 1920, 761 Krivični predmeti, 98, spis 5, HR-DARI.

51. Consiglio dei Rettori, Minutes from Rector Council's meeting, November 6, 1920, cass. 243-1920, verb. cons. rett. 13, AFV.

52. Questura, Report of expulsions from the city, August 8, 1919, cass. 34, prot. 5156, AFV.

53. Danilo L. Massagrande, ed., *I verbali del Consiglio Nazionale Italiano di Fiume e del Comitato Direttivo 1918–1920* (Rome: Società di studi fiumani, Archivio Museo storico di Fiume, 2014), 513.

54. Comando della politizia miliatre italiana, Report on anti-legionnaire graffiti, November 23, 1920, cass. 243-1920, II/b/17 c.1, AFV.

55. Questura, Review of expulsion file, September 27, 1920, 541 Općina Rijeka 1918–1945, Prezidijalni Spisi: 210/1919, HR-DARI.

56. For an example of the police force complaining that it needed more funds to enact expulsions, as had been the case in Hungarian times, see Police request for more funds to enact expulsions, January 31, 1919, cass. 29, prot. 869, AFV.

57. Matteo Biljanich, Petition to have Pasquale Lushinovich banished, February 9, 1919, 1108 Opći spis 1919, 536, spis 1, HR-DARI.

58. Paula Peurača, Report on attempt to bribe policeman, January 11, 1919, 1108 Opći spis 1919, 783, HR-DARI.

59. Ignazio Levi, Application for pertinency, April 1, 1919, 541 Općina Rijeka spis, Opći spisi L13/1919, 8132/19, HR-DARI. Olga Levi's place of birth is listed as "Karlstadt" in the petition, which almost certainly refers to the Croatian city Karlovac and not the German city Karlstadt am Main. The name Constantinople is used in the original document instead of Istanbul.

60. Ibid. This file contains all the communications between Fiume and Istanbul on the Levi pertinency change for the years 1919–1920.

61. Lorenzo Klevisser, Application for pertinency, May 5, 1919, 541 Općina Rijeka spis, Opći spisi L95/1919, 11327/19, HR-DARI.

62. For example, see petitions by Kurt Herzberg, Application for pertinency, June 23, 1919, 541 Općina Rijeka spis, Opći spisi L95/1919, 14955/19, HR-DARI; and Rodolfo Krestan, Application for pertinency, October 3, 1919, 541 Općina Rijeka spis, Opći spisi L95/1919, 24970/19, HR-DARI. Sometimes the provisional government appears to have intentionally stalled processing pertinency applications even when there is no sign that missing documentation from people's places of pertinency was the root of the problem. For example, see the 1919 petitions of café owner Alessandro Roth, homemaker Giorgia Giovanna Maidich, and merchant Bernardo Festő, who all were only awarded pertinency in 1923, though they had lived most of their lives in Fiume. Files available in 541 Općina Rijeka spis- Opći spisi L13/1919, HR-DARI.

63. Filippo Lenassi, Application for pertinency, April 2, 1919, 541 Općina Rijeka spis, Opći spisi L13/1919, 8174/19, HR-DARI. Here Lenassi names the place of his pertinency "Adelsberg," not Postojna.

64. For examples of other applications that passed through quickly and without need for further documentation thanks to "Italian feelings" and good relations with members of the provisional government, see Kranjevich, Emilio, Pertinency application, October 14, 1919, 541 Općina Rijeka spis- Opći spisi L95/1919: 26377/19, HR-DARI; Luigi Ceresato, Pertinency application, September 11, 1919, 541 Općina Rijeka spis- Opći spisi L13/1919, HR-DARI; Emilio Passalacqua, Petition for pertinency so can vote, September 11, 1919, 541 Općina Rijeka 1918–1945 Opći spisi L57/19 kut. I: Passalacqua, Emilio, HR-DARI; Mayor awards pertinency to Alessandro Pedretti (chauffeur), October 9, 1919, cass. 196/1 Atti 82, AFV.

65. Giovanni Liliak, Application for pertinency, August 14, 1919, 541 Općina Rijeka spis, Opći spisi L13/1919, 19037/19, HR-DARI.

66. Ibid. I have been unable to ascertain what the "Italian school of Melana" refers to. It is most likely that this was a girls' school of higher education in the region that today goes by a different name.

67. Consiglio nazionale italiano, Request to Inter-Allied command that Danubius and Whitehead factories employ Fiume pertinent workers, Fiume, May 31, 1919, cass. 241-1919, prot. 3582, AFV.

68. Atti del Comando, Law decreeing expulsion from Fiume of all non-pertinents who took up residency after October 30, 1918, February 27, 1920, 3, HR-DARI.

69. Protest to Italian National Council against inflow of Hungarian refugees, June 29, 1919, cass. 241-1919, prot. 4144, AFV. The full petition reads: "Unemployment in the city has arrived at proportions, if not alarming, certainly grave. It's true that Fiume spends 600 thousand crowns a month for the unemployed, to which sum one must add the considerable costs in the money and clothing distributed to those of the population without means: comprehensively, between subsidies and charity, the city sustains an expenditure of 10 million crowns per year! With things like this and with the employment crisis set to continue for some time even after the political questions are resolved, how is it acceptable that Fiumians are forced to submit to incredibly tough sacrifices to share their meager bread not only with the foreigners that the Hungarian government induced to come here from every part of Hungary and Croatia to subdue the [local] urban component, but also with those who by disregarding the law have landed here in the last months to take advantage of our unfortunate condition?"

70. Camera di commercio e d'industria, Request to Fiume mayor that business licenses be denied to three Hungarians merchants, December 29, 1918, 179 Trgovačko–Obrtnička Komora 1918, kut. 231 spis 2786, HR-DARI.

71. Addetti italiani al Tramvia elettrico, Petition demanding the substitution of Yugoslav-Croatian Tram Inspectors and Controllers, January 20, 1919, cass. 241-1919, prot. 604.a, AFV.

72. Petition demanding Lagher lose his license, April 24, 1919, cass. 241-1919, prot. 2876, AFV. "(German Jew)" was written in the original anonymous note.

73. Comando Corpo d'Occupazione Interalleato, Police report rejecting Carlo Luppis' request for readmission to Fiume, January 8, 1919, cass. 241-1919, prot. 88, AFV.

74. Consiglio nazionale italiano, Government report of prisoners of war held in Trieste camp requesting readmittance to Fiume, March 7, 1919, cass. 241-1919, prot. 1860, AFV.

75. Consiglio nazionale italiano, Testimonies and government reports regarding accusations that Croats discriminated against in applying for industrial licenses, March 12, 1919, cass. 241-1919, prot. 1718, AFV.

76. Servizi pubblici, Response to petition to have Yugoslav and Croatian tram employees replaced, February 17, 1919, cass. 241-1919, prot. 604.b, AFV.

77. Ibid.

78. Petition demanding Lagher lose his license, April 24, 1919, cass. 241-1919, prot. 2876, AFV. In this statement, Lagher's place of birth is listed as "Leopoli," not Lviv, as was common at the time. Lagher was a member of the family whose experiences during the Fascist anti-Semitism campaigns in Fiume and eventual Holocaust experiences are described in Silvia Cuttin, *Ci sarebbe bastato* (Bologna: Epika, 2011).

79. Ibid.

80. Camillo Lavini, Application for pertinency, September 21, 1919, 541 Općina Rijeka spis, Opći spisi L13/1919, 22710/19, HR-DARI.

81. The Italian sailor and follower of D'Annunzio, Alessandro Chilodi, made this reasoning explicit in the pertinency application he submitted for himself and his two friends, Tito Fabbrini and Mario Peragallo, by saying they desired to obtain "citizenship to the free city of Fiume purely with the scope of [exhibiting] greater solidarity and italianità [Italianness]." Alessandro Chilodi, Pertinency petition, October 14, 1919, 541 Općina Rijeka spis- Opći spisi L13/1919, HR-DARI. Their petition was ignored just as all the other such applications were.

82. Particularly ambitious in its efforts to increase the number of Italians registered as Fiume pertinents was the Battaglione "Firenze" Compagnia Mitraglieri Fiat stationed in Trsat, which sent in dittoed pertinency applications, including petitions from illiterate soldiers who signed their name with an *X*.

83. Camillo Lavini, Application for pertinency, September 21, 1919, 541 Općina Rijeka spis, Opći spisi L13/1919, 22710/19, HR-DARI.

84. Magistrato civico, Instructions sent to head of Fiume Volunteers Legion on how to apply for pertinency, January 27, 1920, 541 Općina Rijeka spis, Opći spisi L95/1919, 18155/19, HR-DARI.

85. Nicolò Biasi, Summary of efforts undertaken to restructure local Fiume police force, April 1, 1919, cass. 241-1919, prot. 3533, AFV.

86. Ibid.

87. Anonymous note to police of contraband tobacco and wine trade, March 20, 1920, 761 Krivični predmeti 1920, 126 spis 1, HR-DARI.

88. Consiglio nazionale italiano, Rejection of application by Veneto elementary school teacher for position within Fiume school system, June 24, 1919, 541 Općina Rijeka 1918–1945, Opći spisi 17228, D22/1911, HR-DARI.

89. Antonio Grossich, Request that Inter-Allied Occupation forces resolve subsidies for Italian soldiers and their families living in Fiume, May 21, 1919, cass. 241-1919, prot. 3366, AFV.

90. Ibid.

91. Ibid.

92. Giuseppe Prosperi, Application for pertinency, October 28, 1919, 541 Općina Rijeka spis, Opći spisi L95/1919, 27824/19, HR-DARI.

93. Atti del Comando, Law decreeing expulsion from Fiume of all non-pertinents who took up residency after October 30, 1918, February 27, 1920, 3, HR-DARI.

94. Orsetti, Warning about dangerous behavior of legionnaires, October 11, 1920, cass. 50, prot. 351, AFV.

95. Questura, Request for more monetary support to control prostitution, November 29, 1920, cass. 243-1920, II/b/3 cc.12, AFV.

96. Questura, Complaint of Carmelo Ninfa's illegal activities as member of police, June 8, 1920, cass. 40, prot. 2822, AFV.

97. Giuseppe Maranini, *Lettere da Fiume alla fidanzata* (Milan: Pan, 1973), 42–43.

98. Margherita Bydeskuty née Diracca, Court testimony, August 13, 1920, 761 Krivični predmeti 1920, 208 spis 10, HR-DARI.

99. Stefania Stefan née Diracca, Appeal trial testimony, August 20, 1920, 761 Krivični predmeti 1920, 208 spis 24, HR-DARI.

100. Court case against Dante Greiner for charges of sexually abusing his niece Lilly Greiner, October 2, 1920, 761 Krivični predmeti 1920, 163, spis 56, HR-DARI; emphasis in the original.

101. Anna Lenaz, Complaint to police, April 28, 1919, 1108 Opći spis 1919, 810, spis 1, HR-DARI.

102. Giuseppe Werk, Testimony to police, January 21, 1919, 1108 Opći spis 1919, 726, spis 2, HR-DARI.

103. Police testimony of British soldier smuggling, December 25, 1918, 1108 Opći spis 1919, 534, spis 1/1, HR-DARI.

104. Andrea Wilhelm, Court testimony, February 22, 1919, 112 Gradjanski i Krivični predmeti 1918, 1198, spis 7, HR-DARI; Police report, March 23, 1919, 1108 Opći spis 1919, 614, spis 1, HR-DARI; Police report, January 27, 1919, 1108 Opći spis 1919, 44, HR-DARI.

105. Silvio Sucich, Police testimony, March 18, 1919, 1108 Opći spis 1919, 735, HR-DARI.

106. Ibid.

107. Maurizio Wechsler, Police testimony, March 18, 1919, 1108 Opći spis 1919, 735, HR-DARI.

108. Giuseppe Jerina, Police testimony, December 8, 1919, 112 Gradjanski i Krivični predmeti 1918, 1216, spis 28, HR-DARI.

109. Ibid.

110. Nicolò Rudan, Police testimony, May 30, 1919, 1108 Opći spis 1919, 826, HR-DARI.

111. Ibid.

112. Police report on blackmarket Italian military clothing, May 16, 1919, 1108 Opći spis 1919, 864, HR-DARI.

113. Nicolò Serko, Confession to having stolen Italian colonel's uniform, April 1, 1920, 761 Krivični predmeti 1920, 170, HR-DARI.

114. Ibid.

115. Salvatore Bellasich, Summary of Nicolina Raimondi's dismissal, November 18, 1922, 541 Općina Rijeka 1918–1945, Opći spisi 24696, D53/1922, HR-DARI.

116. For Valacchini-Vlakancic's full file, see Consiglio scolastico, Kvarnerske pokrajine dosej Raimondi Valacchini Nicolina, 44 Školsko nadzorništvo, HR-DARI. Before her official Italianized name change, she also commonly spelled her last name "Vlacancich" instead of her father's Vlakancic.

117. Nicolina Vlacancich, Name change application, April 9, 1920, cass. 39, prot. 1506, AFV.

118. Salvatore Bellasich, Summary of Nicolina Raimondi's dismissal, November 18, 1922, 541 Općina Rijeka 1918–1945, Opći spisi 24696, D53/1922, HR-DARI.

119. Questura, Police report for arrest of Francesco Pospek, March 22, 1919, 1108 Opći spis 1919, 684, HR-DARI.

120. In her examination of how Muslims were incorporated into the newly forming Kingdom of Serbs, Croats, and Slovenes, Emily Greble notices a similar trend as what Fiumians tried to employ, writing, "Postwar governments regularly appropriated imperial structures and concepts, allowing for the persistence of legal pluralism and quasi-sovereign regions through the 1940s. They also created hierarchies of citizenship that were not dissimilar to the differentiated rights we associate with empire." Emily Greble, "The Uncertain 'Wilsonian Moment' for Muslims in Yugoslavia: Reframing Historiographical Conversations through Minority Experiences," within the forum "Trasformazioni e transizioni imperiali sulla scia della Grande guerra (1917–1923)," *Passato e presente* 2019, n. 106, 35–36.

5. A Sense of Self

1. Delegato alle finanze, Report on usage of Hungarian language in Fiume tobacco factory's correspondence [in Hungarian and Italian], January 21, 1920, cass. 44, prot. 418, AFV. Thanks to Ivan Berend and Kati Radics for the translation from Hungarian to English.

2. Consiglio nazionale italiano, Directive that only Italian language materials to be used by state offices, July 9, 1919, cass. 33, prot. 4387, AFV.

3. Ibid.

4. Giovanni Giuriati, Directive that Habsburg uniforms should be made to disappear from Fiume city streets, September 25, 1919, cass. 242-1919, prot. 6104, AFV.

5. Direzione della Manifattura Tabacchi, Response to government about viability of new directive only to use Italian-language stationary, August 18, 1919, cass. 34, prot. 5287, AFV.

6. Delegato alle finanze, Report on usage of Hungarian language in Fiume tobacco factory's correspondence, January 21, 1920, cass. 44, prot. 418, AFV.

7. Consiglio nazionale italiano, Directive that only Italian language materials to be used by state offices, July 9, 1919, cass. 33, prot. 4387, AFV.

8. Direzione della Manifattura Tabacchi, Disciplinary investigation of Béla Szécsey, January 25, 1920, cass. 44, prot. 561, AFV.

9. Ibid.

10. Sezione poste telegrafi e telefoni, Update on status of substituting monolingual Italian office supplies, August 9, 1919, cass. 34, prot. 5120, AFV.

11. Ibid.

12. Dipartimento Ferrovie e Magazzini, Update on status of substituting monolingual Italian office supplies, August 12, 1919, cass. 34, prot. 5169, AFV.

13. Direzione di Finanza, Update on status of substituting monolingual Italian office supplies, August 8, 1919, cass. 34, prot. 5138, AFV.

14. Comitato direttivo, Instructions to railway offices on how to avoid usage of Hungarian in public communications, March 10, 1919, cass. 30, prot. 1523, AFV.

15. Consiglio scolastico, Paperwork for teacher's medical leave [in Hungarian], March 11, 1919, cass. 30, prot. 1766, AFV.

16. Rosalia Toplek, Letter attached to abandoned 5-month-old child [in Croatian], May 22, 1920, 761 Krivični predmeti 1920, 161 spis 1, HR-DARI.

17. Addetti italiani al Tramvia elettrico, Petition demanding the substitution of Yugoslav-Croatian tram inspectors and controllers, January 20, 1919, cass. 241-1919, prot. 604.a, AFV.

18. Tribunale, Court reports on theft in hotel "Città di Fiume," June 16, 1920, 761 Krivični predmeti 1920, 196, HR-DARI.

19. Questura, Police report on possible molestation of 10-year-old girl Wally Vucenovich, April 20, 1920, 761, Krivični predmeti 1920, 134, HR-DARI.

20. Consiglio nazionale italiano, Reminder to notary Gelletich of illegality of using Hungarian in public documents, March 14, 1919, cass. 30, prot. 1812, AFV.

21. Consiglio nazionale italiano, Directive that only Italian language materials to be used by state office, July 9, 1919, cass. 33, prot. 4387, AFV.

22. Ferlan Ruggero, Employment application, July 17, 1920, cass. 43, prot. 3583, AFV.

23. Sergio Cella, "Bellasich, Salvatore," in *Dizionario Biografico degli Italiani* (Rome: Treccani, 1970), http://www.treccani.it/enciclopedia/salvatore-bellasich_%28Dizionario-Biografico%29/.

24. Edoardo Susmel, *La marcia di Ronchi: Centoquarantanove tavole fuori testo con numerosi documenti inediti* (Milan: U. Hoepli, 1941), 22.

25. Undoubtedly the most famous and thought-provoking text on the importance of flags is Michael Billig, *Banal Nationalism* (London: Sage, 1995), where Billig emphasizes the "flagging" of banal (everyday or cold) nationhood in modern, developed, and stable western nation-states as opposed to the "hot" nationalism of new or extremist national movements. More recently, most new work has analyzed how the creation and reappropriation of flag cultures can unlock the tenor of experienced national feeling. For example, see Thomas Hylland Eriksen and Richard Jenkins, *Flag, Nation and Symbolism in Europe and America* (London: Routledge, 2007). For the Fiume case, see the forthcoming article by Ivan Jeličić, "Redefining Fiumians and Italianity: The Ambiguities of the National Building Process in the Former Habsburg-Hungarian Corpus Separatum, 1914–1921" (unpublished manuscript, 2019).

26. Consiglio scolastico, Minutes, December 8, 1919, 42 Školsko vijeće Rijeka 1919, Opći Spis 19, HR-DARI.

27. Some examples of these flag-waving loyalty oaths include Federico Gelletich, Loyalty oath, January 17, 1919, cass. 29, prot. 237, AFV; and Giorgio Fésüs, Loyalty oath, January 2, 1919, cass. 29, prot. 12, AFV.

28. Comitato direttivo, Request for Italian flags, March 26, 1919, cass. 31, prot. 2117, AFV.

29. Riccardo Dina, Letter thanking Fiume National Council for the city's hospitality, August 30, 1919, cass. 242-1919, prot. 5588, AFV.

30. Club Ausonia, Information for August 15 dance, August 13, 1920, 541 Općina Rijeka 1918–1945, Opći spisi 16064, E145/1917, HR-DARI.

31. Consiglio scolastico, Minutes, December 8, 1919, 42 Školsko vijeće Rijeka 1919, Opći Spis 19, HR-DARI.

32. Ibid.

33. Comitato direttivo, Denial of passport for Marco Crentini, April 14, 1919, cass. 31, prot. 2036, AFV.

34. Pietro Diracca, Pre-trial testimony, August 24, 1920, 761 Krivični predmeti 1920, 208 spis 24, HR-DARI.

35. Ibid.

36. Susmel, *La marcia di Ronchi*, 21.

37. Consiglio scolastico, Minutes, December 14, 1919, 42 Školsko vijeće Rijeka 1919, Opći Spis 19, HR-DARI. On December 14, 1918, one school principal reported that on that day alone (one of the coldest of the year), forty-nine students in his school had arrived barefoot.

38. Consiglio scolastico, Minutes from Boys' Civic Elementary School "Edmondo De Amicis," January 9, 1920, 42 Školsko vijeće Rijeka 1920, Opći Spis 87, HR-DARI.

39. Consiglio scolastico, Monthly report from the Girls' Civic Elementary School on via Maylaender, February 5, 1919, 42 Školsko vijeće Rijeka 1919, Opći Spis 21, HR-DARI.

40. Rodolfo Fiumani, Request for clothing subsidy, March 26, 1920, cass. 46, prot. 1853, AFV.

41. Scuola elementare dello Stato di Piazza Scarpa, Final report on 1918–1919, June 29, 1919, cass. 33, prot. 4221, AFV.

42. Ibid.

43. Cesare Finzi, Letter indicating shipment of 4,000 Italian flags, 40 autographed copies of D'Annunzio pamphlet, and 1,000 bulletins of Italian war victory to be distributed amongst Fiume primary schools, December 19, 1918, cass. 28, prot. 337, AFV.

44. Salvatore Bellasich, Request to Benito Mussolini to organize sending Fiume flags, October 15, 1919, cass. 242-1919, prot. 6484, AFV.

45. Some examples include: Stefania Türr, Florentine Irredentist activist's letter describing her efforts to help Fiume be united to Italy, December 12, 1918, cass. 241-1919, prot. 253, AFV; Capo della Sottosezione Propaganda, Reports Italian flags gifted to Fiume from Milan propaganda office, September 12, 1919, cass. 34, prot. 5882, AFV; Consiglio scolastico, Monthly report from the Girls' Civic Elementary School indicating Naples gift of Italian flag, Fiume, May 17, 1919, 42 Školsko vijeće Rijeka 1919, Opći Spis 65, HR-DARI; Sindaco di Pirano (Istria), Letter indicating gift of Italian flag to Fiume, September 13, 1919, cass. 242-1919, prot. 5933, AFV; Verona Nationalist Organization, Letter indicating gift of Italian flags en route to Fiume, November 26, 1918, cass. 28, prot. 134, AFV; Associazione XXX Ottobre (Trieste), Offer to organize Trieste-Fiume bike race and to gift Fiume with large Italian flag, December 30, 1918, cass. 29, prot. 93, AFV; Società Elettrica alto Milanese, Offer of Italian flags to be sent

to Fiume, December 13, 1918, cass. 29, prot. 96, AFV; and Ubaldo Comandini, Telegraph to Fiume Italian National Council offering Italian flag from high school in Rome, February 18, 1919, cass. 241-1919, prot. 1264, AFV.

46. Some examples concerning flag production include Consiglio nazionale italiano, Order to pay Unione Cooperativa di Milano 5917.50 lire for fabric order to produce Italian flags, June 21, 1919, cass. 43, prot. 2429, AFV; Receipt of payment to M. Weiss for fabric order for 7491.20 corone to produce Italian flags, April 16, 1919, cass. 31, prot. 2594, AFV; Oscarre Millich, Receipt for fabric order of 1134 lire and 1360 Corone to produce Italian flags, April 7, 1919, cass. 31, prot. 2627, AFV; and Consiglio nazionale italiano, Receipt of payment to M. Weiss for fabric order for 9640.83 Corone to produce Italian flags, July 8, 1919, cass. 33, prot. 4333, AFV. For an example of tailors' requests for payment, see Mario Giurissevich, Request for payment from Italian National Council for sewing together Italian flags, June 25, 1919, cass. 33, prot. 4548, AFV.

47. Eredi Gorup, Complaint about damages to Hotel Europa because of flags, October 21, 1919, cass. 35, prot. 6559, AFV; Consiglio nazionale italiano, Report of Hotel Europa's request for reimbursement for damages caused from flag placement, May 21, 1919, cass. 32, prot. 3373, AFV.

48. Borislavo Gjurić, Police statement, April 17, 1919, 1108 Opći spis 1919, 813 spis 3, HR-DARI; Nicolò Kuprešanin, Police statement, April 17, 1919, 1108 Opći spis 1919, 813 spis 2, HR-DARI; Questura, Discussion of plot to steal flag from Municipal building, April 17, 1919, 1108 Opći spis 1919, 813 spis 1, HR-DARI.

49. Ibid.

50. Report of skirmish between soldiers and civilians over disrespect to Italian flags and uniforms, March 26, 1920, cass. 196/4, Atti 498, AFV.

51. Lina Dolezal also went by the names Nina and Dina.

52. Consiglio nazionale italiano, Fiume state policy for those unemployed after the war who could prove full employment in 1914, March 3, 1919, 3, predmet 1, str. 16–18, HR-DARI. For another way to understand what three hundred crowns was worth, figures in February 1920 on maximum prices for goods indicate that that amount could get you ten pairs of "luxury leather shoes," six "luxury silk shirts for women," or "12 large bottles of olive oil." Commissione al controllo dei prezzi, Maximum price controls for food stuffs, clothing, and paper products, February 27, 1920, cass. 39, prot. 1118, AFV.

53. Enrico Jugo, Court testimony, January 21, 1920, 761 Krivični predmeti 1920, 118 spis 53, HR-DARI.

54. Commissione al controllo dei prezzi, Maximum price controls for food stuffs, clothing, and paper products, February 27, 1920, cass. 39, prot. 1118, AFV.

55. Lina Dolezal, Court testimony, January 19, 1920, 761 Krivični predmeti 1920,118 spis 6, HR-DARI.

56. Enrico Jugo, Court testimony, January 21, 1920, 761 Krivični predmeti 1920, 118 spis 53, HR-DARI. Jugo purchased a Fiume city flag to hang alongside his Italian national flag, and he indicated that he did not like the quality of the first one he was offered and so was then offered a second, indicating that supplies of flags were varied.

57. Olindo Padoani, Court testimony, January 15, 1920, 761 Krivični predmeti 1920, 118 spis 31, HR-DARI.

58. Ibid.

59. Giovanna Cappa, Court testimony, January 15, 1920, 761 Krivični predmeti 1920, 118 spis 32, HR-DARI.

60. Enrichetta Domich, Court testimony, January 15, 1920, 761 Krivični predmeti 1920,118 spis 30, HR-DARI.

61. Ibid.

62. For information on pre-WWI name-change politics in the Kingdom of Hungary, see Ágoston Berecz, *Empty Signs, Historical Imaginaries: The Entangled Nationalization of Names and Naming in a Late Habsburg Borderland* (New York: Berghahn Books, 2020).

63. Edoardo Csabrian, Petition to have spelling of last name updated, February 24, 1919, cass. 30, prot. 1459, AFV.

64. State resistance to allowing changes in spelling because of local habits affected those even at the highest ladders of the social spectrum. Apparently, a similar case had occurred in Fiume in which a state's attorney was forced to change his name from Szapáry to Czapáry because even though his birth certificate listed him as Szapáry, no legal documentation could be provided to show that central authorities had permitted his forefathers to change the spelling of his name. See "Kristo o Kristoffy?," *La bilancia*, January 12, 1906.

65. Emma Zboženský, Request for being added to electoral lists, with Zboženský used by applicant instead of Zbozensky, September 14, 1919, 541 Općina Rijeka 1918–1945, Opći spisi L57/19, kut. III: Zbogensky, Emma, HR-DARI. For another example of a Fiume pertinent who fought Italianization of his last name in daily office work, see Celestino Zuzulich, Request for being added to electoral lists, with Zuzulich used by applicant instead of Zuzzulich, September 10, 1919, 541 Općina Rijeka 1918–1945, Opći spisi L57/19, kut. III: Zuzzulich, Celestino + Elvira, HR-DARI.

66. Municipio di Trieste, Response to Fiume government explaining cannot deliver decrees to Antonio and Maria Michelich, September 12, 1919, 541 Općina Rijeka 1918–1945, Opći spisi L57/19, kut. II: Michelich, Antonio + Maria, HR-DARI.

67. "Kristo o Kristoffy?"

68. Maura E. Hametz, *In the Name of Italy: Nation, Family, and Patriotism in a Fascist Court* (New York: Fordham University Press, 2012).

69. Giovanni Lukinčić, Application for pertinency, December 5, 1919, 541 Općina Rijeka spis, Opći spisi L13/1919, 30804/19, HR-DARI. In his application the applicant actually spelled his last name with diacritics but then put in parentheses afterward, "(Luchincich)."

70. Questura, Report on disrespect to Fiume police by Lieutenant Colonel Margonari, July 1, 1920, cass. 41, prot. 3188, AFV. There are countless such reports of Italians hurling epithets stating that Fiumians were "doubtful Italians" or "just a bunch of Croats." For another example, see Nicolò Supin, Report on disrespect shown to Fiume police by Lieutenant Giovanni de Domenico, February 18, 1920, cass. 39, prot. 1009, AFV.

71. Questura, Confirming Italian nationality of Bruno Fuerst, August 31, 1920, cass. 43, prot. 4575, AFV; Confirming Italian nationality of Giovanni Blasich, March 5, 1920, cass. 43, prot. 1255, AFV; Confirming Italian nationality of Letizia Ramous, January 30, 1920, cass. 43, prot. 576, AFV.

72. Delegato agli interni, Letter to Italian Captain Antonio Priolo of passport office regarding Yugoslav sentiments of Polonio-Balbi family, July 14, 1920, cass. 41, prot. 3408, AFV.

73. Deputazione fiumana, Fiume Deputation's memorandum presented to Woodrow Wilson in Rome, January 3, 1919, cass. 241-1919, prot. 415, AFV.

74. As had been the case in the prewar period, all state and private applications and testimonies continued to use family names as one of the primary means of identification. The primacy of family names as an organizing principle in terms of the Fiume administration's relations with the wider populace can be seen in the 1920 law that required rations cards

only to be valid for households that all shared the same family name as the head of household. See Questura, New rules for ration cards, May 5, 1920, cass. 40, prot. 2278, AFV.

75. Consiglio nazionale italiano, Name-change law, March 27, 1919, cass. 41, prot. 2140, AFV.

76. For discussions of how public place names were changed in 1919–1920, see Consiglio nazionale italiano, List of proposed name changes for streets, schools, quays, and parks, March 24, 1919, cass. 31, prot. 2030, AFV.

77. For an excellent discussion of the goals, strategies, and procedures of states' nationalizing campaigns regarding family names, see James C. Scott, John Tehranian, and Jeremy Mathias, "The Production of Legal Identities Proper to States: The Case of the Permanent Family Surname," *Comparative Studies in Society and History* 44, no. 1 (2002): 4–44.

78. For a fascinating handbook explaining how the Italian Fascist name-change laws were enacted, see Aldo Pizzagalli, *Per l'italianità dei cognomi: Nella Provincia di Trieste* (Trieste: Libreria Treves-Zanichelli, 1929).

79. Consiglio nazionale italiano, Name-change law, March 27, 1919, cass. 41, prot. 2140, AFV.

80. Giovanni Marussich, Name-change application, January 22, 1919, cass. 30, prot. 1182, AFV.

81. Throughout the late nineteenth and twentieth centuries, Italian nationalists claimed that the majority of Slavic-heritage naming practices of the eastern Adriatic were actually the result of Slavic-speaking priests trying to denationalize Italians by registering names with the Slavic -*ch* or -*ć* instead of the Italian -*ino*, all three indicating the diminutive or "son of."

82. Eight other fathers in Fiume demonstrated a similar commitment to Italianizing their surnames just as they had celebrated the Italian national campaign through the selection of their children's names, though the ancestries they tried to wipe out from their last names were not just Slavic but also German. The most common first names in these cases were Dante, Italo/Italia, and, in 1918, Redenta/Redento (redeemed).

83. Apparently, some other fathers had applied a similar Italian nationalist strategy to the naming of their children, and officials used this information in the postwar period to "confirm someone *italianissimo.*" See, for example, Eugenio Coseleschi, Investigation of why Quarnero workers expelled from city, April 25, 1920, cass. 40, prot. 2136, AFV.

84. The complete file of name-change applications can be found in 541 Općina Rijeka 1918–1945, Opći spisi L19/19, HR-DARI.

85. Ufficio parrocchiale di Fiume, Church refusal to recognize name-change from Kotscken to Rossini, November 19, 1921, 541 Općina Rijeka 1918–1945, Opći spisi L19/19, HR-DARI.

86. Francesco Ursić, Name-change application, February 4, 1920, cass. 38, prot. 519, AFV. Thanks to Ivan Jeličić for pointing out the funny grammatical mistake. "Da Fiume" or "Di Fiume" would be the grammatically correct versions to indicate "from Fiume."

87. Ettore Lust, Name-change application, May 17, 1920, 541 Općina Rijeka 1918–1945, Opći spisi L19/19, HR-DARI.

88. Pizzagalli, *Per l'italianità dei cognomi.*

89. All of these cases are in the April 1919 name-change files held at 1919, 541 Općina Rijeka 1918–1945, Opći spisi L19/19, HR-DARI.

90. Consiglio nazionale italiano, Directive that only Italian language materials to be used by state offices, July 9, 1919, cass. 33, prot. 4387, AFV. The reluctance to change surnames

was not based on feudal reasons; most of the Italian National Council was made up of middle-class professionals.

91. There is a growing literature on Fiume's prewar Italian nationalist and autonomist, but *not* its annexationist, civic and political culture. See Giovanni Stelli, *Storia di Fiume: Dalle origini ai giorni nostri* (Pordenone, Italy: Edizioni biblioteca dell'immagine, 2017); Ljubinka Karpowicz, "Biografia politica di un autonomista: Ruggero Gottardi," *Quaderni: Centro di Ricerche storiche-Rovigno* (1983–1984): 39–64; Ljubinka Karpowicz, "La concezione della nazione e dello Stato nell'interpretazione degli autonomisti fiumani (Contributo allo studio del movimento autonomista di Fiume nel 1899–1918)," *Quaderni: Centro di ricerche storiche-Rovigno* (1988–1989); *L'autonomania fiumana (1867–1947) e la figura di Riccardo Zanella, Atti del convegno* (Trieste: Edizioni Italo Svevo, 1996); William Klinger, "Negotiating the Nation: Fiume, from Autonomism to State Making (1848–1924)" (PhD diss., European University Institute, 2007); Ivan Jeličić, "Nell'ombra dell'autonomismo: Il movimento socialista a Fiume, 1901–1921" (PhD diss., Universita' degli Studi di Trieste, 2016); and William Klinger, "Dall'autonomismo alla costituzione dello Stato—Fiume 1848–1918," in *Forme del politico: Studi di storia per Raffaele Romanelli*, ed. Emmanuel Betta, Daniela Luigia Caglioti, and Elena Papadia (Rome: Viella, 2012).

92. Scuola elementare dello Stato di Piazza Scarpa, Final Report on 1918–1919 school-year, June 29, 1919, cass. 33, prot. 4221, AFV.

93. Consiglio nazionale italiano, Announcement of reopening of schools, December 10, 1918, cass. 28, prot. 233, AFV.

94. Consiglio scolastico, Discussion of difficulties in reaching students because of current conditions, May 20, 1919, 42 Školsko vijeće Rijeka 1919, Opći Spis 60, HR-DARI.

95. Consiglio nazionale italiano, Announcement of reopening of schools, December 10, 1918, cass. 28, prot. 233, AFV.

96. Consiglio scolastico, Discussion of how to organize reopening of schools with limited space, January 16, 1919, 42 Školsko vijeće Rijeka 1919, Opći Spis 18, HR-DARI.

97. Ibid.

98. Direzione scuola elementare femminile di V. Sem Benelli, Request for American troops to be relocated, January 10, 1919, cass. 29, prot. 115, AFV.

99. Dirigenti delle scuole elementari di Fiume, Demand that soldiers be removed from schools otherwise will send their children to Croatia, October 20, 1919, 42 Školsko vijeće Rijeka 1919, Opći Spis 202, HR-DARI.

100. Cosimo Battistini, Plea for soldiers to be removed from elementary school, September 29, 1919, 42 Školsko vijeće Rijeka 1919, Opći Spis 172, HR-DARI.

101. Ibid.

102. Civica Scuola Elementare di Cosala, Demand that soldiers be removed from school, February 18, 1920, 42 Školsko vijeće Rijeka 1920, Opći Spis 70, HR-DARI.

103. Ibid.

104. Consiglio scolastico, Demand that soldiers be removed from schools otherwise will send their children to Croatia, January 13, 1920, 42 Školsko vijeće Rijeka 1920, Opći Spis 37, HR-DARI.

105. Silvino Gigante, Explanation why student expelled, May 19, 1919, 42 Školsko vijeće Rijeka 1919, Opći Spis 59, HR-DARI.

106. Corpo insegnante dell'Istituto Tecnico Leonardo da Vinci, Minutes, November 25, 1920, 42 Školsko vijeće Rijeka 1920, Opći Spis 1920, Riječko Nacionalno vijeće 27, HR-DARI.

107. Consiglio scolastico, Discussion of why student attendance diminished, December 10, 1919, 42 Školsko vijeće Rijeka 1920, Opći Spis 80, HR-DARI.

108. Consiglio scolastico, Discussion of difficulties in reaching students because of current conditions, May 20, 1919, 42 Školsko vijeće Rijeka 1919, Opći Spis 60, HR-DARI.

109. Consiglio scolastico, Discussion of problems with school attendance, May 4, 1920, cass. 48, prot. 2375, AFV.

110. Ibid.

111. Salvatore Bellasich, Discussion of problems with reopening schools, November 19, 1919, cass. 242-1919, prot. 6971, AFV.

112. Cosimo Battestini, Suggestions to Fiume school board on how to increase patriotism among students and their families, June 11, 1919, 42 Školsko vijeće Rijeka 1919, Opći Spis 85, HR-DARI.

113. Consiglio scolastico, Monthly report from the Girls' Civic Elementary School on via Maylaender, February 5, 1919, 42 Školsko vijeće Rijeka 1919, Opći Spis 21, HR-DARI.

114. Comitato di propaganda, Letter from propaganda department to Italian National Council, January 18, 1919, cass. 241-1919, prot. 727, AFV.

115. Maggior Generale Comandante della Divisione Ceccherini, Commitment to help city schools improve, January 20, 1920, cass. 48, prot. 508, AFV; Cosimo Battestini, Suggestions to Fiume school board on how to increase patriotism among students and their families, June 11, 1919, 42 Školsko vijeće Rijeka 1919, Opći Spis 85, HR-DARI.

116. Antonio Grossich, Discussion of how book on Fiumian history will be produced, April 8, 1919, cass. 241-1919, prot. 2435, AFV.

117. Dirigenze delle scuole elementari dello Stato, Change in elementary school curriculum, January 29, 1919, cass. 29, prot. 741, AFV. Interestingly enough, the Italian National Council ended this decree by adding that the new law was made not because of "small-minded political intolerance, but in the interests of those students who, remaining in Fiume, will need to continue their studies in Italian."

118. Francesco Grazioli, Discussion of future of Hungarian schools in Fiume, July 18, 1919, cass. 242-1919, prot. 5126 + allegati, AFV.

119. Consiglio scolastico, Discussion of many challenges in teaching, February 11, 1919, 42 Školsko vijeće Rijeka 1919, Opći Spis 20, HR-DARI; Stefano Tuchtan, Discussion of problem teaching mixed language classrooms, February 7, 1919, 42 Školsko vijeće Rijeka 1919, Opći Spis 23, HR-DARI.

120. When the Hungarian schools were closed, the number of private Hungarian schools and the number of private tutors exploded immediately. Initially this was allowed, but as time passed it became an increasingly fraught issue for the Italian National Council. For example, see Alessandro Urbanek, Discussion of private Hungarian schools and tutors, December 7, 1919, cass. 36, prot. 7352, AFV; and Discussion of private Hungarian schools and tutors, January 20, 1920, cass. 48, prot. 671, AFV.

121. Consiglio nazionale italiano, List of teachers sent to Florence summer school plus approval for funds transfer, July 8, 1919, cass. 33, prot. 4338, AFV.

122. Stefano Tuchtan, Request for additional Italian courses for Fiume teachers, December 27, 1919, 42 Školsko vijeće Rijeka 1920, Opći Spis 5, HR-DARI.

123. Consiglio nazionale italiano, Request for free travel passes for 85 Fiume teachers attending Italian summer school in Opatija, August 8, 1919, cass. 34, prot. 5086, AFV.

124. Consiglio scolastico, Additional Italian language, literature, history, and geography courses for teachers, February 16, 1920, 42 Školsko vijeće Rijeka 1920, Opći Spis 62, HR-DARI.

125. Magistrato civico, Response to Methodist organization wishing to open a school in Fiume, May 17, 1920, 42 Školsko vijeće Rijeka 1920, Opći Spis, spis 188, HR-DARI.

126. Ibid.

127. Ibid.

128. Edoardo Susmel, Description of why Fiume-produced Hungarian language textbook preferable, November 22, 1911, 22 Opći spisi, D41/1912, br. 6385/1911, HR-DARI; Silvino Gigante, Description of why Fiume-produced Hungarian language textbook preferable, October 21, 1910, 22 Opći spisi, D40/1912, br. 2, HR-DARI.

129. Conferenza ordinaria pedagogico-didattica del corpo insegnante, Discussion of whether to approve Hungarian-produced textbook, December 9, 1911, 42 Školsko vijeće Rijeka, kut. 36, br. 100–101, HR-DARI.

130. Consiglio scolastico, Minutes, December 8, 1919, 42 Školsko vijeće Rijeka 1919, Opći Spis 19, HR-DARI.

131. Consiglio scolastico, Discussion of new geography book, school trips, and gymnastics courses, April 13, 1912, 42 Školsko vijeće Rijeka, knj. 23, HR-DARI; Antonio Fonda, Discussion of status for new Fiume-produced geography textbook, March 9, 1913, 22 Opći spisi, D58/1912, HR-DARI.

132. Consiglio scolastico, Lesson plan for geography, September 30, 1912, 42 Školsko vijeće Rijeka, kut. 37, br. 395, HR-DARI.

133. Consiglio scolastico, Lesson plans, October 29, 1912, 42 Školsko vijeće Rijeka, kut. 37, br. 396, HR-DARI.

134. Consiglio scolastico, Lesson plans, March 11, 1913, 42 Školsko vijeće Rijeka, kut. 38, br. 70/1913, HR-DARI.

135. Consiglio scolastico, Lesson plans and examination results, September 9, 1913, 42 Školsko vijeće Rijeka, kut. 39, br. 283/1913, HR-DARI.

136. Edoardo Susmel, Discussion of new geography textbook, May 13, 1913, D15/1913, 22 Opći spisi, HR-DARI.

137. For a request for topographic maps and maps of Hungary, see Consiglio scolastico, Request for maps, October 3, 1912, 42 Školsko vijeće Rijeka, kut. 37, br. 398, HR-DARI. For a request for geographic maps of Europe, see Consiglio scolastico, Request for teaching materials, November 7, 1913, 42 Školsko vijeće Rijeka, kut. 39, br. 362/1913, HR-DARI.

138. Consiglio scolastico, Discussion of class trip to source of Fiumara River, June 19, 1912, 42 Školsko vijeće Rijeka, kut. 37, br. 408, HR-DARI. The river's source is located in a cave in the mountains nineteen kilometers north of Fiume.

139. Consiglio scolastico, Discussion of new geography book, school trips, and gymnastics courses, April 13, 1912, 42 Školsko vijeće Rijeka, knj. 23, HR-DARI.

140. Consiglio scolastico, Minutes, December 8, 1919, 42 Školsko vijeće Rijeka 1919, Opći Spis 19, HR-DARI.

141. Consiglio scolastico, Minutes, May 19, 1920, 42 Školsko vijeće Rijeka, Opći Spis 1920, spis 186, HR-DARI.

142. Ibid.

143. Consiglio scolastico, Discussion of how to organize reopening of schools with limited space, January 16, 1919, 42 Školsko vijeće Rijeka 1919, Opći Spis 18, HR-DARI.

144. Consiglio scolastico, Minutes, May 19, 1920, 42 Školsko vijeće Rijeka, Opći Spis 1920, spis 186, HR-DARI.

145. It is interesting to note that in the section on Italian geography, almost all the emphasis is put on northern and central Italy, with little attention paid to the South. Ibid.

146. Consiglio scolastico, Minutes, December 14, 1919, 42 Školsko vijeće Rijeka 1919, Opći Spis 19, HR-DARI.

147. Ibid.

148. Comitato di propaganda, Letter from propaganda office to Italian National Council, January 18, 1919, cass. 241-1919, prot. 727, AFV.

149. For a complete description of the celebration at the Plasse school, see Maria Voncina, Letter to city magistrate defending her patriotic decisions for Plasse school celebration, April 14, 1919, 42 Školsko vijeće Rijeka 1919, Opći Spis 33, HR-DARI.

150. Consiglio scolastico, Minutes, May 9, 1919, 42 Školsko vijeće Rijeka 1919, Opći Spis 46, HR-DARI.

151. Maria Voncina, Letter to city magistrate defending her patriotic decisions for Plasse school celebration, April 14, 1919, 42 Školsko vijeće Rijeka 1919, Opći Spis 33, HR-DARI.

152. Ibid.

153. Rinaldo Caddeo, *Inni di guerra e canti patriottici del popolo italiano* (Milan: Casa Editrice Risorgimento, 1915), quotes taken from "Stroffette Cantate a Pirano" and "Canto di Laurana," though there are hundreds of other such examples from the pre- and post-WWI period.

154. Maria Voncina, Letter to city magistrate defending her patriotic decisions for Plasse school celebration, April 14, 1919, 42 Školsko vijeće Rijeka 1919, Opći Spis 33, HR-DARI.

155. Consiglio scolastico, Request for teaching materials, November 7, 1913, 42 Školsko vijeće Rijeka, kut. 39, br. 362/1913, HR-DARI. In Voncina's 1913 supply orders, she specified that her school needed "an electric typewriter, maps of Europe, the Austro-Hungarian Monarchy and Hungary, a compass, a printing press with moveable type to teach printing, and for the library two volumes: the Songs of Castelvecchio by Pascoli and the Carduccian Anthology."

156. Comitato di propaganda, Letter from propaganda office to Italian National Council, January 18, 1919, cass. 241-1919, prot. 727, AFV.

157. Ibid.

158. Stefano Tuchtan, Request for additional Italian courses for Fiume teachers, December 27, 1919, 42 Školsko vijeće Rijeka 1920, Opći Spis 5, HR-DARI.

159. Gábor Egry also notes that in post-WWI Greater Romania the nationalizing naming campaigns need to be more carefully studied to understand the many local power dynamics involved, beyond "just" the national question. See Gábor Egry, "Navigating the Straits: Changing Borders, Changing Rules and Practices of Ethnicity and Loyalty in Romania after 1918," *Hungarian Historical Review* 2, no. 3 (2013): 449–476.

160. Salvatore Bellasich, Request to Benito Mussolini to organize Italians to send Fiume flags, October 15, 1919, cass. 242-1919, prot. 6484, AFV.

Conclusion

1. The figure of Riccardo Zanella dominates the historiography of early twentieth-century Fiume autonomism and today he is treated in some circles in Rijeka and Italy as an anti-Fascist, anti-communist, liberal, multicultural localist (though there is much one could question about such a characterization). For more on Zanella by historians, see Amleto Ballarini, *L'Antidannunzio a Fiume: Riccardo Zanella* (Trieste: Italo Svevo, 1995); *L'Autonomania fiumana (1867–1947) e la figura di Riccardo Zanella, Atti del convegno* (Trieste: Italo Svevo,

1996). For examples of how Zanella is being reconsidered in today's press, see Damir Cupać, "Tko je bio Riccardo Zanella, ponosni Fiuman, zbog kojeg se i HDZ-ovci pozivaju na antifašizam?," *Novi list*, June 1, 2019; Andrea Marsanich, "L'autonomista Zanella 'ritorna' a Fiume," *Il piccolo*, June 2, 2019.

2. For a wonderful article tracking all the reasons for Fiume's economic disaster before 1945, see Stefano Petrungaro, "Una cruciale periferia: Fiume," in *Porti di frontiera: Industria e commercio a Trieste, Fiume e Pola tra le guerre mondiali*, ed. Laura Cerasi, Rolf Petri, and Stefano Petrungaro (Rome: Viella, 2008).

3. Paul Miller and Claire Morelon, eds., *Embers of Empire: Continuity and Rupture in the Habsburg Successor States after 1918* (New York: Berghahn Books, 2018).

4. Some exciting new work is under way to uncover these histories. See especially the research unit put together by Gábor Egry called Negotiating Post-imperial Transitions: From Remobilization to Nation-State Consolidation, a Comparative Study of Local and Regional Transitions in Post-Habsburg East and Central Europe. One of the first articles to push for research in post-imperial Habsburg legacies is by Sascha O. Becker et al. and has the wonderful title of "The Empire Is Dead, Long Live the Empire! Long-Run Persistence of Trust and Corruption in the Bureaucracy" (University of Warwick Working Paper Series No. 40, 2011). Other fascinating pieces that led the pack in putting these structurally oriented post-imperial histories together include the many books and articles by Gábor Egry on post-Hungarian Slovakia and Transylvania; Miller and Morelon, *Embers of Empire*; and Roberta Pergher and Marcus M. Payk, eds., *Beyond Versailles: Sovereignty, Legitimacy, and the Formation of New Polities after the Great War* (Bloomington: Indiana University Press, 2019). Conference presentations commemorating the 1918 centennial indicate that many scholars are starting to rethink the histories of the early successor states precisely along these post-imperial lines. For the regions discussed in this book, forthcoming work by Marco Bresciani, Ester Capuzzo, Vanni D'Alessio, Emily Greble, Maura Hametz, Ivan Jeličić, Borut Klabjan, Jernej Kosi, John Paul Newman, Ágnes Ordasi, Máté Rigó, Tamara Scheer, Rok Stergar, Iryna Vushko, Natasha Wheatley, and Matthew Worsnick is worth particular mention, among others. I only hope these burgeoning works reanchor what we know and how we understand what was to come.

5. New Jersey Italian and Italian American Heritage Commission, "Primo Levy," lesson 3 in "Italians and the Holocaust," unit 7 of Italian Heritage Curriculum, 2019, https://www.njitalianheritage.org/wp-content/uploads/2019/10/12-PrimoLevi-L.pdf.

6. Alessandra Farkas, "Palatucci, tutte le ombre sulla vita dello 'Schindler italiano,'" *Corriere della sera*, May 23, 2013; Patricia Cohen, "Italian Praised for Saving Jews Is Now Seen as Nazi Collaborator," *New York Times*, June 20, 2013.

7. The best fair-minded history of this scandal is Marco Coslovich, *Giovanni Palatucci: Una giusta memoria*, Bibliotheca (Atripalda: Mephite, 2008). There are dozens of English-language articles published by major US and UK news sources that summarize the scandal for the interested reader.

8. For a beautiful, careful reconstruction of Jewish life in interwar and Fascist-era Fiume, see Sanja Simper, *Židovi u Rijeci i liburnijskoj Istri u svjetlu fašističkog antisemitizma (1938.–1943.)* (Zagreb: Židovska Vjerska Zajednica Bet Israel U Hrvatskoj, 2018).

9. Cohen, "Italian Praised for Saving Jews."

Acknowledgments

A good friend of mine said, "Well, try to avoid too much gallows humor in those acknowledgments." She was right to warn me. The temptation is real. So, to avoid going too dark, I will try to stay light and mention briefly, but with feeling, some of the people who made this book possible.

Boris Zakošek, head archivist at the Croatian National Archives in Rijeka, is one of the main reasons that I could write a book like this. His sociological mind, his passion for history, and his persistence led to the moments I love most in this book. He and I do not agree about everything regarding Rijeka's past, but we do agree about one very important thing: people matter. I thank him for helping me feel the people of Fiume we found together in the archives. Mladen Urem, head librarian at the Croatian National Archives in Rijeka, never stopped trying to find ways to aid me, and he did it with humor. The coffee machine in the archive is not the best, yet I gladly drank its sludge if it meant I could relax for a bit with these two sweet, generous, intelligent colleagues. I have embarrassed them relentlessly over the years with my gratitude; now I've decided to take it up a notch. *Hvala vama!*

Alessandro Tonacci, the head archivist at the Vittoriale, has saved me so many times we now make a joke of it. The last time I saw him, just months before I completed revisions of the manuscript, he said, "Dominique, we love having you here . . . but your luck once you get here . . . maybe it's safer if you stay away?" I cannot imagine staying away, alas, because that would mean I could not spend time thinking and laughing with him and Roberta Valbusa (the other archivist, who probably scanned almost every sheet of paper at the Vittoriale for me, bless her heart). Some of my fondest memories will always be the days we tried to understand the Fiumian dialect used in testimonies given by tram conductors in 1919. Thank goodness we were alone, because the sights and sounds of us trying to "pronounce things Fiumian" to understand what words those dialectal spellings indicated really would bring blushes. Toward the end of my research, I had the great pleasure of meeting Federico Carlo Simonelli, who has proved a stimulating interlocutor about all things Fiume, as well as an expert in identifying what in the world was going on in the magnificent photography collection the Vittoriale possesses and which they were gracious enough to allow me full access to. This is all to say, my time at the Vittoriale and the support I have received there have astounded me. *Grazie!*

The staffs at the University Library in Rijeka and the University of Miami have proved relentless in trying to find what I sought. The same is true (though for shorter stints) for the Bodleian Library in Oxford, the State Library in Berlin, Johns Hopkins Special Collections, the American Academy in Rome, the Rome Library of Modern and Contemporary History, the National and University Library in Zagreb, and the Library of Congress in Washington, DC. Emiliano Loria at the Fiume Museum in Rome and Tea Perinčić at the Maritime and History Museum in Rijeka have also been absurdly generous with their time and expertise.

One nice thing about this book is that I met a whole world outside the Venetian-Triestine-Dalmatian one I had known before. And I am grateful for it. Vanni D'Alessio was my first friend (and remains my closest) in Rijeka. He took me in, forced me to take time off, teased me relentlessly, and stayed up late talking with me about Rijeka and Istria. Later I met Ivan Jeličić, a man so knowledgeable and uncompromising when it comes to historical research that I often forget that I am almost twice as old as he is. He is also funny, which makes the many hours we have brainstormed together not *too* dorky. I know for a fact that without these two interlocutors, this book would not be what it is.

The late William Klinger, the vivacious Francesca Rolandi, the spunky Mia Orlić, the analytical Marco Bresciani, and the uncompromising Natka Badurina also stimulated me to ask new questions. You meet the greatest people working in and around the Rijeka archives.

This book took as long to write as it did to research, and without a generous band of readers, it would have been a much paler thing. Bruce Carruthers, Vanni D'Alessio, Gábor Egry, Alison Frank Johnson, Scott Heerman, Ivan Jeličić, Pieter Judson, Robert Nemes, and Ágnes Ordasi read everything and provided endless corrections and wonderful ideas for revision, most of which I took. These people made their busy lives even busier to help. Wow.

The ever-careful and cheerful Martha Schulman helped me edit, grace be to God. Isabelle Lewis made about thirty revisions to try to figure out how to map Fiume. Ashley Moore did a phenomenal job at catching all the pesky errors in the text and endnotes that somehow I did not see. And, finally, my editor Kathleen McDermott has proved incredibly useful at showing me how to tease out the point. Funding from the University of Miami, the American Council of Learned Societies, and the National Endowment for the Humanities made the researching, writing, and revising possible.

I cannot name all the others who have supported me in my career over the last ten years. The History Department at the University of Miami (thanks to the fearless leadership of Mary Lindemann), the American Academy in Rome, Victoria de Grazia, István Deák, Larry Wolff, my fellow editors at *Contemporary European History* and *Central European Studies*, the entire National Endowment for the Humanities World War I in the Middle East Seminar, Columbia University's Interdisciplinary Center for Innovative Theory and Empirics (INCITE) community, and the oodles of universities and conference organizers who have invited me to share my work and brainstorm together: all these people and institutions (and there are so many more that I don't know where to start listing) have my gratitude.

There's a core group of friends who have lived so much with me that if I don't give them at least a shout-out, I probably wouldn't recognize this book as mine. Mustafa Aksakal, Lia Avant, Simone Begani, Krista

Bentson, Ivan and Kati Berend, Michael Bernath, Merike Blofield, Laura Bonagiunti, Lâle Can, Andrea Cohen, Lucy Corin, Tanja de Coster, Pietro D'Agostino, Roberto D'Agostino, Matthias Dietrich, Annelien de Dijn, Aimee Genell, Alexander Geppert, Jenna Gibbs, Krista Goff, Arne Grafweg, Emily Greble, Laura Gunther, Anna Kendrick, Bill McAllister, Romina Molina, Brenna Munro, Charles and Sabina Neu, Tommaso Ortino, and Angelo Sampieri have brought laughter and love to me over these last tough years. To them and the many, many more I can't thank right now (but you know who you are): knowing you has been a lifesaver for me. I cherish you all.

The year I started working on this project, my beloved stepfather, Rolf Rudestam, had a stroke and died unexpectedly. While I was finishing the last chapter, my mother and partner in crime and cards, French Steele Prescott, became very ill and eventually died. The day I celebrated my first peer review on the manuscript, the man who taught me to giggle, my father Peter Hanns Reill, tripped and died suddenly. A few months before receiving the copyedits, the COVID-19 pandemic began. Over the arc of this book, I lost most of my family. Actually, I lost my favorite people. The only thing I can take heart from is that they knew this book so well. They were part of it. I'm glad this thing we made together has a life beyond.

Illustration Credits

185   Courtesy of Fondazione Il Vittoriale degli Italiani—Archivio Iconografico
190   Author's collection
212   Courtesy of Fondazione Il Vittoriale degli Italiani—Archivio Iconografico
219   Courtesy of Fondazione Il Vittoriale degli Italiani—Archivio Iconografico
226   Courtesy of Fondazione Il Vittoriale degli Italiani—Archivio Iconografico

Index